THE TRANSNATIONAL CONSTRUCTION OF MAYANNESS

The Transnational Construction of Mayanness

Reading Modern Mesoamerica through US Archives

EDITED BY
**Fernando Armstrong-Fumero
and Ben Fallaw**

UNIVERSITY PRESS OF COLORADO
Denver

© 2023 by University Press of Colorado

Published by University Press of Colorado
1624 Market Street, Suite 226
PMB 39883
Denver, Colorado 80202

ASSOCIATION
of UNIVERSITY
PRESSES
The University Press of Colorado is a proud member of
the Association of University Presses.

The University Press of Colorado is a cooperative publishing enterprise supported, in part, by Adams State University, Colorado State University, Fort Lewis College, Metropolitan State University of Denver, University of Alaska Fairbanks, University of Colorado, University of Denver, University of Northern Colorado, University of Wyoming, Utah State University, and Western Colorado University.

ISBN: 978-1-64642-425-2 (hardcover)
ISBN: 978-1-64642-426-9 (paperback)
ISBN: 978-1-64642-427-6 (ebook)
https://doi.org/10.5876/9781646424276

Library of Congress Cataloging-in-Publication Data

Names: Armstrong-Fumero, Fernando, editor. | Fallaw, Ben, 1966– editor.
Title: The transnational construction of Mayanness : reading modern Mesoamerica through US archives / edited by Fernando Armstrong-Fumero and Ben Fallaw.
Description: Louisville, Colorado : University Press of Colorado, [2023] | Includes bibliographical references and index.
Identifiers: LCCN 2022062225 (print) | LCCN 2022062226 (ebook) | ISBN 9781646424252 (hardcover) | ISBN 9781646424269 (paperback) | ISBN 9781646424276 (ebook)
Subjects: LCSH: Mayas—Ethnic identity. | Mayas—Civilization. | Mayas—Cultural assimilation. | Mayas—Archival resources. | Cultural fusion—Yucatán Peninsula—History—20th century. | Indians of Central America—Archival resources. | Transnationalism—Social aspects—Yucatán Peninsula—History. | Transnationalism—Social aspects—United States—History. | United States—Civilization—Latin American influences—Archival resources. | United States—Civilization—Indian influences—Archival resources.
Classification: LCC F1435.3.E72 T73 2023 (print) | LCC F1435.3.E72 (ebook) | DDC 305.897/42—dc23/eng/20230120
LC record available at https://lccn.loc.gov/2022062225
LC ebook record available at https://lccn.loc.gov/2022062226

Cover photographs by Fernando Armstrong-Fumero

Contents

Figures

Acknowledgments

This volume had its origins in a series of conversations between the two editors and contributor Julio Hoil Gutiérrez at the XV Reunión Internacional de Historiadores de México in Guadalajara in 2018. Since then, it has evolved to incorporate previously collected material, new research, and new conversations. For these, we'd like to offer the following thanks.

Our research has drawn on a number of key US-based archives, to whose staff we are deeply indebted. These include the American Philosophical Society, the American Antiquarian Society, the Harvard Peabody Museum, and the Carnegie Institution of Washington, DC. Special thanks go to Michèle Morgan, PhD Museum Curator of Osteology and Paleoanthropology at the Peabody Museum of Archeology and Ethnology of Harvard University. Some of Fallaw's research for this volume was conducted under a National Endowment of the Humanities Grant FT-61649-14. Likewise, some of Armstrong-Fumero's work was sponsored by a Library Fellowship at the American Philosophical Society. The Office of the Provost of Colby College generously provided a subvention towards the publication of this volume. More generally, we are both indebted to a broader community of Yucatecan and Mayanist scholars whose insights, anecdotes, and generous criticism have helped to put flesh on the documentary bones of this work.

Both of us have benefited from the work of students in the completion of the manuscript. Sheila Hernandez of Smith College did wonderful work on the translation of Hoil Gutiérrez's chapter into English and general copyediting for the initial review submission. Meredith Whitman of Colby College helped immensely with compiling, formatting, and editing the volume. María Martínez and Avery Hudson of Colby helped with the final stages.

As the manuscript reached its final stages, we were lucky to have invaluable input and support from the University Press of Colorado. We'd like especially to thank the two anonymous external reviewers for their generous and insightful comments. Very special thanks go to Allegra Martschenko for her constant support and for managing to keep the whole project on such a fast timetable in the midst of a pandemic.

This was a collective undertaking that involved all of our collaborators, and we are extremely grateful to the innumerable ways they contributed. This volume came together amid the COVID-19 pandemic. Each of our authors persevered through disruption in fieldwork, limited access to institutional resources, challenging childcare situations, and so much more to deliver superb essays on what turned out to be a remarkably fast timetable. Without the possibility of meeting in person, everyone made the most of digital communications, including the zoom conference we organized in January 2021. After all of this, we are very proud of this volume as editors, and so grateful to all of you for making this happen.

Finally, we would like to thank our family members who put up with us during the process of writing this book. Ben Fallaw is immensely appreciative of his wife, Mónica, and daughter, Amy, who accompanied him on several research trips to Mérida. Fernando Armstrong-Fumero is grateful to his parents, Dafne and Fernando, who were a vital lifeline to the world outside of New England during the depths of the pandemic.

THE TRANSNATIONAL CONSTRUCTION OF MAYANNESS

1

Introduction

FERNANDO ARMSTRONG-FUMERO AND BEN FALLAW

A full-scale cast of a Mayan stela from Copán, Honduras, stands before the ivied walls of Harvard's Peabody Museum. Works of art like this one, and the institution that brought it "home" to 11 Divinity Avenue, embody the intersections of science and the US global ambitions that are at the heart of this volume. As historian Andrew Bell has observed (2018), this appropriation of Mayan cultural heritage as metonym for Americanness is consistent with an evolving imperial project in which the ideological work of archaeology intersected with an increasingly assertive foreign policy that stressed US dominance over its culturally distinct and diverse southern neighbors. With more than a century of hindsight, this is a particularly poignant moment in a longer history of encounter in which transnational engagements with Maya culture are always shaped by larger geopolitical events and narratives.

This book is an attempt to ground this larger history in a series of specific encounters that have left significant traces in various US-based archives as well as in the local life worlds of different groups of Mayan people. Each of the essays in this book focuses on a particular site and moment of encounter between western, predominantly Anglo-American travelers, and diverse peoples—Mayan and non-Indigenous alike—from Central America and Mexico. The travelers represent a diverse collection of capitalists, scientists, and tourists. Their local interlocutors are equally diverse in terms of ethnic identity, language, and socioeconomic status. But a common thread joining these encounters is how each contributed to a

https://doi.org/10.5876/9781646424276.c001

different series of interpellations of the Mayan peoples of the region, as ethnological research subjects, medicalized bodies, laborers, and a component of cultural tourism. In each case, aspects of this encounter can be documented through various US-based archives that are relatively understudied in ethnographies and histories that focus on primary materials that can be collected "in country" in Mexico and Central America. Thus, the essays in this book offer an invitation for interdisciplinary Mayanist studies that simultaneously explore the transnational histories of Indigenous culture and expand the range of sources that are available for research.

By the 1990s, "transnationalism" was a pervasive component of Mayanist anthropology, from studies of migrants in exile from the Civil War in Guatemala (Burns 1993), to discussions of the place of Indigenous agricultural production in global markets (Fischer and Hendrickson 2001), to analyses of the Ejército Zapatista de Liberación Nacional's (Zapatista Army of National Liberation; EZLN's) global political strategies (Nash 2001). Transnationalism continues to inspire anthropologists such as Rebecca Galemba (2018), who examines the intersection of smuggling, ethnicity, and nationalism on the Guatemala-Mexico frontier. Historians working in the Maya region have been slower to cross national boundaries in their research, though authors like Catherine Nolan-Ferrell have demonstrated the deep links between cross-border populations in Mexico and Guatemala that have been absent from previous historiography (2012, 12; see also Fink 2003). But whether scholars arrived at this conclusion earlier or later, there is a cross-disciplinary consensus that the social, economic, and cultural dynamics that have shaped the lives of generations of Mayan peoples must be traced across national as well as regional boundaries.

As will become clear to the reader, the particular iteration of "transnationalism" that is the focus of the essays in this volume is somewhat narrower and more targeted than larger circuits of migration, trade, and exchange that different authors have explored. In essence, we focus on the kinds of phenomena that take place in what Mary Louise Pratt famously characterized as a "contact zone" (1992). That is, each of the essays in this volume focuses on specific sites and moments of transcultural interaction marked by struggles and negotiations over resources, territory, and prestige. At the heart of these zones of contact is the deep and evolving relationship of US capital, NGOs, state officials, and the diverse societies of Mexico and Central America, a relationship that pervaded the production of knowledge and cultural representations that range from industrial techniques and notions of public health to archaeology and tourism.

As the chapters of this book illustrate, our perspective on this evolving historical dynamic can be greatly enriched by turning to primary sources that are found in the United States. These range from documentary materials in US archives, to ephemeral materials published for US readerships, to the ethnography of different production techniques that North American investors and travelers developed in tandem with Mayan laborers in Mexico and Central America. These sources are not simply a body of data. They are a material or living embodiment of the complex and often asymmetrical relationship between members of local Indigenous communities and foreign travelers, researchers, and capitalists. Although these different archives record relationships between US residents and Mayan peoples, we turn the historical perspective of Mayanist studies back on the "gringos" who played different roles in shaping, studying, marketing, and consuming Indigenous cultures.

This introduction will consist of four broad sections. First, we will outline discussions of the history of United States interventions in the politics and economies of Mexico and Central America, emphasizing how these interventions shaped the lives of rural Maya-speaking communities. Drawing from some of the classic insights of dependency theory, this discussion will provide a general template for the forms of economic and cultural exchange at the heart of this volume. The second section will explore how parallel and complementary trends in anthropology and different interdisciplinary studies have charted cultural exchanges that flow through channels that were first built with US capital, diplomacy, and military intervention. From there, we will turn to the history of some archives that are housed in the United States, both to highlight the rich documentary and ethnographic legacies that are available for the study of these historical relationships, and to contextualize the essays in this volume. Finally, we turn to how each chapter in this volume builds on these overarching themes and offer some possible avenues for future scholarship.

DEPENDENCY THEORY AND MAYA STUDIES

In the 1970s and 1980s, scholars in the United States and Latin America were deeply influenced by Andre Gunder-Frank (1967), Fernando Henrique Cardoso, Enzo Faletto, and Marjory Urquidi (1979), and Immanuel Wallerstein (1979). These canonical *dependistas* attributed Latin America's poverty, conservative social order, and chronic political problems to its position on the underdeveloped periphery of a world system dominated by the Global North (Salvucci 1996b). Gunder-Frank's notion (1967, esp. 124) that the "problem of the Indian" lay not in social and geographical isolation—as Robert Redfield would have it—but in structural economic position vis-à-vis domestic elites and within the global system resonated with students of Mayan peoples.

We are not adopting dependency theory as our primary theoretical approach but instead use it to historically contextualize and critique scholarly literature on the region. We are aware that many academics have challenged the underlying assumptions of dependency theory that can deny agency to Indigenous people (and other

Latin Americans as well) (Salvucci 1996a). Criticism of Cardoso and Falleto's depiction of Latin American countries as "non-nations" dominated by a comprador bourgeoisie class has been especially fierce since the end of the Cold War. The study of commodity chains common in more recent scholarship allows for the possibility of Latin American countries to escape reliance on a global economy rigged by the Center (Topik, Marichal, and Frank 2006, 6–7, 9).

Read against these critiques, we find the approach of William Roseberry (1993, 334) especially useful. He criticized the reductionist, structuralist approach of classical dependency theorists for relying heavily on sociological categories drawn from Karl Marx, Vladimir Lenin, and Alexander Chayanov in which "both the ejidos and the Mayans finally disappear into the structural categories of comfortable, middle, and poor peasants." Roseberry reminds us that archival and ethnographic research that developed since the 1990s has allowed us to account for the power of structure while at the same time recognizing the agency exercised by Indigenous people (1993, 334). For example, in the 1980s and 1990s, Anglophone historical scholarship on the Yucatán peninsula's Mayan peoples tended to focus on three events. These are the Caste War of 1847, the creation of an export-oriented henequen economy during the liberal dictatorship of Porfirio Díaz (1877–1910), and Yucatán's role as a crucial "revolutionary laboratory" under radical reformist governors Salvador Alvarado (1915–18) and Felipe Carrillo Puerto (1922–24). Through all of these processes, the expansion of US capital in the peninsula contended with different forms of local agency that ranged from the interests of local landowning and political elites to the armed resistance of some Indigenous groups that remained essentially autonomous until the 1920s and 1930s.

The power centers of Boston, New York, and Washington, DC, might not be the sole or even primary drivers of economic development in the Maya area, but examining archives in those cities does offer significant insights that are often missed by ethnographic and archival approaches that focus exclusively on primary materials drawn from Latin America. Gilbert Joseph and Allen Wells reshaped our understanding of Yucatán's economic and political history by turning to the archives of the US-based multinational corporation International Harvester (Wells 1985; Joseph 1988). They argued that collusion between this powerful North American fiber corporation and the dominant clique of Yucatán's regional oligarchy created a sort of informal empire in Yucatán and strengthened the hold of the plantocracy at the cost of keeping about 80,000 Yukatek Maya people trapped in debt servitude. What is most significant about their work, at least from the perspective represented in this volume, is that this connection between a US corporation and the quotidian lives of rural Indigenous people in Mexico was only brought into relief through the reading of sources not previously subjected to serious academic research.

Joseph's and Wells's work had theoretical impacts on Mexicanist historiography beyond the rereading of the Yucatecan economy, despite the fact that another US-trained historian, Diane Roazen-Parrillo (Roazen-Parrillo and Carstensen 1983), used the same archives to challenge this interpretation. Mexican and US scholars might have applied dependency theory to Yucatán's monocrop economy in different ways, but they tended to agree that the Porfirian creation of a plantation economy devastated the older subsistence practices of much of the Maya-speaking peasantry, substituting them with different regimes of labor closely tied to foreign capital or markets (Ortiz Yam 2013). For instance, the conclusion to an influential interdisciplinary volume on Yucatán published in the 1980s argued that the Mayan peasantry escaped near-slavery on henequen plantations via revolutionary land reform, only to find themselves earning low wages ultimately supported by federal spending. Put another way, dependency on a henequen industry reliant on US capital and markets was replaced by dependency on Mexico City's developmentalist spending and ersatz social welfare programs delivered through a corruption-ridden bureaucracy (Brannon 1991). The market-driven reforms that removed these federal subsidies in the 1980s resulted in "ejidos without ejidatarios" (Baños Ramírez 1996).

In different regions across what is traditionally referred to as "the Maya Area," the legacies of foreign economic intervention created different political and economic configurations around crops and other natural resources in different ecological niches. Such is the case of the chicle economy that flourished in the forests that straddle the Mexico-Guatemala border and span into the former British colony of Belize. Here, thousands of Indigenous and non-Indigenous chicleros formed the base of an extractive economy whose primary customers were US chewing-gum companies. In a similar vein to Joseph and Wells, Michael Redclift's *Chewing Gum: The Fortunes of Taste* (2004) links the advertising campaigns and social trends that popularized gum chewing in the US to larger circuits of transnational investment and national economic development. These, in turn, shaped political organizations in Mexico that ranged from state-sanctioned cooperatives to the personal fiefdom that was held for decades by the Indigenous strongman General Francisco May Pech (Redclift 2004, see also Mathews and Schultz 2009).

In the Maya highlands that crosscut the border between Mexican Chiapas and Guatemala, the lives of rural people were likewise shaped by export-directed economies in which US markets and investors played a central role. In the eastern and the coastal regions of Guatemala, members of the Hispanic elite and middle classes (referred to variously as Creoles and Ladinos) benefited from growing exports such as coffee and other crops via railroads and Pacific ports. In the Guatemalan highlands, however, most Mayan communities survived pressure from a strengthening liberal state and land-hungry landowners by seeking to limit contact with outsiders and preserve the authority of the cofradia/cargo system. Contrary to Eric Wolf's classic description (1957), these communities were never entirely "closed." Studies of the K'iche' town of Quetzaltenango and Kaqchikel town of Tecpan found widespread collaboration between Indigenous elites and Ladino outsiders; the former gaining access to credit and markets as well as buttressing their own position atop a patriarchal, conservative social order (Grandin 2000; Esquit Choy 2002, 2010). Nevertheless, different strategies of corporate governance allowed these communities to maintain a strong degree of political and cultural autonomy through much of the nineteenth century, even as Guatemala's agrarian economy shifted towards export-oriented production.

By the late nineteenth and early twentieth centuries, debt, demographic growth, coercive break up of communal lands, vagrancy laws, and tax burdens forced many Mayan Guatemalans into the labor market, particularly into export-oriented agriculture. The expansion of commercial agriculture (especially coffee) during this period had an uneven impact across Guatemala's different regions. While the more arable soil of the central highlands allowed Kacquikel smallholders to effectively control their own land base, communities to the north and west tended to occupy lower-quality lands and thus had fewer opportunities to participate in more lucrative agricultural markets.[1] Some Mayan people resided on plantations as resident *colonos*, others worked daily on nearby fincas, and still others migrated to work on commercial estates or in towns for long periods. This last form of employment evolved into annual labor migration described by Rigoberta Menchú in her autobiography (Menchú 2010, 21–27, 33–37, 38–42, 87–90).

The role of US-based trusts in the development of commercial agriculture in Guatemala offers us both commonalities and contrasts to Yucatán. While International Harvester (and smaller competitors) were politically marginalized after the Mexican Revolution, United Fruit Company (UFCO) reached the peak of its power in Central America during the first half of the twentieth century. As Wells points out, International Harvester never sank capital into infrastructure and land to create a true enclave in Yucatán comparable to those the UFCO carved out in a number of Latin American and Caribbean countries (1998, 109). In Guatemala, UFCO capital transformed vast areas of the Atlantic lowlands (specifically, the Motagua Valley in Izabal Province) and then Pacific lowland areas into banana enclaves. These were linked to each other by the International Railways of Central America (or IRSA), whose head, Minor C. Keith, was known as the Green Pope. These foreign-owned conglomerates exercised a strong influence over many heads of nations around the Caribbean, including a string of Guatemala presidents, from Manuel Estrada Cabrera (1898–1920) to Jorge Ubico (1931–1944). Although some Mayan people worked for the UFCO, its impact on the Mayan communities of Guatemala was mainly indirect. United Fruit's two lowland enclaves and rail-road corridors largely bypassed lands held by Mayan communities, and attempts to impress Mayan people to build the northern railroad line that would form the backbone of the Motagua Valley estates failed after thousands fled horrific work conditions (Dosal 49–51, 121; C. Cardoso 1991). Ultimately, UFCO had to rely on Afro-descendant immigrant labor from the US South, Belize, and especially Jamaica (see Colby 2011). The company had a long history of pitting Black, Hispanic, and Indigenous labor in Central America against each other to impede class-based orga-nizing (Bourgois 1989, 109, 222–23).

Nevertheless, the UFCO profoundly shaped the histories of Guatemala's Mayan communities through its influence on national policy in Guatemala (Dunkerley 1991, 120–22). Most infamously, UFCO played a key role in prompting the United States government to engineer the 1954 coup that prevented the nationalization of 200,000 acres of land by the Jacobo Árbenz Guzmán administration. Just as in the Delahuertista movement that toppled Felipe Carrillo Puerto's populist regime in Yucatán, rural Mayan people did not rise up en masse to fight in support of the pop-ular reformist regime. In fact, the conservative leaders of the K'iche' community of Quetzaltenango generally supported the counterrevolution of 1954 because Arbenz's agrarian reform opened up rifts within the community, empowering a new, younger generation of leaders (Grandin 2000, 217–18). Unlike the failed 1923–24 coup in Mexico, the overthrow of Arbenz led to a rollback of existing reforms and decades of reactionary terror. It is difficult to imagine a 1954 coup without UFCO, and it was this traumatic event that triggered Guatemala's descent into decades of civil war that claimed the lives of 200,000 people, mostly from diverse Mayan ethnic groups.

The experience of Mayan peoples of Chiapas presents some ecological and social parallels to that of the Mayan peoples of Guatemala. Beginning in the 1880s, the expansion of coffee exports in Chiapas motivated Hispanic elites (also known as Ladinos) that dominated the state government to expand their control over lands and Indigenous labor. Liberal laws backed by the force of the Porfirian state enabled white and mestizo landowners to seize the land owned collectively by Mayan com-munities, while a combination of taxes, vagrancy laws, labor drafts, and debt forced Indigenous subsistence agriculturalists into the labor market. As in Guatemala, for-eign investors—US and German—often played key roles in developing coffee fincas.

As in Guatemala, some highland Chiapanec communities responded to these pressures by minimizing contact with outsiders and strengthening internal gover-nance through a cofradia-cargo system. This form of internal governance controlled seasonal wage labor by its members on coffee fincas (Washbrook 2012, 160–77). This helps explain why Porfirian landowners complained that Chiapas' state gov-ernment was lax in enforcing debt peonage compared to other Mexican states and

Guatemala. As a result, coffee planters in the state's Soconusco region had to rely on relatively expensive labor, with some landowners purchasing coffee fincas on both sides of the national border in order to facilitate the drafting of Indigenous laborers from Guatemala to work on Chiapan estates (Washbrook 2012, 338–41). Many landowners also relied on labor brokers to bring Indigenous workers from the highlands (Washbrook 2012, 343).

As it had elsewhere in Mexico, in Chiapas the revolution brought a series of often-contradictory effects to the dynamics between Indigenous communities, local elites, and transnational capital. By the mid-1930s, landowners increasingly had to acknowledge the political gains of rural agriculturalists under the 1917 Constitution, above all the expansion of the national agrarian reform that accelerated under President Lázaro Cárdenas del Río (1934–40). In many ways, the main beneficiaries of Cárdenas' reforms were not Mayan workers but Ladino and bilingual Indigenous mediators (Rus 1994; Lewis 2005). But the post–World War II growth in international demand for coffee and tropical fruit led the Mexican government to shift its priorities and once again support large-scale private agribusiness in Chiapas. Federal policies that depressed the price of basic consumer goods further impoverished the Indigenous peasants that produced them. Having lost opportunities to gain control over their own lands and weakened in their ability to negotiate with large-scale private landowners, thousands of Tzeltal and Tzotzil peasants colonized lands in the lowlands of the Lacandon Forest, where they entered into further conflicts with cattle ranchers and non-Indigenous settlers. All of these social, demographic, and economic factors coalesced into the pressures that ultimately resulted in the neo-Zapatista uprising of 1994 (Collier and Quateriello 2005, 29–36).

With decades of hindsight, it is fair to say that dependency theory and its various latter-day iterations helped to build a consensus on the importance of transnational linkages in the historiography of the Maya area. Whether it was through the formation of direct enclave economies by the US-based corporations, financial control over local landowning elites, pressure on national governments, or simply the formation of large markets for export goods, transnational influences emanating from US capital played a central role in the postcolonial history of rural societies in much of Mexico and Central America. The Indigenous communities that were the focus of twentieth-century Mayanist anthropology were located in some of the regions most affected by these transnational forces. These insights have broader implications within the discipline of history, which we hope to address in this volume. While many historians of the US have trumpeted the need to move past exceptionalism and parochialism, there has been an uneven recognition of how linkages to Latin America—and particularly Mexico—have shaped the social and economic development of the United States (Bayly et al. 2006; Bender 2006; Russo 2006). Jessica Kim's *Imperial*

Metropolis (2019) exemplifies some of the most exciting recent work in this direction. Kim applied William Cronon's notion of hinterlands to examine Los Angeles' imbrication in northwest Mexico from the period of accelerated development during the Porfiriato through the revolution's armed and reconstructive phases.

Kim's focus on Los Angeles as a nexus for cultural and economic exchange was an inspiration for this project, which grew out of a series of conversations regarding the many ties binding Massachusetts to the Maya lands. These range from the early economic interventions in the henequen industry by Peabody & Company and Plymouth Cordage to the Bostonian origins of the United Fruit Company. As several chapters in this volume will show, it is impossible to dissociate the intervention of the American Antiquarian Society of Worcester, Harvard, and the Peabody Museum—all foundational institutions for modern Maya studies—from this larger context of global Massachusetts. To better understand the parallel histories of transnational capitalism and cultural production, it is useful to examine how the more cultural dimensions of transnational contacts have been explored by incorporating English-language materials into Mayanist studies by anthropologists and scholars in a number of humanistic interdisciplines.

TRACING CULTURE ACROSS BORDERS

Just as the archives of International Harvester helped to ground dependency theory in the history of a specific transnational circuit of commodity and capital, other documentary collections tell the story of evolving cultural connections between the Maya area and the US. Rather than privileging either political economy or cultural factors, we second William Roseberry's (1998) call to put them in dialogue and debate with one another. In this section, we delve into how parallel and complementary trends in anthropology and allied disciplines have probed cultural exchanges that flow through multiple channels. We are especially interested in how interventions of US capital, diplomacy, and military power have created distinct paths where "close encounters" (Joseph, LeGrand, and Salvatore 1998) between Mayan people and US American officials, scientists, businesspeople, and tourists take place. We recognize that research drawing on US-based archives made early, if relatively marginal, contributions to Mayanist studies in the mid-twentieth century. These include biographies of influential figures in the field of anthropology based on their unpublished diaries and archived letters. Here, two figures who stand out are Wolfgang Von Hagen, an amateur naturalist and historian who wrote at length about John Lloyd Stephens and about Frederic Catherwood (Von Hagen 1947), and Robert L. Brunhouse, a trained historian and university professor who penned biographies of Sylvanus Morley (1973) as well as a general work on early Mayanist archaeologists (1971).

While some of these biographical works are widely read and have gone through multiple editions, they have remained peripheral to broader discussions in history and anthropology. This status is due, in no small part, to the decline in the prestige of biography as a genre of academic historiography over the course of the twentieth century. More recent examples, such as Ian Graham's book (2002) on Alfred Maudslay, continue to be written by working archaeologists as a tribute to mentors or particularly revered figures in the discipline. But monographs like this find a limited readership among recent generations of anthropologists, who are often wary of "hagiographic" accounts of figures whose theoretical agendas and personal politics have been problematized within the discipline since at least the 1970s.

Notwithstanding the biographical genre's loss of academic prestige, historians such as Mary Kay Vaughan have recently sought to revive it as a means of exploring historical processes through the frame of an individual's career (see Vaughan 2014). Similar arguments could be made for a number of key figures in Mayanist anthropology who worked to form academic institutions in tandem with the expansion of US power in the early twentieth century. Take Alfred Tozzer, celebrated as a founder of US Mayanist studies, who has not yet been the subject of a major published biography. Tozzer is known for his classic ethnography of the Lacandon Mayan people of Chiapas (1907), for some of the first archaeological field work at Tikal, for linguistic research, and for the publication of a meticulously annotated English translation of Bishop Diego de la Landa's *Relación de las cosas de Yucatán*. His publications are only one part of his largely unknown role in shaping Maya Studies during the early twentieth century. Tozzer was a consummate bureaucratic insider—chairing Harvard's Anthropology Department for years, directing Franz Boas's International School of American Archaeology and Ethnology in Mexico in 1914, and helping place his students in key positions in the archaeological projects of the Carnegie Institution of Washington (CIW). A closer examination of Tozzer's career would yield a better understanding of the growth of US presence and influence in Mexico and Central America. As a young scholar, Tozzer helped document US consul Edward H. Thompson's controversial dredging of Chichén Itzá, and he reluctantly smuggled a precious jade out in a specially prepared padded waistcoat (McVicker 2005, 127–28). After military service in World War I, he directed a regional branch of the Office of Strategic Services, the forerunner of the CIA, during World War II. (Lothrop 1955; Phillips 1955). These connections between Maya archaeology, espionage, and the consolidation of US hegemony over the Western Hemisphere in the twentieth-century figure in several chapters in this book.

Although formal biographies are less common today, reflections on the context and legacies of intellectual figures from the late nineteenth and early twentieth centuries still figured in some significant trends in the Mayanist anthropology of the last several decades. The diaries, correspondence, and other personal documents of early twentieth-century archaeologists were rediscovered in the 1980s and 1990s amidst a series of disciplinary agendas associated with anthropology's "crisis of representation." Paul Sullivan's discussion of encounters between Sylvanus Morley and descendants of the Cruzo'ob Maya in *Unfinished Conversations* (1991) and Quetzil Castañeda's analysis of CIW archaeologists and the residents of the town of Pisté in *In the Museum of Maya Culture* (1996) are good examples of this trend. Critiques of the theoretical paradigms that were published in the classic texts of early twentieth-century anthropology had been common since the 1960s (see Goldkind 1965). Authors such as Sullivan and Castañeda, however, turned to the same unpublished documentary materials that had been available to Brunhouse and Von Hagen, intending to reconstruct the intercultural dialogue between US academics and various Indigenous interlocutors. In this regard, the revival of interest in the biographies of major intellectual figures is consistent with the broader interest in critical intellectual history that rose in tangent with the "Writing Culture" critiques of anthropology in the late 1980s and 1990s (see Marcus and Clifford 1987).

These hybrids of intellectual and social history created important synergies among Anthropology and American studies, ethnic studies and related interdisciplines since the 1990s. One of the signature achievements of these interdisciplines has been the ability to trace common analytical threads that link the experiences of very different populations through parallel phenomena such as colonial racialization and global circuits of goods and capital. So, for example, authors have drawn parallels between discourses of race in the work of the mid-nineteenth-century Yucatecan intellectual Justo Sierra O'Reilly and his US contemporaries (Brickhouse 2004, see also Silva Gruesz 2002). This comparative theoretical framing has influenced a wave of scholars such as Paul Worsley and Rita Palacios (2019), Gloria Elizabeth Chacón (2018), and Arturo Arias (2018), who have situated contemporary Maya-language literatures in the context of comparative identity politics and international literary production.

Despite examples like these, it is fair to say that research on Mayan peoples has tended to figure more in regionally grounded anthropological and historical scholarship than in the kind of transnational or multisited project that marks much work in the interdisciplinary "studies" model. In many cases, as in the popular field of border studies, this can be seen as a missed opportunity. Following Gloria Anzaldúa's classic work (1987), literary and interdisciplinary scholars have developed powerful theoretical frames that have been adopted by students of border phenomena across the humanities and social sciences. But, perhaps ironically, the transformation of the national boundary defined by the Rio Grande / Río Bravo into a metonym for "the border" tends to overlook complex transnational phenomena that occur throughout the Maya area. In this regard, works such as a recent collection on the maritime history of the Gulf of Mexico, which documents incidents such as the mid-nineteenth-century collaboration between independent Texas and separatists in the Yucatán peninsula are a notable exception (see Sledge 2019).

Although it is less often cited in interdisciplines such as American Studies, there has been some important historical work on the Guatemala-Mexico border, most of which has focused on its porousness, and its role in state formation in both countries. The separatist movement of the mid-nineteenth-century Cruzo'ob Maya people has been better understood by looking at its international dimensions, from the fluid national identity of settlements along the northern border of Guatemala (see Schwartz 1990) to ties between those same groups and British merchants working out of Belize (Dumond 1997; Rugeley 2009). Still understudied, similar histories exist for interactions between Mayan peoples, national Hispanic elites, and different international agents along the complex series of borders that divide Mexico, Guatemala, Belize, El Salvador, and Honduras. Further exploration would undoubtedly enrich the substantive empirical base that informs the larger theoretical project of understanding the human experience of "borders." Given the role of the United Fruit Company and other US corporate interests in the economic development of this region, US-based documentary sources have a meaningful role to play in this historiography.

Despite these promising synergies, some earlier academic debates remind us of tensions that have emerged when Mayanist studies engage with broader theoretical currencies from the humanities. Matthew Restall, for example, has observed how theorists who have been influential in interdisciplinary cultural studies, such as Tzvetan Todorov and Walter Mignolo, have often employed essentialist tropes in characterizing pre-Hispanic civilization, leading to analyses that grossly simplify the encounter between Indigenous and European cultures (Restall 2003). In some of his most widely cited works on the nature of writing and conquest, Mignolo makes significant factual errors, including mixing terms from Mayan languages that are as historically distinct from one another as English and Russian to refer to a generalized tradition of writing among ancient and colonial Mayan people.[2] Similarly, Todorov (1999) applied post-Structuralist analysis of signs and their interpretations to argue that the sixteenth-century Aztecs were culturally incapable of perceiving the true motives of the Spanish conquerors. These last assertions were pulled into an acrimonious debate between anthropologists about the writing of conquest and the use of popular theories of "the Other" to denigrate the agency and even intellectual ability of non-western peoples (Borofsky 1997).

Academic conflicts like these should not imply that the kind of comparativism used by American studies and related interdisciplines does not have much to contribute to discussions of the Maya area, or that this research should be dominated by traditionally trained historians and anthropologists. However, they do underscore the potential problem of substituting current theoretical trends for more "disciplined" skill sets such as expertise in Indigenous languages or in-depth knowledge of national historical traditions. Restall's critique of authors such as Mignolo and Todorov reflects his own intellectual trajectory as a member of the "New Philology," a school of UCLA-based scholars who trained extensively in the reading of Indigenous language texts that are inaccessible to scholars in more traditional (i.e., western-focused) humanistic traditions. Ironically, projects that sought to incorporate Indigenous texts into global literary history without this grounding included errors that underscore the historical hierarchy between European languages and those of formerly colonized peoples. The need for a rigorous engagement with Indigenous languages has become even more pressing as several generations of native Maya language speakers have played a more prominent role in international scholarship (Montejo 2005; Otzoy 2008; Xinico Batz 2015; Castillo Cocom 2004).

Similar forms of grounding are central to the essays in this volume. Each represents an engagement with contemporary theoretical agendas that stress global capital, intercultural encounters, and other aspects of the transnational relationship between Mexico, Central America, and the United States. In each case, however, these agendas emerge organically from established research projects in Mexico or Central America and situate their transnational connections in substantive ethnographic and documentary materials. We consider this dual grounding, which focuses on both site-specific history or ethnography and transnationally sourced documents, to be essential for a nuanced and rigorous interpretation of the centuries-long interactions and relationships between different groups of Mayan people and US Americans. This foundation is at the heart of the expanded notion of the archive that we touched upon earlier in this introduction. In the following section, we will look more closely at the historical formation of some of the sources for this dual grounding that are available in the United States, how those sources were constituted, and some ways in which they have been used in the past. This description, then, forms a basis for a more targeted discussion of the specific ways that our contributors have incorporated knowledge derived from US archives.

ARCHIVES AS TRANSNATIONAL ARTIFACTS

As we discussed in the previous section, a solid grounding in the nuanced knowledge of the languages, ethnography, and history of Mesoamerica is essential for the development of empirically rich and theoretically nuanced interdisciplinary Mayanist studies. In the case of this volume, part of that grounding is to be found in the use of US-based archival sources that have until now often been peripheral to Mayanist history and ethnography. As we will discuss in the next section, several of the authors in this volume use materials that are more representative of ethnography and cultural studies than traditional historiography. Nevertheless, they play similar function to U.S.-based documentary archives that embody different forms of engagement between U.S. travelers and different Mayan communities in Mexico and Central America. Before turning to these specific studies, however, we will briefly discuss the formation of some of the more standard text-based archives that will figure in these chapters. Stated in broad terms, this process reflects a gradual transition from the writing and collecting activities of amateur archaeologists and diplomats to an increasingly professionalized terrain of academics and Foreign Service personnel. This process of professionalization occurred in tandem with the expansion of US economic and political hegemony that we discussed in the second section.

Several collections associated with what we will refer to as "antiquarian organizations" embody the origins of interest in Mesoamerica among US intellectuals in the early nineteenth century, when studies of antiquities and colonial texts dovetailed with the continental imaginaries of the emergent republic. Institutions including the American Philosophical Society (APS) of Philadelphia and the American Antiquarian Society (AAS) of Worcester, Massachusetts, accumulated colonial-era texts, artifacts ranging from ceramics to sculpture, and contemporaneous descriptions of ancient sites. These antiquarian collections include some of the earliest internationally sourced documents relevant to the study of ancient Mesoamerica. The venerable APS, for instance, harbors correspondence between Anglo-American intellectuals and their Mexican and Central American contemporaries dating back to the late eighteenth century. This includes 1830s correspondence between P. S. Du Ponceau, pioneering French-American linguist and president of the APS, and various Guatemalan and Mexican interlocutors regarding Mayan philology. These exchanges between intellectual societies led to the APS's early acquisition of what are now extremely rare printed and manuscript materials such as the eighteenth-century *Gaceta de Guatemala* and the original text of Guillermo Dupaix's description of Maya ruins. Already, the connections between scholarship and political or economic expansion are evident. The Dupaix manuscript was donated to the APS in 1830 by US diplomat Joel Poinsett, a figure whose scholarly forays in Latin America have long been overshadowed by his controversial meddling in Mexican politics (Belohlavek 1985, 20–21, 215–20). In the age of national independence and Manifest Destiny, these collections offered a means of reconstructing the ancient history of civilization in the New World, a project as ideologically crucial to Anglo-American authors as it was to their contemporaries in former Spanish colonies (Keen 1971). It is no accident that Poinsett, pioneer gringo diplomat in Latin America and an assertive advocate of republican forms of government in the region, was also cofounder of the National Institute for the Promotion of Science and Useful Arts (NIPSUA). An antecedent of the Smithsonian, NIPSUA reflected the Jeffersonian dream of a United States-centric "empire of liberty," and its branches included "American History and Antiquities" (Rippy 1935, 211).

These close ties between the collection of Mesoamerican antiquities and US commercial and political expansion are reflected in the frequent mingling of scholarly and diplomatic pursuits evident in correspondence by elite US American interlopers in the Maya area. This activity is not at all surprising considering that Mayan peoples (and the material traces of their past) occupied some of the routes coveted by the US entrepreneurs hoping to establish a pathway between the Atlantic and Pacific Oceans, be this by road, railroad, or canal. The roots of US intervention in the isthmus have a clear connection to earlier diplomatic and commercial endeavors that were closely tied to the history of Mayanist archaeology. Often referred to as the "father" of Maya archaeology in the United States, John Lloyd Stephens represented his country as a diplomat in Central America when he and his illustrator Fredrick Catherwood composed their famous *Incidents of Travel* during 1839–43. By meticulous descriptions and Catherwood's illustrations, Stephens refuted claims by Europeans like Jean-Frédéric Maximilien de Waldeck that the builders of the abandoned cities in Central America and southern Mexico were connected to the Old World. Stephens advanced the idea that the ancient Maya city-states were part of a "native" tradition of civilization inherited by the United States after independence from Great Britain (Evans 2004, 37, 45). Stephens and his publisher (Harper and Brothers) correctly anticipated the US market for beautifully illustrated accounts of an ancient "American" civilization (Evans 2004, 49).

Stephens's commercial ambitions for Maya culture were not limited to publishing. He attempted to purchase Palenque and monuments from Copán, in large part to deny them to European buyers. As the Mexican philosopher Juan Ortega y Medina noted, the Monroe Doctrine had an archaeological corollary (Evans 2004, 55; Ortega y Medina [1953] 2015). In 1849, Stephens collaborated in the foundation of the Panama Railway Company, one of the first large-scale attempts to create a transisthmian passage. He was not the only early nineteenth-century antiquarian involved in these efforts. After the Mexican-American War and the Gold Rush made the United States a Pacific power and a transisthmian route a strategic necessity, the United States dispatched Ephraim George Squier to Central America. Squier was already an accomplished scholar, and his career reads like a roadmap of Manifest Destiny. He published on the "Mound People" of the Mississippi Valley before posting to Central America, where he continued his scholarship on the pre-Contact past of Indigenous people in the 1850s before moving on to Peru. Like many nineteenth-century scholars, he combined belief in Anglo-Saxon superiority with a love for the pre-Contact past of Indigenous peoples (Gobat 2018, 33).

Given the depth and breadth of United States intervention in the politics of Mexico and Central America, state-commissioned travelers such as Poinsett, Stephens, and Squier left relatively light footprints in the official state archives of their native country. The ad hoc nature of US American foreign policy through the nineteenth and early twentieth centuries (Belohlavek 1985) allowed US agents broad leeway in determining the scope of their mission. This is perhaps best exemplified by the pithy communiqué with which Stephens ended his attempt to establish relations with the soon-to-be defunct Central American Union in 1839: "After a diligent search, no government was found." Stephens then essentially abandoned his diplomatic mission and resumed archaeological studies (Stephens [1841] 1969, 127).

The archival trail left by US agents in Mexico and Central America becomes much easier to follow at the beginning of the twentieth century. At this time the United States began expanding and professionalizing diplomacy and intelligence gathering in the region because of the geopolitics of the Panama Canal Zone, the uncertainties brought about by the Mexican Revolution, and the build-up to World War I. This increased intervention enables scholars of the early twentieth century to draw on materials in the US State Department as well as military agencies like the Office of Naval Intelligence to chronicle the operations of US American spies such as the archaeologist Sylvanus Morley (Harris and Sadler 2003). From the early twentieth century onward, official US archives become an especially rich resource for understanding the larger political and economic dynamics that shaped growing US influence in the region.

As noted in "Dependency Theory and Maya Studies," historians such as Gilbert Joseph have drawn on the US State Department archives to better understand different techniques of US intervention in the late nineteenth and early twentieth centuries and the rationale that guided them. In a highly influential study, Joseph (1988) revealed how the United States sought to control Yucatecan henequen production from 1915 to 1922, when World War I reduced global supply and Mexico's new revolutionary regime sought to inflate prices and thus increase revenue. A reading of US State Department archives informed by new methodological and theoretical perspectives discloses how henequen policy focused more on commodity prices and US corporate consumers than its impact on poor Mayan workers on henequen plantations. They also reveal the racism of Yankee diplomats that informed US foreign policy toward parts of Mesoamerica with large Indigenous populations.[3]

Just as the closing of the nineteenth century saw a greater bureaucratization of US foreign policy, increasing financial autonomy and institutionalization profoundly changed museums. Although the process was uneven, what are now understood to be professional archaeological practices replaced the gentlemanly pursuits that had created antiquarian collections a century earlier. Rather than an assemblage of artifacts and texts gleaned through individual members' adventures and personal correspondence with Latin American interlocutors, collections associated with public museums and universities resulted from a longer, institutionally supported investment in research by full-time academics. By extension, the archives associated with these institutions tend to include detailed descriptions of sites as well as administrative documentation of expenses incurred by different projects. They continue to be consulted by archaeologists as a source of the "raw data" about the sites that generated well-known artifact collections and early canonical studies. Just as importantly for historians, these archives include detailed documentation of life, labor, and politics in the times and places where Anglo-American researchers worked. In particular, they can include substantial amounts of previously unpublished quasi-ethnographic data on the Indigenous communities on or near whose lands these scholars worked.

By the beginning of the twentieth century, similar archives were created by philanthropic institutions like the Carnegie Institution and the Rockefeller Foundation. Insofar as they organized large-scale and long-term research and kept detailed records of the process and results, there are intriguing parallels to museum archives. However, these foundations were not built around museums, and their projects did not generally include the kind of collection efforts that characterized the Peabody at Harvard or the American Museum of Natural History (AMNH) in New York. How this shift changed the work of Anglo-American anthropologists is evident in a feud between the CIW and several museums in the 1920s. Representatives of the AMNH accused Sylvanus Morley, then directing the CIW project at Chichén Itzá, of using the fact that the institute had no intention of removing artifacts from Mexico to drive a wedge between the postrevolutionary government and the more established museums. Morley's superiors pressured him to avoid creating conflicts with his US American colleagues, but the "new" way of working with the governments of Mexico and Central America would essentially transform the transnational dynamics of archaeological work in the twentieth century.[4]

Besides altering the relationship between US researchers and national governments in ways that would shape modern archaeology, the Rockefeller and Ford Foundations would also come to play the kind of ancillary function to US diplomacy that Cold War–era political scientists generally referred to as "soft power" (see Berman 1983). To the extent that they figure in the exercise of US cultural and political hegemony over Latin America, the context and content of these foundation archives often dovetail with the information that can be gleaned from the archives of early transnational corporations such as the United Fruit

Company or International Harvester. In many cases—and particularly in the case of UFCO—these corporations facilitated the work of North American archaeologists and anthropologists, from providing introductions to key political figures to transport to crucial logistical support. At the same time that these corporations enabled international research on the past of the Maya area, they were profoundly remaking the economies of the region during the nineteenth and early twentieth centuries. This involvement makes documents regarding their in-country operations invaluable for historical researchers.

The UFCO, like Massachusetts-based Peabody cordage brokers, eagerly supported the CIW's work. Even before the start of major projects at Chichén Itzá and other sites, UFCO employees, such as the physician Moise Lafleur, often accompanied archaeologists into the field. As Carnegie established a stronger foothold in the region, UFCO contributions to archaeology involved the expenditure of even more financial and political capital. In 1934, for example, United Fruit intervened to obtain permission for the CIW to transport Anglophone Afro-Caribbean laborers to replace natives of the Guatemalan Petén (whom CIW archaeologist Alfred Kidder considered "drunk and lazy") at the excavation of Uaxactún. This essentially reproduced the pattern of labor importation that UFCO had used in its commercial agricultural ventures. It also gave the CIW an exemption to strict Guatemalan labor law.[5]

In other cases, United Fruit played a more direct role in defining archaeological research agendas. UFCO's controversial president Sam Zemurray funded self-taught archaeologist and CIA agent John M. Dimick's restoration of the archaeological site of Zaculeu. The accompanying academic study was published by UFCO's Middle American Information Bureau. Dimick praised UFCO's "public service" and saluted Zaculeu as restoring to the Mayan people of Guatemala their past—and making a highland Maya site finally reachable by US tourists (United Fruit Company 1947, 1). The close, continuing relationship between United Fruit and the CIW is evident in Dimick's hiring of Kidder to serve as a consultant on the Zacaleu project (United Fruit Company 1947, 32; Price 2016, 228).

This project seeks to show how such previously hidden ties between UFCO and other powerful US-based corporations allowed Yankee scholars to play such an important role in the first decades of the professional Mayanist studies. We also hope to highlight how the asymmetries in resources that divide US American scholars from our Mexican and Guatemalan colleagues still exist—albeit in different forms. It is worth noting that this volume came together during the height of the COVID-19 pandemic, at a time when many of our colleagues and we were asking questions about the long-term resilience of projects that required international travel to in-person research sites. Not only were many of these institutions located in our own "neighborhood" of the northeastern states, but US institutions are also far more likely to have large numbers of primary documents available in digitized form than their Latin American peers. These differences heightened our awareness of inequalities in access to basic material between scholars in the Global North and South.

Digitalization projects notwithstanding, many of these US archives contain extensive material that can only be utilized in person. While US scholars have privileged access to external grants and in-house funding that allows them to travel abroad, Mexican and Guatemalan researchers often face daunting financial and bureaucratic obstacles in accessing US resources. At the time of writing, Mexican scholars wishing to visit the US must wait a year for an interview to get a visa. Even the scanning of primary sources has not equalized access. For instance, genealogical information from Mexican civil and baptismal registries and US immigration records are behind paywalls. US Americans can access US census information gratis on the US National Archives website and via many public libraries; Mexicans have to pay to access some 220 million Mexican documents—many of which are not accessible otherwise.[6] Perhaps the crowning irony involves the out-of-print volumes that were published in very small editions in Central America and Mexico and that are accessible to most scholars in the United States through the interlibrary loan but impossible to obtain in their countries of publication.

Aside from offering reasons for reflecting on the deep and complex relationship between gringo scholars, Mayan peoples, and the Hispanic populations of Mexico and Central America, these US-based archives present an ethical challenge for Mayanists who live and work in this country. Working to make these materials accessible to broader international publics would improve the long and often fraught relationships that have shaped the careers of generations of US-based Mayanists. In telling some of the stories that can be found in those archives, the essays in this volume take the first step in making them accessible. Working toward broader shifts in how research is funded and how global access to primary sources can be more equitable needs to be part of a much longer collective project.

EIGHT ESSAYS ON THE TRANSNATIONAL HISTORY
OF GRINGOS AND MAYAN PEOPLES

This introduction along with several of the essays in this volume frequently refer to "Mayanness" as a series of discourses and identities that emerged through transcultural encounters that often involve US-based researchers, capitalists, and tourists. This term refers to the fact that different cultural phenomena attributed to peoples in Mexico and Central America are not necessarily the product of centuries-long "Indigenous" development but often reflect the ideologies of national elites and foreigners who sought to legitimate various economic and political projects in the region. Still, as we observed earlier, it would be wrong to assume that nonelite Maya speakers were simply passive recipients of this process of interpolation. In this regard, the diverse forms of Mayanness that appear in our chapters reflect the different social, political, and economic dynamics that presided over key contact zones at different moments in the history of Mexico and Central America.

It is to this point that we as editors have resisted imposing a strict lexicon of terms for different ethnic or social categories on the contributing authors. Outside of some very broad parameters, the use of terms such as "Mayan," "Indigenous," *indígena*, and "gringo" in each chapter will reflect different disciplinary practices as well local and microregional realities that might be distinct to that particular case study. The latter reflects a long-standing reality of Mesoamerican studies, in which the very diversity of regional cultures and social structures belies neat reductions. For example, the dichotomy between "Indigenous" and "Ladino" that holds for much of the highlands of Guatemala and Chiapas, and that has contributed to a vast literature on "ladinoization," is difficult to reconcile with the ethnic categories of the Yucatán peninsula and other parts of the Maya lowlands. Likewise, the term "gringo," which tends to be associated with citizens of the United States, often refers to a much broader category of non-Hispanic foreigners, which will become evident in some of the substantive chapters of this study.

A third dimension of this local or microregional diversity involves a category of actors that we can refer to broadly as "Hispanic mediators." By this term we refer to persons native to Mexico and the Central American countries and are identified as members of the dominant Hispanic culture, that serve as indispensable (and often invisible) intermediaries between foreign scientists, tourists and investors, and local Indigenous communities. This relationship has a long role in the history of Mayanist research, particularly in the Yucatán peninsula. There, regional elites had turned to the archaeological and linguistic heritage of the peninsula as a source of regional identity since at least the 1840s. These native philologists and antiquaries were indispensable for European and North American travelers who had limited knowledge of the region's geography, to say nothing of the then little-studied languages (see Von Hagen 1947; Armstrong-Fumero 2018; chapters 2 through 5 in this volume).

In contrast to their Yucatecan contemporaries, who had turned to Indigenous heritage as a source of regional identity since at least the 1840s, the white landowning elite of Chiapas and highland Guatemala showed little early interest in the formal study of Maya culture. The fact that numerous Maya languages are spoken in Chiapas and Guatemala, while only one—Yukatek Maya—is spoken in the Mexican states of Campeche and Quintana Roo as well as Yucatán helps us understand these regional differences. Mérida's relative size and prosperity compared to San Cristóbal, and the city of Guatemala likely play a role as well. By the beginning of the twentieth century, there were some important exceptions, such as the chiapaneca Rosario Castellanos, whose novels were immersed in Maya folkways and language. A more internationally prominent figure was Adrián Recinos, the Guatemalan diplomat and philologist whose translations of texts in K'iche' and Kaqchikel were the standard reference for US scholars for decades.

Although the role of these Hispanic intermediaries is often downplayed in the writing of "classic" Anglo-American authors, many of the most famous early works in Mayanist anthropology would have been impossible without their "native" expertise in Indigenous languages. One such mediator, Alfonso Villa Rojas, will figure in three chapters of this book. Born in Mérida in 1897, Villa Rojas was working as the federal schoolteacher in the community of Chan Kom when he made the acquaintance of US scholars affiliated with the CIW project at Chichén Itzá. Despite that CIW scholars had conducted some early anthropological studies and tended to christen pre-Hispanic sites with names in highly simplified Yukatek Maya, none had more than a rudimentary knowledge of the language. This turned Villa Rojas, a more-or-less native speaker, into an indispensable resource for Carnegie ethnographers such as Robert Redfield. Villa Rojas built on these collaborations by studying anthropology at the University of Chicago thanks to his CIW patrons before returning to Mexico. After rising to a high rank in the Mexican bureaucratic agency known as the Instituto Nacional Indigenista (National Indigenist Institute), Villa Rojas played a prominent role in anthropological research in the state of Chiapas and in the work of academic institutions in Mexico City. Between the 1940s and 1960s, he continued to be a very valuable contact for US researchers hoping to work in Mexico, even as the agendas of state-sponsored research in Mexico increasingly diverged from that of many international scholars.

Focusing encounters between a gringo patron of early Mayanist studies in Yucatán and elite Hispanic intermediaries in the 1860s and 1870s, chapter 2, by Julio Hoil Gutiérrez, opens this volume with some of the historical precursors of the transnational relationships that brought Villa Rojas into the CIW orbit two generations later. Hoil focuses on the little-studied figure of Stephen Salisbury III, scion of a family of Massachusetts business magnates and longtime director of the Worcester-based AAS. After hiring a stand-in recruit to escape conscription into the Union Army during the Civil War, Salisbury embarked on an extended trip through Yucatán, where he socialized extensively with members of the Hispanic planter elite, particularly the influential Casares family. His letters home and diaries not only document a poorly understood period in the history of Mayanist archaeology but also provide an especially rich and intimate portrait of the affective bonds between members of two very different elites. As Hoil points out, this challenges the emphasis on armed conflict and nationalistic tensions that marks the historiography of US-Mexico relations in the mid-nineteenth century. It also highlights the early role of interelite friendships and cultural diplomacy in the development of transnational Mayanist studies.

Salisbury's interactions with Casares and other members of the Yucatecan Hispanic elite helped generate a series of social networks that expanded to another stalwart Massachusetts institution, the Peabody Museum of Harvard University. By the 1920s, early graduates of Harvard's program in anthropology contributed to the development of the Carnegie Institution of Washington project at Chichén Itzá, which would be a laboratory and training ground for a generation of Mayanist anthropologists. In chapter 3, Armstrong-Fumero examines the private writings of two key figures of the Carnegie era, Sylvanus Morley and Robert Redfield, emphasizing how each characterized their own role as a gringo researcher in Mexico. Morley was at once jovial and gregarious when interacting with Mexicans and deeply racist. He genuinely enjoyed socializing with and entertaining his elite Yucatecan interlocutors, even as his commentary to fellow Harvard Men betrayed imperialist attitudes inherited from Rooseveltian expansionism. Redfield's writing is rife with expressions of elitism, though his reserve toward many of his Yucatecan interlocutors was matched by constant doubts about his ability to "fit in" with older scholars who were wedded to more traditionally colonial research. His isolation was compounded by a lack of spoken ability in Yukatek Maya, which made him dependent on the aid of Alfonso Villa Rojas and a small group of bilingual Mayan people. As Armstrong-Fumero argues, the attitudes towards "native" research subjects and gringo peers that emerge in the writings of Morley and Redfield embody a series of intellectual and ethical problematics that still occurs in the training and careers of US-based Mayanists.

One of the pervasive concerns of Sylvanus Morley and the early Carnegie archaeologists was to maintain positive professional and social relationships with Mexican intellectuals and politicians who permitted and supported their operations in the field. In chapter 4, "American Idols," Ben Fallaw picks up on the story of the "Carnegie Era" from the perspective of Yucatecan politics, specifically during the gubernatorial term of Bartolomé García Correa (1930–34). An inheritor of Felipe Carrillo Puerto's populist legacy, García Correa contributed to the incorporation of Yucatán's radical socialist party into the predecessors of the long-ruling "official" party known as the Partido Revolucionario Institucional (PRI), even as he faced opposition from regional political elites who derided his purported Indigenous and African heritage. At the same time, the governor's association with Mayan heritage often became a point of reference in his interactions with CIW archaeologists and their collaborators, just as the narrative of Maya civilization that emerged from the US American project at Chichén Itzá suited his propagandistic ends. García Correa's interaction with the industrial and cultural elites of New York and the West Coast offers us a glimpse into the kind of informal diplomacy facilitated by the nexus between the CIW and the state government of Yucatán. These were, in essence, mid-twentieth-century iterations of the kinds of cultural diplomacy practiced by Stephen Salisbury III, and that would continue to evolve in the following decades. After the Mexican Revolution, gringos had to rely more on Mexican political and intellectual elites and less on members of the old Hispanic Yucatecan upper class as mediators.

This dynamic resulted in part from the growth of the modern bureaucratic apparatus that managed archaeology, cultural policy, and Indigenous education in Mexico after the revolution (1910–20). Matthew Watson's contribution to this volume, chapter 5, covers most of the Mexican ruling party's so-called Golden Age (1940–68). This chapter shifts geographic focus from Yucatán to the highlands of Chiapas to examine a crucial turning point in the complex relationship between Anglo-American Mayanists and their Mexican peers. In 1957, Harvard's Evon Z. Vogt Jr. launched the decades-long Harvard Chiapas Project in collaboration with representatives of Mexico's Instituto Nacional Indigenista (National Indigenist Institute; INI), which had founded a series of research and educational projects meant to incorporate Indigenous Chiapanecs into Mexico's "national" Hispanic culture. Watson demonstrates how Vogt sought to reconcile his own research project with the developmentalist ends of the INI. As the Harvard Chiapas Project evolved over its first decade of operation, Vogt's pivot from the explicit study of culture change to "basic research" on cultural and economic life essentially reduced the INI's intervention into a variable in a descriptive study of a living Mayan peoples. As Watson argues, this emphasis essentially naturalizes the modernizing role of the Mexican state while maintaining the image of neutral observation and documentation that Vogt sought for his ethnographic project.

Our next two chapters, by two pairs of contributors, share three important themes: recovering Mayan bodies, analyzing the materiality and physicality of Mayan labor, and "fixing" labor by binding Mayan workers into transnational networks centered on sugar and medical knowledge. In "Distilling the Past through the Present," chapter 6, Jennifer P. Mathews and John R. Gust show how archaeology can shed light on Xuxub and San Eusebio. These were two sugar plantations on Yucatán's north coast during the heyday of nineteenth-century liberalism. Matthews and Gust's innovative approach also draws on an "archive" in the form of the knowledge and practices of twenty-first-century artisanal distillers in the United States that have revived nineteenth-century-distilling technology. Although the two estates produced sugar for Mexico's domestic market, these agroindustrial centers depended on imported distilling technology and a host of other products from the United States that were sold to Indigenous workers to create debt. US credit, technology, and manufactured goods were an integral part of the plantation society that subordinated Maya workers.

A roughly analogous racialized hierarchy is analyzed in "*Indígenas* and International Influences of Modern Medicine in Twentieth-Century Guatemala," chapter 7. David Carey, Jr., and Lydia Crafts read US-based archives from an anthropologically informed perspective to show how pharmaceutical and biomedical research hinged both on close collaboration with Guatemalan non-Indigenous medical specialists and on control over Indigenous bodies. Both chapters 6 and 7 reveal a variety of forms of resistance by Maya people. In Guatemala, curanderos, *comadronas* (midwives), bonesetters, and other practitioners of traditional medicine fought back against attempts to criminalize nonbiomedical practice. On Yucatán's Caribbean littoral, Mathews and Gust suggest, the absence of physical remains of housing might well indicate Mayan workers' preferences to avoid accepting permanent peonage on sugar-producing estates in spite of attempts to ensnare them in debt through the sale of goods—many of them imported—in the tienda de raya (see also Gust and Mathews 2020).

Carey and Crafts reveal how Hispanic elites could invoke science from the Global North to legitimize their claims over Indigenous bodies. During the Porfiriato in Yucatán, medical treatises authored by elite Yucatecans on the malnutrition and disease associated with the spread of henequen in the late nineteenth and early twentieth-century yield insight into how then-contemporary science legitimized the dehumanizing treatment of Mayan peons. Rather than consider how hacendados' restrictions on the right to plant diversified milpas, hunt, and forest-garden caused poverty and illness among the Mayan workers residing on henequen estates, elite Yucatecan biomedical practitioners invoked a concept from scientific racism and social Darwinism to blame "racial decay." Their solution was to construct a modern hospital—ironically the location of the state archives of Yucatán today—to nurse Mayan patients back to physical and mental health to return to the henequen fields (García Quintanilla and Millet Cámara 1992, 56–59, 61–62). Tellingly, the discourse of science reduced the Maya body to just a pair of laboring hands (García Quintanilla and Millet Cámara 55–59).

No discussion of the history of transnational exchanges of capital, resources, and culture between the United States and Maya area would be complete without a discussion of tourism. In Mexico, tourism emerged as a core economic activity in the last third of the twentieth century, displacing increasingly marginal forms of agricultural exports and import-substitution industries. Cultural tourism gained importance in Guatemala in the decades since the formal end of the Civil War in 1996. Today, this multi-billion-dollar industry accounts for one of the greatest infusions of export dollars into the economies of Mexico and Central America, even as US and native capitalists often compete for control of particularly lucrative sites and routes. As chapters by M. Bianet Castellanos and Matilde Córdoba Azcárate show, this new industry is also contributing to emergent archives that document the latest phases of this centuries-old national exchange.

Focusing on the guidebooks of Cancún and the Mexican Caribbean geared toward foreign tourists, Castellanos, in chapter 8, notes how nonacademic representations of the regional landscape appeal to the expectations of US audiences by representing vast expanses of populated space as if they were "empty" of anything but isolated ruins and beach attractions. Echoing the classic settler colonialist trope of terra nullius, these pictorial representations essentially erase the contemporary Indigenous presence and the nineteenth-century legacy of armed Maya resistance to represent a region ripe for "discovery" by white adventurers. Castellanos contrasts these "classic" touristic representations with those associated with more contemporary representations of community-driven, sustainable tourism. As she argues, while hierarchies of power remain in the practice and representation of tourism, changing consumer expectations and local practices can work to transform older paradigms that rely more heavily on classic settler colonial tropes.

In chapter 9, our last contribution, Córdoba Azcárate explores new forms of knowledge production about Mayan peoples in the very recent history of inland tourism. She adopts an innovative methodology that blends ethnography with a close reading of gray literature generated by tourism industries and research into "archives" of information defined in a less conventional manner. This last category embraces the internet and specialized knowledge created and exchanged among a transnational community of cultural promoters, employees of large corporations, and politically connected entrepreneurs. Members of this community represent themselves as experts on Maya history and culture and are attuned to the high-end market for wellness and leisure branded as "Maya." This chapter reads the "novel popular archives" created by this community, analyzing how they commodify and contribute to the (conventionally defined) archives and other sources of information consulted by scholars of the Maya Area. By examining the selective restoration of two well-known tourist haciendas, Córdoba Azcárate closely examines how Mayanness created for consumption by the affluent tourist is shaped by transnational capital and private-public collaborations that are at once neoliberal and nepotistic. This chapter poses an important question for the future of Mayanist studies: How will we study representations of the idea of "The Maya" when "tourism entrepreneurs and stakeholders, urban planners, designers and architects, and bankers and global corporations in the hospitality industry" (chapter 9) define Mayanness?

Taken together, our contributors suggest how a range of new methodologies and theoretical approaches can be applied to a variety of public and private archives based in the US, as well as to unconventional para-archives involving actors in the Global North, to productively expand Mayanist studies. Before participating in this volume, most of our authors never would have considered that artisanal distilleries and for-profit online genealogical services can open new vistas on the Maya past. Insofar as the experience of generations of Mayan peoples have been shaped by direct or indirect contacts with US capital, research, and diplomacy, many important facets of the modern history of Maya people are to be found north of the Rio Grande / Río Bravo. Making these sources familiar and accessible to a large international community of scholars is, we believe, one of the most pressing tasks for the future of Maya studies. It is our hope that the various methodological, conceptual, and theoretical explorations in the chapters that follow will offer some productive avenues for this larger project.

NOTES

1. We gratefully acknowledge David Carey Jr. for pointing this out.

2. See, e.g., the use of the K'iche' term *vuj* to refer to hieroglyphic manuscripts in colonial Yucatán in Mignolo's *Darker Side of the Renaissance* (1995). Mignolo also seems not to recognize the very significant phonetic content of lowland Maya hieroglyphic traditions as he generalizes the logographic or ideographic nature of Mesoamerican writing systems (70–77).

3. See, for instance, February 15, 1928, Consul Fayette J. Flexer, "Political Summary for the State of Tabasco for the Year 1927," Records of the Department of State Internal Affairs of Mexico 1910–29, roll 96 as discussed in Fallaw's chapter 4 in this volume. In a similar vein, Kim shows how US-Mexican relations on the border were molded by a dialogue between US and Mexican elites about the assumed inadequacies of people of Indigenous descent by drawing on US-based archives (2019, 49–56).

4. CIW Archives AV Kidder Corr. NB VI and VII, 1928 and 1932. A general description of this approach is detailed in a memo prepared for Merriam, possibly by Kidder on 13 April 1932. A letter, also from Kidder to Merriam, details frustration regarding Morley's "crowing" about the CIW's uniquely philanthropic relationship to the Mexican government, and is dated February 9, 1928.

5. July 10, 34, Kidder to Merriam, AV Kidder Corr, 1934–35 NB VII March 13, 2012.

6. See the census records website: https://www.archives.gov/files/research/census/#:~:text=Ancestry.com%20is%20available%20free,libraries%2C%20otherwise%20by%20subscription.&text=Visit%20State%20Archives%20or%20State,of%20the%20microfilm

%20from%20us; https://www.ancestry.com/corporate/blog/ancestry-mexico-launches-with
-more-than-220-million-searchable-mexican-historical-records.

REFERENCES CITED

Anzaldúa, Gloria. 1987. *Borderlands / La Frontera*. Berkeley: Aunt Lute Books.

Arias, Arturo. 2018. *Recovering Lost Footprints*. Vols. 1 and 2. Albany: SUNY Press.

Armstrong-Fumero, Fernando. 2018. "Hacienda Domesticity and the Archaeological Sublime: Sentiment and the Origins of Heritage Management in Yucatán, Mexico." *Archaeologies: Journal of the World Archaeology Congress* 14 (1): 115–41.

Baños Ramírez, Othon. 1996. *Neoliberalismo, reorganización y subsistencia rural: El caso de la zona henequenera de Yucatán: 1980–1992*. Mérida: Universidad Autónoma de Yucatán.

Bayly, C. A., Sven Beckert, Matthew Connelly, Isabel Hofmeyr, Wendy Kozol, and Patricia Seed. 2006. "AHR Conversation: On Transnational History." *American Historical Review* 111 (5): 1441–64.

Bell, Andrew. 2018. "'100% American': The Politics and Culture of Maya Archaeology in the World War I Era." Society for Historians of American Foreign Relations Annual Meeting, Philadelphia, June 21–23.

Belohlavek, John M. 1985. *Let The Eagle Soar!: The Foreign Policy of Andrew Jackson*. Lincoln: University of Nebraska Press.

Bender, Thomas. 2006. *A Nation among Nations: America's Place in World History*. New York: Hill and Wang.

Berman, Edward. 1983. *The Ideology of Philanthropy: The Influence of the Carnegie, Ford and Rockefeller Foundations on American Foreign Policy*. Albany: State University of New York Press.

Borofsky, Robert. 1997. "Cook, Lono, Obeyesekere, and Sahlins." *Current Anthropology* 38 (2): 255–82.

Bourgois, Philippe. 1989. *Ethnicity at Work: Divided Labor on a Central American Banana Plantation*. Baltimore: Johns Hopkins University Press.

Brannon, Jeffrey. 1991. "Conclusion: Yucatecan Political Economy in Broader Perspective." In *Land, Labor, and Capital in Modern Yucatán: Essays in Regional History and Political Economy*, edited by Jeffrey Brannon and Gilbert Joseph, 1–9. Tuscaloosa: University of Alabama.

Brickhouse, Anna. 2004. *Transnational Literary Relations and the Nineteenth-Century Public Sphere*. Cambridge: Cambridge University Press.

Burns, Allan. 1993. *Maya in Exile: Guatemalans in Florida*. Philadelphia: Temple University Press.

Cardoso, Ciro. 1991. "The Liberal, Era, c. 1870–1930." In *Central America since Independence*, edited by Leslie Bethel, 37–67. New York: Cambridge University Press.

Cardoso, Fernando Henrique, Enzo Faletto, and Marjory Mattingly Urquidi. 1979. *Dependency and Development in Latin America*. Berkeley: University of California Press.

Carnegie Institution for Science. Various dates. Historical Archive, Chevy Chase, MD.

Castañeda, Quetzal. 1996. *The Museum of Maya Culture*. Minneapolis: University of Minnesota Press.

Castillo Cocom, Juan A. 2004. "Lost in Mayaland." In Special issue, "The Maya Identity of Yucatán, 1500–1935," edited by Q. E. Castañeda and Ben Fallaw. *Journal of Latin American Anthropology* 9 (1): 179–86.

Chacón, Gloria Elizabeth. 2018. *Indigenous Cosmolectics: Kab'awil and the Making of Maya and Zapotec Literatures*. Chapel Hill: University of North Carolina Press.

Colby, Jason M. 2011. *The Business of Empire: United Fruit, Race and US Expansion in Central America*. Ithaca, NY: Cornell University Press.

Collier, George, and Elizabeth Quateriello. 2005. *Land and the Zapatista Rebellion in Chiapas*. 3rd ed. Oakland, CA: Food First Books.

Cronon, William. 1992. *Nature's Metropolis: Chicago and the Great West*. New York: W. W. Norton.

Danien, Elin. 1999. "Robert Burkitt and George Byron Gordon: An End and a Beginning." In *Assembling the Past: Studies in the Professionalization of Archaeology*, edited by Alice B. Kehoe and Mary Beth Emmerichs. Albuquerque: University of New Mexico Press.

Dosal, Paul. 1993. *Doing Business with Dictators: A Political History of United Fruit in Guatemala, 1899–1944*. Wilmington, DE: Scholarly Resources.

Dumond, Don. 1997. *The Machete and the Cross: Campesino Rebellion in Yucatan*. Lincoln: University of Nebraska Press.

Dunkerley, James. 1991. "Guatemala since 1930." In *Central America since Independence*, edited by Leslie Bethell, 119–57. New York: Cambridge University Press.

Esquit Choy, Edgar. 2002. *Otros poderes, nuevos desafíos: Relaciones interétnicas en Tecpán y su entorno departamental, 1871–1935*. Guatemala, CA: Instituto de Estudios Interétnicos.

Esquit Choy, Edgar. 2010. *La superación del indígena: La política de la modernización entre las élites indígenas de Comalapa, siglo XX*. Guatemala City: Instituto de Estudios Interétnicos, Universidad de San Carlos de Guatemala.

Evans, R. Tripp. 2004. *Romancing the Maya: Mexican Antiquity in the American Imagination, 1820–1915*. Austin: University of Texas Press.

Fink, Leon. 2003. *The Maya of Morganton: Work and Community in the Nuevo New South*. Chapel Hill: University of North Carolina Press.

Fischer, Edward, and Carol Hendrickson. 2001. *Tecpan Guatemala: A Modern Maya Town in Global and Local Context*. New York: Routledge.

Galemba, Rebecca. 2018. *Contraband Corridor: Making a Living at the Mexico-Guatemala Border*. Stanford, CA: Stanford University Press.

García Quintanilla, Alejandra, and Luis Millet Cámara. 1992. "Milpa y henequén, salud y enfermedad en la hacienda henequenera a finales del siglo XIX." In *La modernización de la nueva milpa en Yucatán: Utopía o realidad*, edited by Daniel Zizumbo Villareal Daniel Zizumbo Villareal, Christian Rasmussen, Luis Manuel Arias Reyes, and Silvia Terán Contreras, 53–63. Mérida: CICY/DANIDA.

Gobat, Michel. 2018. *Empire by Invitation: William Walker and Manifest Destiny in Central America*. Cambridge, MA: Harvard University Press.

Goldkind, Victor, 1965. "Social Stratification in the Peasant Community: Redfield's Chan Kom Revisited." *Social American Anthropologist* 67 (4): 863–84.

Graham, Ian. 2002. *Alfred Maudslay and the Maya: A Biography*. Norman: University of Oklahoma.

Grandin, Greg. 2000. *The Blood of Guatemala: A History of Race and Nation*. Durham, NC: Duke University Press.

Gunder-Frank, Andre. 1967. *Capitalism and Underdevelopment in Latin America: Historical Studies of Chile and Brazil*. New York: Monthly Review Press.

Gust, John, and Jennifer Mathews. 2020. *Sugar Cane and Rum: The Bittersweet History of Labor and Life on the Yucatan Peninsula*. Tucson: University of Arizona Press.

Harris, Charles, and Louis Sadler. 2003. *The Archaeologist Was a Spy: Sylvanus G. Morley and Office of Naval Intelligence*. Albuquerque: University of New Mexico Press.

Joseph, Gilbert. 1988. *Revolution from Without: Yucatán, Mexico, and the United States, 1880–1924*. 2nd ed. Durham, NC: Duke University Press.

Joseph, Gilbert, Catherine Legrand, and Ricardo Salvatore, eds. 1998. *Close Encounters of Empire: Writing the Cultural History of US-Latin American Relations*. Durham, NC: Duke University Press.

Keen, Benjamin. 1971 *The Aztec Image in Western Thought*. New Brunswick, NJ: Rutgers University Press.

Kim, Jessica. 2019. *Imperial Metropolis: Los Angeles, Mexico, and the Borderlands of American Empire, 1865–1941*. Chapel Hill: University of North Carolina Press.

Lewerth, Catherine. 1949. "Source Book for a History of the Rockefeller Foundation." Unpublished manuscript. 21 vols.

Lewis, Stephen. 2005. *The Ambivalent Revolution: Forging State and Nation in Chiapas, 1910–1945*. Albuquerque: University of New Mexico Press.

Lothrop, S. K. 1957 "Alfred Marston Tozzer, 1876–1954." *American Anthropologist* 57 (3): 614–18.

Marcus, George, and James Clifford, eds. 1987. *Writing Culture: The Politics and Poetics of Ethnography*. Berkeley: University of California Press.

Mathews, Jennifer, with Gillian P. Schultz. 2009. *Chicle: The Chewing Gum of the Americas. From the Ancient Maya to William Wrigley*. Tucson: University of Arizona Press.

McVicker, Mary. 2005. *Adela Breton: A Victorian Artist Amid Mexico's Ruins*. Albuquerque: University of New Mexico Press.

Menchú, Rigoberta. 2010. *I, Rigoberta Menchú: An Indian Woman in Guatemala*. London: Verso Books.

Mignolo, Walter. 1995 *The Darker Side of the Renaissance: Literacy, Territoriality and Colonization*. Ann Arbor: University of Michigan Press.

Montejo, Victor 2005. *Maya Intellectual Renaissance*. Austin: University of Texas Press.

Nash, June. 2001. *Maya Visions: The Quest for Autonomy in an Age of Globalization*. New York: Routledge.

Nolan-Ferrell, Catherine. 2012. *Constructing Citizenship: Transnational Workers and Revolution on the Mexico-Guatemala Border, 1880–1950*. Tucson: University of Arizona Press.

Ortega y Medina, Juan. (1953) 2015. "Monroísmo arqueológico: Un intento de compensación de americanidad insuficiente." In *Obras de Juan A. Ortega y Medina*, 3. Literatura viajera. Ed. María Cristina González Ortiz y Alicia Mayer. Mexico City: UNAM.

Ortiz Yam, Inés. 2013 *De milperos a henequeneros en Yucatán, 1870–1930*. Mexico City: El Colegio de México.

Otzoy, Irma 2008. "Indigenous Law and Gender Dialogues." In *Human Rights in the Maya Region*, edited by Pedro Pitarch, Shannon Speed, and Xochitl Leyva, 171–86. Durham, NC: Duke University Press.

Phillips, Philip. 1955. "Alfred Marston Tozzer, 1876–1954." *American Antiquity* 71 (1): 72–80.

Pratt, Mary Louise. 1992. *Imperial Eyes: Travel Writing and Transculturation*. New York: Routledge.

Price, David. 2016. *Cold War Anthropology: The CIA, the Pentagon, and the Growth of Dual Use Anthropology*. Durham, NC: Duke University Press, 2016.

Redclift, Michael, 2004. *Chewing Gum: The Fortunes of Taste*. New York: Routledge.

Restall, Matthew 2003. "A History of the New Philology and the New Philology in History." *LARR* 38 (1): 113–34.

Rippy, J. Fred. 1935. *Joel R. Poinsett: Versatile America*. Durham, NC: Duke University Press.

Roazen-Parrillo, Diane, and Fred V Carstensen. 1983. "International Harvester, Molina y Compania, and the Henequen Market: A Comment." *Latin American Research Review* 18 (3): 197–203. http://www.jstor.org/stable/2503030.

Roseberry, William. 1993. "Beyond the Agrarian Question in Latin America." In *Confronting Historical Paradigms: Peasants, Labor, and the Capitalist World System in Africa and Latin*

America, by Frederick Cooper, Florencia E. Mallon, Steve J. Stern, Allen F. Isaacman, and William Roseberry, 318–36. Madison: University of Wisconsin Press.

Roseberry, William. 1998. "Social Fields and Cultural Encounters." In *Close Encounters of Empire: Writing the Cultural History of US-Latin American Relations*, edited by Frederick Cooper and Allen F. Isaacman, 515–24. Durham, NC: Duke University Press.

Rugeley, Terry. 2009. *Rebellion Now and Forever: Mayas, Hispanics, and Caste War Violence in Yucatán, 1800–1880*. Stanford, CA: Stanford University Press.

Rus, Jan 1994. "The 'Comunidad Revolucionaria Institucional': The Subversion of Native Government in Highland Chiapas, 1936–1968." In *Everyday Forms of State Formation*, edited by Gilbert Joseph and Daniel Nugent, 265–300. Durham, NC: Duke University Press.

David Russo. 2006. *American History from a Global Perspective*. Westport, CT: Praeger.

Salvucci, Richard J. 1996a. "Introduction." In *Latin America and the World Economy: Dependency and Beyond*, edited by Richard Salvucci, xiii–xiv. Lexington, MA: D. C. Heath.

Salvucci, Richard J. 1996b. "Core and Periphery? Colonial Beginnings." *Latin America and the World Economy: Dependency and Beyond*, edited by Richard Salvucci. Lexington, MA: D. C. Heath.

Schwartz, Norman. 1990. *Forest Society: A Social History of Peten, Guatemala*. Philadelphia: University of Pennsylvania Press.

Silva Gruesz, Kirsten. 2002. *Ambassadors of Culture: The Transamerican Origins of Latino Writing*. Princeton, NJ: Princeton University Press.

Sledge, John S., ed. 2019. *The Gulf of Mexico: A Maritime History*. Columbia: University of South Carolina Press.

Stephens, John Lloyd. (1841) 1969. *Incidents of Travel in Central America, Chiapas and Yucatán*. Vol. 2. New York: Dover.

Sullivan, Paul. 1991. *Unfinished Conversations: Mayas and Foreigners between Two Wars*. Berkeley: University of California Press.

Todorov, Tzvetan. 1999. *The Conquest of America: The Question of the Other*. Oxford: Oxford University Press.

Topik, Steven, Carlos Marichal, and Zephyr L. Frank. 2006. "Introduction." In *From Silver to Cocaine: Latin American Commodity Chains and the Building of the World Economy, 1500–2000*. Durham, NC: Duke University Press.

Tozzer, Alfred. 1907. *A Comparative Study of the Mayas and the Lacandones*. New York: Archaeological Institute of America by MacMillan.

United Fruit Company. 1947. *Zaculeu: Restoration by United Fruit Company*. New York: Middle American Information Bureau.

Vaughan, Mary Kay. 2014. *Portrait of a Young Painter: Pepe Zúñiga and Mexico City's Rebel Generation*. Durham, NC: Duke University Press.

Von Hagen, V. 1947. *Maya Explorer: John Lloyd Stephens and the Lost Cities of Central America and Yucatan*. Norman: University of Oklahoma.

Wallerstein, Immanuel. 1979. *The Capitalist World Economy*. New York: Cambridge University Press.

Washbrook, Sarah. 2012. *Producing Modernity in Mexico: Labour, Race, and the State in Chiapas, 1876–1914*. Oxford: Oxford University Press.

Wells, Allen. 1985. *Yucatán's Gilded Age: Haciendas, Henequen, and International Harvester, 1860–1915*. Albuquerque: University of New Mexico.

Wells, Allen. 1998. "Henequen." In *The Second Conquest of Latin America: Coffee, Henequen and Oil during the Export Boom, 1850–1930*, edited by Steven C. Topik and Allen Wells, 85–201. Austin: University of Texas Press.

Wolf, Eric. 1957. "Closed Corporate Peasant Communities in Mesoamerica and Central Java." *Southwestern Journal of Anthropology* 13 (1): 1–18.

Worsley, Paul, and Rita Palacios. 2019. *Unwriting Maya Literature: Ts'íib as Recorded Knowledge*. Tucson: University of Arizona Press.

Xinico Batz, Sandra. 2015. "Bajo el disfraz de ladina." La Hora. Accessed November 27. https://lahora.gt/bajo-el-disfraz-de-ladina/.

2

Yucatecan High Society and Stephen Salisbury III

The Origins of Social Ties between Elites from Yucatán and Massachusetts

JULIO CESAR HOIL GUTIÉRREZ

TRANSLATED BY SHEILA HERNANDEZ

The historiography of US-Mexico relations has been dominated by discussions of diplomatic, political, and military conflict.[1] Classic studies have focused on the expansionist and annexationist projects of the United States and the loss of sovereignty and of tangible heritage by Mexico. In 1847, Mexico lost half of its national territory to the United States. For many authors, this geographical loss provides a lens for understanding the evolution of modern archaeology. During the last quarter of the nineteenth century and first decade of the twentieth, American consuls sent more than 30,000 archaeological pieces to the United States. Thus, US expansionism seemed to have had grave and parallel effects on Mexico's territory and archaeological heritage.

However, targeted regional studies that focus on more particular engagements between keys social actors from the two countries can offer an alternative, and in many cases more nuanced, perspective on these processes. Given this historiographic panorama, we must ask ourselves: Were formal political institutions and economic exchanges the main or only point of engagement between Mexico and the United States in the nineteenth century? And were these engagements primarily at the level of nation state-to-nation state interaction? Charting a somewhat different path, I will focus on interactions that take place on a region-to-region scale and that involve members of distinct social sectors rather than formal political institutions.

The main goal of this chapter is to analyze the affective and social ties between the Massachusetts business magnate Stephen Salisbury III and Yucatecan elites during

https://doi.org/10.5876/9781646424276.c002

the former's visit to the state between December 1861 and May 1862. These relationships continued until his death in the early twentieth century and shaped Yucatecan archaeology. This understudied period and figure can demonstrate how an important channel of transnational exchange took place through social and cultural interaction between members of relatively small regional societies. This analysis recasts the question of US-Mexican relations using a different scale, different points of geographical contact, and different series of social actors from those that have figured in much of the literature. It seeks to fill historiographic gap with a case study focused on specific ties between elites from Yucatán and the state of Massachusetts.

Many of the incidents that are discussed here reveal the friendly relationships that Salisbury had forged during his first, five-month stay in Yucatán. These relationships formed the background for his social and cultural activities in the city of Mérida, and in various haciendas, towns, and ancient Mayan ruins. All of this information came from letters that Salisbury wrote to his family members, mostly to his aunt and father, during his time in Yucatán. These are now part of the Salisbury Family Papers Collection in the archives in the American Antiquarian Society (AAS) in Worcester, Massachusetts.

TRADITIONAL INTERPRETATIONS OF US-MEXICO RELATIONS IN THE NINETEENTH CENTURY

The modern historiography of US-Mexico relations has tended to accentuate the political-territorial and military conflicts that took place between 1836 and 1848. Some of these conflicts led to tragic outcomes for Mexico, such as the repeated violation of its national sovereignty and eventual loss of almost half of the territory that it had claimed upon independence from Spain. These outcomes have captured the attention of Mexican historians who were interested in explaining these painful historical moments for their nation. Abundant research has provided reasons for the hostility between Mexico and the United States during this time, as well as the political, economic, and territorial effects on both countries. They have painted an image of a political-military interaction that was highly asymmetrical, one in which Mexico was always at a disadvantage.

This narrative of US-Mexico relations hinges on the assumption that the nation-state is the primary scale at which these cross-border dynamics function. That is, it has focused on foreign policies, expansionism, and territorial conflict that are primarily visible through formal federal institutions that function at the national level. This focus has in turn tended to downplay the role of local actors on a local scale.

This literature tends to frame the Texas Revolution of 1836, the resolution of the conflict with the Treaties of Velasco, and the subsequent annexation of the short-lived republic into US territory as the roots of military hostilities that would simmer for decades. These culminated in the Mexican-American War in 1847, which threatened Mexico's very existence as a nation-state due to the occupation of its capital. When the Treaty of Guadalupe-Hidalgo was signed in February 1848, it ended the war and Mexican sovereignty over nearly half of its territory, which was annexed by the United States. Mexico's internal political turmoil coupled with the United States' ambitious expansionism sparked the most important lines of research in this field, seeking to explain the animosity between both countries and the darkest period in Mexico's independent history.[2]

Nineteenth-century Yucatán provides an important counterexample of transnational dynamics on a regional scale. Recent literature has highlighted a series of political and diplomatic tensions that emerged from the traffic of Mayan antiquities by US diplomats who were stationed in Yucatán. In this case, loss of cultural heritage at the hands of US museums and universities can be seen as a regional microcosm of the threats to national sovereignty that are embodied by Mexico's territorial losses between 1836 and 1848. In many cases, the theft of antiquities was perpetrated by consular officers who took advantage of their official position to avoid major legal consequences beyond the occasional public denunciation. Often, they did so with the complicity of Mexican officials with whom they had extensive interactions. The nature of relations between these actors and Yucatecan elites has some distinct characteristics that are particularly evident in the interactions between the Massachusetts industrialist Stephen Salisbury III and his friends and interlocutors in the peninsula.

Some of the most important explorations of Yucatán's ancient Mayan cities between the 1870s and the end of the nineteenth century were promoted by a group of Bostonians who were affiliated with major institutions such as the American Antiquarian Society of Worcester and the Harvard Peabody Museum. Stephen Salisbury III was a prominent member and president of the AAS from 1887 to 1905. By promoting archaeological predation as one of their goals, these institutions had harmful effects on Mexico's tangible cultural heritage. Nevertheless, the consolidation of these institutions in the eastern part of the United States contributed to global awareness of the Mayan peoples and to the creation of the region of study that is known today as the Maya area. Since the establishment of this region as a focus of global interest in the last quarter of the nineteenth century, it has become the archaeological workshop for US American societies, museums, and universities (Palacios 2012).[3] In that regard, the intervention of the Bostonians in Yucatán's ancient Mayan cities shone a light on Mayan archaeology, even as the activities of the American consuls of Yucatán led to the eradication of significant parts of the historical and material record.

Between 1880 and 1914, American consuls Louis Henry Aymé and Edward Thompson illegally sent thousands of archaeological pieces to the United States. While Aymé was consul, he participated in a number of illegal activities such as excavating Mayan ruins, making molds and taking photographs of monuments, and sending barrels full of ceramic and clay fragments to the United States for analysis. One of his shipments to New York—containing pieces of clay, bone, and obsidian fragments—was confiscated at the port of Progreso, Yucatán (Sellen 2005, 151–59). Because of this, Aymé was removed from his position and Edward Thompson took his place. From the time of his appointment as consul in 1885 until his dismissal in 1907, Thompson dedicated himself to exploring and extracting archaeological pieces from Mayan ruins. This activity included extended visits to the archaeological sites of Labná and Chichén Itzá. As has been widely documented, Thompson illegally exported thousands of archaeological objects to the United States, which then ended up in the Mesoamerican collections of the Peabody Museum, Field Museum of Chicago, and AAS. While he was US consul for the state of Yucatán, he bought the Hacienda Chichén, located a few meters away from the center of the ancient Mayan site of Chichén Itzá. It was there that the most infamous looting of Yucatán's archaeological heritage took place: the extraction of thousands of archaeological Mayan pieces from the Sacred Cenote. It has been estimated that Thompson collected (or looted) more than 30,000 archaeological objects, most of which ended up in the United States. Undoubtedly, Thompson did not act on his own, instead receiving support and sponsorship from the AAS, the Peabody Museum, and other prestigious American institutions (Palacios 2015; Castro 2016).[4]

It is in this context that Stephen Salisbury III's intervention becomes particularly relevant. His personal fascination with Mayan archaeology led to the financing of some of the first major excavations in the region during his years as director of the AAS. Beginning in 1887, he financed the work of the Franco-American archaeologist Augustus Le Plongeon (Izard 2004, 15), and later those of Thompson. Salisbury likewise played an indirect role in the importation of antiquities. This personal interest first developed during his stay in Yucatán between December 1861 and May 1862. This would be his first encounter with both contemporaneous Yucatecan culture and archaeological sites such as Uxmal. In this regard, the relatively brief visit of a key social actor, and his interactions with members of the regional elite, contributed to a series of amateur excavations that would feed directly into the emergence of professional archaeology in the area at the beginning of the twentieth century.

As I noted earlier in this section, the grave consequences of the conflicts generated by the secession of Texas and the war of 1847 have dominated many discussions of US-Mexican relations in the nineteenth century. In contrast, existing literature on the interactions of Mexican elites with academics and institutions from the United States during the same period point to a series of region-to-region interactions that have relatively little to do with interests of the two nation-states as whole. In the latter cases, the primary US-based actors are philanthropic, and academic institutions such as the Harvard Peabody Museum and the AAS. Rather than being based on territorial expansion and the acquisition of productive assets, this dynamic was characterized by an expanding, and mostly illegal, traffic in antiquities that built the collections of these institutions. This was often facilitated by US consular officers and by regional elites who were motivated by distinctly local interests.

In the case of Salisbury and the AAS, early patronage of amateur excavations by Augustus le Plongeon and Edward Thompson both built major collections in the United States and anticipated the more professional research that emerged decades later. In this context, the documentary record of Salisbury's first interactions with members of Yucatán's landed elite provides interesting insight into the experiences and interpersonal relationship that formed the perspective of the region that he brought to his tenure as head of the AAS from 1887 to 1905. The materials help to explain both the formation of his own passion for Mayanist archaeology and the circumstances that allowed him to organize projects in the succeeding decades.

This chapter proposes that the diverse ties between the American Stephen Salisbury III and Yucatecans in the second half of the nineteenth century show that the US-Mexico relationship had many other facets and that the two countries also enjoyed moments in history marked by harmony. Salisbury gradually established intimate, cultural, economic, and even affective ties with various sectors of Yucatecan high society that lasted until the day of his death in November 1905. During his first and longest stay, between December 1861 and May 1862, he laid the foundation for those solid and permanent relationships. Because of the complexity of the topic and because it is about such a crucial period of history that contributed to many US-Mexico ties afterward, this chapter addresses only the beginning of the relationship between Stephen Salisbury III and Yucatecan elites. In other words, it attempts to sketch a historical portrait of Salisbury's first visit to Yucatán.

A BIOGRAPHICAL OUTLINE OF STEPHEN SALISBURY III
AND THE REASONS FOR HIS TRIP TO YUCATÁN

I will be presenting an outline of the most significant events in the life of Stephen Salisbury III in order to contextualize his trip to Yucatán. This summary does not do justice to his later intellectual and philanthropic contributions, which have been documented by other authors. First, I will briefly discuss the legacy of Stephen

Salisbury II, Salisbury III's father, and how he greatly influenced the philanthropic and intellectual interests of his son. These interests then became one of Salisbury III's main reasons to go to Yucatán.

Stephen Salisbury II was a major force in agricultural, industrial, and social development of Worcester, Massachusetts. He constructed homes for workers, as well as factories. Thanks to these entrepreneurial activities, Salisbury accumulated a fortune and became an economically powerful and influential figure in Massachusetts. In addition, he held important political positions in his state such as representative in the General Court from 1838 to 1839, and then state senator from 1846 to 1847. In the world of finance, he was president of two banks.

Like other nineteenth-century business magnates, Stephen Salisbury II also dedicated part of his life to philanthropy. In 1840, the AAS appointed him as one of its members. Because of his outstanding work as a representative of the institution, the AAS then appointed him as president in 1854, a position he held until his death in August 1884. During this time, Salisbury II promoted publications and collaborated with other institutions interested in antiquities such as Harvard University. He financed and founded an extensive and valuable documentary archive safeguarded in the AAS's Antiquarian Hall. Besides these historical and antiquarian interests, Stephen Salisbury II also excelled in cultivating exotic plants in greenhouses and in developing machines to plow his fields. These accomplishments led him to become a member of the Worcester Agricultural and Horticultural Society. In short, Salisbury II was a "Collector of Culture" (Izard 2004).[5]

An only child, Stephen Salisbury III was born in March 1835. He grew up in an entrepreneurial, political, philanthropic, and cultural atmosphere that his father created throughout his life. His mother, Rebekah Scott Dean, died when he was only twelve. His father would remarry twice over the course of his life.

Stephen Salisbury III graduated from Harvard University in 1856. Since he was twenty-two years old, he took an interest in the affairs of institutions connected to his father's cultural and economic activities. As was common for the youth of the American business elite, he traveled to Europe between 1856 and 1858 to study languages and cultures. He studied German at Friedrich Wilhelm University in Berlin, Germany. In France, he attended conferences at the Faculty of Law of Paris, and he also visited England, Scotland, and Ireland. He then went to Turkey and Greece to study the traditions of its people before returning to Worcester in December 1858. The following year, at the age of twenty-four, he went to Harvard Law School and obtained a bachelor of law in mid-1861 (Worcester Historical Museum 2012). His father's influence led him to develop an admiration for antiquities and to study them as well. Among his other primary interests were Yucatán and its ancient Mayan cities, which he visited at the end of 1861.

Salisbury III's arrival in Yucatán was ultimately a result of the rising tide of war in the United States. The US Civil War had just started in April of that same year due to the secession of Alabama, Florida, Georgia, Louisiana, Mississippi, South Carolina, and Texas from the Union to create the Confederacy in February 1861 and the attack on Fort Sumter in Charleston, South Carolina. For thousands of young New Englanders, this meant that they had to enlist to fight against the Confederacy (Terrazas y Bazante et al. 2012, 399–400). At the age of 26, Stephen Salisbury III felt the patriotic duty to support the Union, even if service proved to be a death sentence. However, his father and one of his aunts convinced him to avoid military service. They were able to send in a substitute in his place thanks to their privileged economic and political position and the concessions of the Conscription Act. Although Salisbury had escaped the immediate threat of conscription, a planned stay in Yucatán would spare him from the possible insults from his peers for not answering Lincoln's call to the nation's youth (Izard 2004).

The diplomatic relationship that already existed between Yucatán and the United States since the middle of the nineteenth century facilitated Salisbury's trip. Because of growing commercial relationships at that time, the US government established a consulate in Mérida, Yucatán. The first American consul to Yucatán was Charles Thomson Jr., appointed on March 3, 1843. At that time, the main port was in Sisal, to the southeast of Yucatán. Like his successors, Thomson served the business interests of investors who sought to profit from the opening of ports in Sisal and Campeche for duty-free imports and exports by the Mexican government. More than a century and a half later, Mérida still has the only US consulate in all of southeastern Mexico.

Given these established commercial and diplomatic links, Yucatán was not an unknown place for the Salisbury family, which made Stephen feel more comfortable with the idea of visiting it. Moreover, he could count on friendships that he already had established with some Yucatecan elites, surely originating from the commercial transactions between Massachusetts and Yucatán. In summary, Stephen Salisbury III's economic status, his cultural pursuits encouraged by his father and the AAS, his interest in antiquities, the presence of a US consulate in Yucatán, the budding relationships with Yucatecans, and above all the Civil War all led to his decision to go to Yucatán.

STEPHEN SALISBURY'S STAY IN YUCATÁN: THE ORIGINS OF HIS FRIENDSHIP WITH ELITE YUCATECANS

The Civil War decade in the United States posed a number of economic difficulties for the state of Yucatán. At the beginning of the 1860s, the region was still recovering from the Caste War, an armed uprising of Yukatek Maya people in response to excessive taxation from civil and religious authorities and to the loss of traditional lands. This crisis was more acute in some parts of the state than in others. The east, particularly around the town of Valladolid, still existed on war footing, with towns, villages and haciendas being largely depopulated and unproductive under the constant threat of rebel attack. The sugar and large-scale cattle production that had emerged during the first half of the nineteenth century had essentially collapsed (Hoil 2019).

In contrast, the northwest of the state, home to the capital city of Mérida, experienced a gradual economic recovery and a return to prewar lifestyles. Free from the immediate threat of rebel attack, many of these communities retained most of their original population. Nevertheless, the specter of the Caste War figured prominently in the mind of its inhabitants and continued to impact the local economy. At the start of the 1860s, many haciendas and other private properties lacked capital or a sufficient base of resident laborers to remain productive and were ultimately sold at bargain prices to the first bidder. The few that remained productive focused their energies on cattle and, to a lesser degree, maize and other rural staples (Bracamonte 1994, 106–18). The henequen production that would generate vast fortunes in the region at the end of the nineteenth century was in the early phases of its development and would not become a booming monocrop industry until the 1870s (Ortiz 2013, 116–56). This was the situation Stephen Salisbury III found in Yucatán.

Even before his arrival in the state, Salisbury had close ties with some members of the Mérida elite. Some Yucatecans had traveled to Massachusetts to visit the Salisbury family while on business trips. Although I have not found a source that pinpoints the exact moment when these relationships started, presumably it happened sometime after the establishment of the American consulate in Mérida and was related to Massachusetts-Yucatán commerce. For example, Salisbury received a letter dated August 1, 1861, from Primitivo Casares during the latter's layover in Lancaster, Jamaica. Casares had left the port of Sisal and was heading toward the United States. In his letter, he told Salisbury that he had received his missive dated June 30, 1861, and that he would arrive in Boston on a Saturday. From there, he would take an express train at 3:00 p.m. toward Worcester. Adding a personal detail, he recounted that he had a good time dancing with some friends at a beach house party. He closed by saying that he regretted not accompanying Salisbury on his trip to Princeton but had decided to spend a final Sunday in Jamaica.[6] Primitivo Casares's trip to Worcester in August 1861 reveals to us the early relationships between the Salisbury family and the Yucatecan elites and how these relationships sparked Salisbury's interest in Yucatán and the Mayan people.

Salisbury arrived in Yucatán on December 6, 1861, and stayed in a house in Mérida. In his journal, he wrote down his multiple activities during his five-month stay in

Yucatán. He was hosted by the Casares family, which strengthened the preexisting relationship between them. The two brothers, David and Primitivo Casares, took it upon themselves to introduce him to the social and intellectual circles of Mérida, accompanying him to dinners, dances, theaters, meetings, and trips. Salisbury's journal showed that the elite Yucatecans warmly welcomed him wherever he arrived. Besides the Casares family, Salisbury became friends with other prominent Mérida families, who hosted him on their country estates.[7] Because of how much time he spent with them, there were occasions when David Casares would send letters to Salisbury asking him to return to the city. In one of them, dated December 21, 1861, Casares wrote that he was glad that Salisbury was enjoying his time with the family where he was staying, but he asked him to come back to Mérida as soon as possible to talk about topics of great interest.[8]

The affective ties that Salisbury had with some members of high Yucatecan society, as well as with the landowners, are reflected in the extensive correspondence between Salisbury III and his family in Worcester and Boston. In one of the many letters that he sent to his aunt in Boston on January 11, 1862, he mentioned how he was enjoying himself and how he liked the people of Yucatán. He described his stay at the Hacienda Chactún, which was propriety of a Mrs. Jesusa "Chucha" Peón, located forty-eight miles from Mérida. He explained that it was about twenty-one square miles, and that it cultivated both sugar and cotton. At the hacienda, Salisbury enjoyed reading books, singing, and dancing with the landowner and some friends from Mérida. In that same letter, he also talked about visiting Mr. Manuel Casares's Hacienda Xcuyum, a few miles from Mérida, where he attended a party. Salisbury concluded his letter saying that he felt very happy in Yucatán and that he was already well acquainted with the best people of Mérida but that his closest friends were in Mrs. "Chucha" Peón's family. It was also during this series of visits that he visited an unspecified Mayan ruin, apparently for the first time.[9] In another letter to his aunt, dated January 22, Salisbury confirmed that he received the letter that she had sent from Boston on November 25, 1861. He told her that during his trip to Mrs. Julia Fajardo's hacienda in Tixcacal, he had a very good time with her family. He sang, danced along with the guitar, read poems, went horseback riding with the ladies of Mrs. Fajardo and Mrs. Peón's family, and went to dinner parties.[10]

Unlike many North American travelers, Salisbury had few complaints about the climate in Yucatán. This disposition reflects, in no small part, the fact that he arrived there in winter. Winter in Yucatán meant warm days and cooler nights. In one of the letters to his mother, Salisbury said that he found this climate agreeable. During one week, a north wind had brought a dust cloud, and for two days it was relatively cool in the morning and during the day the temperature would rise to only seventy-five degrees (twenty-three degrees Celsius).[11] It amused Salisbury that

Yucatecans felt very cold when the temperature dropped a bit. Being used to New England weather, he mentioned to his father in a letter that in Yucatán they called cold what he would call pleasant weather, and that therefore he would not want to imagine what a Yucatecan summer would be like.[12] Yucatecan winters not only facilitated Salisbury's environmental adaptation but also his frequent visits to haciendas, towns, and Mayan ruins. His experience would likely have been different had he visited during the spring or summertime.

Salisbury also quickly became accustomed to Yucatán's social life because of his interest in the cultural practices of foreign peoples. He would attend festivities dedicated to the towns' patron saints. During the end of January, he showed up to festival of the Virgin of Umán, a town located a few miles west of Mérida. There, he stayed with some people from the town and took pleasure in watching the traditional dances that happened twice a day and the bullfights.[13] In February, he went to the festival in Motul, a city located twenty miles east of Merida, accompanied by Mrs. Bruna Casares and her son David. In Motul, he was especially fascinated by the bullfights and the traditional dances.[14]

It is a bit ironic that Salisbury's description of his trip through Yucatán stressed his sense of safety, given the continued presence of armed Indigenous groups in the south and east of the state, to say nothing of the ongoing political unrest in central Mexico. In fact, the Three Years War between Liberals and Conservatives had only ended in January 11 of the previous year. In letters that he sent to his aunt toward the end of February, he told her that he was doing well and was very happy because of how safe it was in Yucatán—free of danger from foreign intervention and foreign people. He mentioned that Yucatán provided a perfect kind of peace and was inhabited by friendly and pacific people. In short, Salisbury felt happy with the Yucatecans, to the extent of participating in their social activities such as the carnival of Mérida. He said in his letter that he attended his first costume ball for carnival with his friends. Among them were Donata, dressed as the mother of the flowers; Prudencia, dressed as Marie Stuart; Guardiana, dressed as a Hungarian; David as Felipe II; and Salisbury himself as the French general of Cherbourg.

Something else that tied Salisbury to Yucatán was his passion for ancient Mayan cities. During his stay, he visited some that were near Mérida and others that were further away, most notably Uxmal. This was one of his first activities in the first weeks that he arrived. In the beginning of January, while he was at Mrs. "Chucha" Peón's Hacienda Chactún, he took the opportunity to explore nearby Mayan ruins, even though he did not specify a site or location by name.[15] In the letter that he wrote to his mother during the middle of March, he told her that in his visit to Uxmal, he collected a large number of seeds for her. He also bought various hammocks and other Mexican curios to give to his friends.[16]

Salisbury's account gives some insight into how by 1861, visits to archaeological sites were a routine leisure activity for Mérida elites. In a letter that he sent to his father in March, Salisbury told him about his trip to Uxmal. He left Mérida with his other friends at around three or four in the morning and traveled in a buggy pulled by three mules while his friends rode horses. During the trip, they stopped at some large haciendas until they arrived in the town of Ticul at nighttime. They were welcomed as guests of Don Felipe Peón, a wealthy landowner in the region. The next day, with a large supply of provisions, they continued their way until arriving at their destination at the hacienda of Uxmal, property of Don Simón Peón, where they ended up staying. In the afternoon, they explored the ruins of Uxmal, which were located barely a mile and a half from the hacienda. Salisbury made drawings, wrote down observations, described buildings, and came to several conclusions about the architectural style of Uxmal. He told his father that he could write a book with all the information he had acquired.[17]

Since his arrival in Mérida, Salisbury had not stopped receiving letters from Worcester and Boston. Some letters informed him about what was going on in the family; others responded to what he said in his previous letters. Out of all the letters that he received, the one that caused the greatest impact and pain was the eighth letter from his father on January 4, 1862, in which Salisbury learned the sad news of the death of his stepsister Georgiana (Georgie), in December 1861.[18] Salisbury responded to his father's letter on February 7 to express the sadness that he felt for Georgie's death. It was a difficult loss to accept due to how suddenly it had occurred when she was actually in good physical health. He confessed that he thought about Georgie constantly and that he had hoped to tell her about his time in Yucatán when he returned to Worcester.[19]

Salisbury also exchanged letters with his aunt in Boston. In one of her letters from January 1862, she confessed feeling scared and sad for Salisbury when he arrived in Mérida, given the political instability of the surrounding regions. She dreamt of seeing him arrive one day with his parents on the steamer "Columbia." She also told him that his father was fine, coughing less than normal, had difficulty writing, and trusted that Salisbury would come back safe and sound.[20] In other letters, dated February 2, she encouraged him to write to her more frequently about his stay in Mérida and the Casares family. In an attempt to cheer up Salisbury, she told him that Frank, Georgie's husband, felt calm but terrified by his wife's death. She regretted that Frank's house was so empty but added that some friends accompanied him during the winter so that he would not feel lonely. She ended the letter with a brief description of the weather in Boston—very cold, even though the sun shone intensely. Salisbury finally concluded his stay in Yucatán in May 1862 and returned to Worcester.

Using the letters that he exchanged with his family, I have tried to reconstruct some of the key moments in Salisbury's social interactions with aristocratic Yucatecans and their emotional and cultural dimensions. During his time in Yucatán, Salisbury laid the foundation for close and long-lasting ties with Merida and members of its upper class. Since his arrival in the city, these people had welcomed him and treated him kindly, as shown by his stays at the haciendas, and his visits to the provincial fiestas and Mayan ruins, as well as his participation in Merida's social activities. In short, the elite Yucatecans became good friends of Salisbury just as he became a good friend to them. He was thankful for the hospitality and kindness from these Yucatecan families that hosted him during his stay. This was only the beginning of the friendly ties between Salisbury and the upper sectors of Yucatecan society. His friendships, his interest in Yucatecan traditions, and his curiosity about ancient Mayan cities kept him connected to Yucatán until his death in 1905.[21]

Salisbury was named "Honorary Conservator" in Yucatán in 1878 for his contributions to archaeology. From 1884 on, he sponsored the travel of US researchers working in the state, supporting the growth of the collections of institutions such as the Peabody Museum and garnering greater publicity for archaeology in post–Caste War Yucatán. These archaeological endeavors developed concurrently to the development of some important financial and business contacts between Yucatán and Massachusetts. In 1871, Salisbury was visited by his friend David Casares to discuss a number of issues regarding business in the state. Salisbury himself returned to Yucatán in 1885, and members of the Mérida elite made frequent visits to Worcester. Evidence also points to Salisbury financing several projects to improve the urban infrastructure of Mérida (Izard 2004, 16–17). This intersection of transnational business interests and transnational archaeology would continue to mark Mayanist anthropology as it evolved during the late nineteenth and twentieth centuries.

CONCLUSION

This chapter focused on how personal interactions between two regional elites, those of New England and Yucatán, established relations that would have long-lasting impacts on the development of archaeological research in the Maya area and of heritage institutions on both sides of the transnational exchange. What is significant is that the connections between Salisbury the Casares family, and his other Yucatecan interlocutors, had little to do with formal foreign policy governing nation state-to-nation state relations between Mexico and the United States.

This finding has two broader implications for the historiography of the nineteenth century. First, it highlights how more regionalist perspectives complicate the narrative of US-Mexico relationships that has focused on large-scale conflicts and territorial expansion. Second, it highlights how a microlevel analysis of interactions between elite social actors from both regions reveals the role of informal networks, academic institutions, and philanthropy in establishing distinct dynamics for transnational exchange.

From this conceptual perspective, and considering the understudied materials that I found in the American Antiquarian Society's (AAS) archive, I have attempted to piece together the origins of the relationship between Stephen Salisbury III and Yucatán elite families during the second half of the nineteenth century. His stay in Yucatán during the early 1860s helped him establish close ties with the several elite families, which he maintained after returning to Worcester. His quick adjustment to the Yucatecan environment as well as the rapid acceptance that he received from many Yucatecans allowed him to integrate himself and get involved in various social and cultural activities inside and outside of Mérida.

As Salisbury's letters have shown, he enjoyed his time in the haciendas and towns near Mérida. However, he was not exempt from living painful moments such as the death of his stepsister and the US Civil War as well. Nonetheless, Salisbury's stay in Yucatán can be defined as the first step in establishing international friendships, learning Yucatecan cultural practices, and becoming fascinated with antique Mayan cities. This highlights the cordial nature of some US-Mexican relations in the mid- to late nineteenth century.

This trip also anticipated the expansion of US interest in the Yucatán peninsula, a process which Salisbury served as patron and sponsor of early on. His visits with his many Yucatecan friends led him to learn much about towns around Mérida and others far from it like Uxmal. After returning to Worcester, Salisbury's contact with pre-Hispanic Maya culture was crucial in starting US research on Maya civilization and ancient Mayan cities in the last quarter of the nineteenth century, especially during his long presidency of the AAS from 1887 to 1905. In other words, the fascination that Salisbury had for the ancient Mayan cities that he explored led antiquarian societies, museums, and universities in the United States to become increasingly invested in studying Maya civilization.

As president of the AAS, Salisbury sponsored archaeological digs in Yucatán, including the work of the British-American archeologist Augustus Le Plongeon in Chichén Itzá. He also financially supported explorations in order to obtain archaeological pieces that would expand the antiquities collection in the AAS. Even before Salisbury assumed the AAS's presidency, the organization had begun obtaining numerous Mayan pieces to expand its antiquities collection through the efforts of Edward Thompson, appointed consul of the United States in Yucatán in 1885. Later, toward the end of the nineteenth century, Salisbury and the AAS withdrew their sponsorship of Thompson. By that time, however, Stephen Salisbury had oriented institutions in the United States toward the study of Mayan civilizations, a direction they would follow during the second half of the nineteenth century and the first half of the twentieth century.

NOTES

1. I would like to thank Dr. Teresa Rojas Rabiela and Richard Leventhal for facilitating the funding for my stay in Worcester, MA, to consult at the AAS. Likewise, I am thankful to my friend and colleague Fernando Armstrong-Fumero for his hospitality during my visit to Massachusetts and for early comments on this project. Finally, I appreciate the ease the AAS offered in consulting documents in the Salisbury Family Papers Collection, as well as for offering local researcher housing during my stay in Worcester.

2. Valadés (1979); Hale (1990); De la Teja (1994); Velasco (1994); Velasco y Thomas (1994); Vázquez (1994); Vázquez (1997); Duval (2000); Eisenhower (2000); De Vega (2001); Meyer y Vázquez (2001); Mayers (2004); Terrazas y Basante et al. (2012).

3. Palacios named this group of people Bostonians because they were people from Boston as well as nearby Worcester and Cambridge. For more information about the Bostonians and their expeditionary work in pre-Hispanic Mayan cities in Yucatán and others in Central America, as well as its archaeological scope and damage to the archaeological heritage of Mexico, see Palacios (2012).

4. Their research has documented accurately and comprehensively Thompson's work in Yucatán, the role of his sponsors in exploring Mayan cities, and the illegal trafficking of thousands of Mayan archaeological pieces to the United States.

5. I would like to thank Holly V. Izard, curator of the Worcester Historical Museum, for personally providing me with her article and for the information she provided in my short talk with her at the museum in 2019.

6. Primitivo Casares to Stephen Salisbury III, August 1, 1861, AAS, box 3, folder 38.

7. AAS, box 67, vol. 6.

8. David Casares to Stephen Salisbury III, December 21, 1861, AAS, box 38, folder 4.

9. Stephen Salisbury III to Catharine Dean Flint, January 11, 1862, AAS, box 38, folder 5.

10. Stephen Salisbury III to Catharine Dean Flint, January 22, 1862, AAS, box 38, folder 5.

11. Stephen Salisbury III to Mary Grosvenor Bangs, January 26, 1862, AAS, box 38, folder 5.

12. Stephen Salisbury III to Stephen Salisbury II, March 17, 1862, AAS, box 38, folder 6.

13. January 26, 1862, AAS, box 38, folder 5.

14. January 30, 1862, AAS, box 38, folder 5.

15. January 11, 1862, AAS, box 38, folder 5.

16. Stephen Salisbury III to Mary Grosvenor Bangs, March 17, 1862, AAS, box 38 folder 6.

17. Stephen Salisbury III to Stephen Salisbury II, March 17, 1862, AAS, box 38, folder 6.

18. Stephen Salisbury II to Stephen Salisbury III, January 4, 1862, AAS, box 38, folder 5.

19. Stephen Salisbury III to Stephen Salisbury II, February 7, 1862, AAS, box 38, folder 5.
20. Catharine Dean Flint to Stephen Salisbury III, January 26, 1862, AAS, box 38, folder 5.
21. Catharine Dean Flint to Stephen Salisbury III, February 2, 1862, AAS, box 38, folder 5.

REFERENCES CITED

Bracamonte, Pedro. 1994. La memoria enclaustrada: Historia indígena de Yucatán, 1750–1994. Mexico City: CIESAS.

Castro, Pedro. 2016. *El fabuloso saqueo del Cenote Sagrado de Chichén Itzá*. Mexico City: Universidad Autónoma Metropolitana–Unidad Itztapalapa.

De la Teja, Jesús. 1994. "La colonización e independencia de Texas: El punto de vista texano." *Mitos en las relaciones México–Estados Unidos*. Mexico City: Fondo de Cultura Económica.

De Vega, Mercedes. 2011 *Historia de las relaciones internacionales de México, 1821–2010*. Mexico City: Ministry of Foreign Relations, General Directorate of the Diplomatic Historical Collection.

Duval H., Dolores. 2000 "Una mirada al expansionismo estadounidense: La legación francesa en México, 1853–1860." *Secuencia: Revista de Historia y Ciencias Sociales* 48 (September–December, Mexico City: Institute of Mora-Conocí): 121–36.

Eisenhower, John D. 2000. *Tan lejos de Dios: La guerra de los Estados Unidos contra México (1846–1848)*. Mexico City: Fondo de Cultura Económica.

Hale, Charles A. 1990. "La guerra con Estados Unidos y la crisis del pensamiento mexicano." *Secuencia: Revista de Historia y Ciencias Sociales* 16 (January–April, Mexico City: Institute of Mora-Conacyt.) 43–62.

Hoil Gutiérrez, Julio Cesar. 2019. "La Guerra de Castas y su impacto agrario en los pueblos del oriente de Yucatán, 1847–1870." *Antrópica: Revista de Ciencias Sociales y Humanidades* 5(10): 283–303.

Izard, Holly 2004. "Collectors of Culture: The Salisburys of Worcester." Presented at the Dublin Seminar for New England Folklife. Worcester Historical Museum, June.

Mayers, David. 2004. "La guerra con Estados Unidos y los disidentes estadounidenses, 1846–1848." In *Secuencia: Revista de Historia y Ciencias Sociales* 59 (May–August, Mexico City: Institute of Mora-Conacyt): 33–70.

Meyer, Lorenzo, and Josefina Zoraida Vázquez. 1989. *México frente a Estados Unidos: Un ensayo histórico (1776–1988)*. Mexico City: Fondo de Cultura Económica.

Ortiz Yam, Inés. 2013 *De milperos a henequeneros en Yucatán, 1870–1930*. Mexico City: El Colegio de México.

Palacios, Guillermo. 2012. "Los Bostonians, Yucatán y los primeros rumbos de la arqueología Americanista estadounidense, 1875–1894." *Historia Mexicana* 62, Núm. 1 (245) (July–September, Mexico City: College of Mexico A.C.): 105–93.

Palacios, Guillermo. 2015. "El cónsul Thompson, los Bostonians y la formación de la Galaxia Chichen, 1893–1904." *Historia Mexicana* 65, Núm. 1 (157) (July–September, Mexico City: College of Mexico A.C.): 167–288.

Sellen, Adam T. 2005. " 'Nuestro hombre en México': Las hazañas del cónsul estadounidense Louis Henri Aymé en Yucatán y Oaxaca." *Península* (Mérida) 1, (0): 151–70. http://www.scielo.org.mx/scielo.php?script=sci_arttext&pid=S1870 -57662005000100007&lng=es&nrm=iso.

Terrazas y Basante, Marcela, Gerardo Gurza Lavalle, Paolo Riguzzi, and Patricia de los Ríos. 2012. *Las relaciones México–Estados Unidos, 1756–2010.* Vol. 1, *Imperios, repúblicas y pueblos en pugna por el territorio, 1756–1867.* Vol. 2, *Destino no manifiesto, 1867–2010.* Mexico City: Universidad Nacional Autónoma de México, Historical Research Institute, North American Research Center / Ministry of Foreign Affairs.

Valadés, José. 1979. *México: Santa Ana y la guerra de Texas.* Mexico City: Ed. Diana.

Various Authors. 1850s–1908. Stephen Salisbury III papers. Part of Salisbury Family Papers. American Antiquarian Society, Worcester, MA.

Vázquez, Josefina Zoraida. 1994 "¿Dos guerras contra Estados Unidos?" *De la rebelión de Texas a la Guerra del 47.* Mexico City: Nueva Imagen.

Vázquez, Josefina Zoraida. 1997. *La intervención norteamericana: 1846–1848.* Mexico City: Ministry of Foreign Relations.

Velasco, Jesús. 1994. "La separación y la anexión de Texas en la historia de México y Estados Unidos." In *De la rebelión de Texas a la guerra del 47,* edited by Josefina Zoraida Vázquez. Mexico City: Nueva Imagen.

Velasco, Jesús, and Benjamín Thomas. 1994. "La guerra entre México y los Estados Unidos, 1846–1848." *Mitos en las relaciones México–Estados Unidos.* Mexico City: Fondo de Cultura Económica.

Worcester Historical Museum. 2012. "The Salisbury Legacy." Salisbury, MA: n.p.

3

Bad Spanish and Worse Maya

On the Performance of Gringohood during the "Carnegie Age"

FERNANDO ARMSTRONG-FUMERO

In a recent book, the historian Mary Kay Vaughan proposes the use of a "new biography" to examine how individuals embody opportunities and external constraints that exist in a particular place and historical moment. She argues that this approach is useful in contextualizing dominant social and discursive structures within the subjective experience of persons who "are not simply written upon by external texts [but] become authors of their own texts" (2015, 4). As I will argue, the informal writings of Sylvanus Morley and Robert Redfield offers insights beyond the personal life histories of two influential figures in Mayanist anthropology. They help understand changes and continuities in how generations of US scholars have articulated their identity vis-à-vis "the field." These evolving identities offer further insight into the shifting roles of anthropology within the complex transnational relationship between Mexico and the United States.

At the heart of this discussion is how Morley or Redfield chose to—or chose not to—incorporate non-English words into their informal English prose. In a now-classic analysis of race discourse in American English, linguistic anthropologist Jane Hill referred to common Spanish-language phrases used in informal English language discourse—like "hasta la vista," "mi casa es su casa" and "no comprendo"—as "mock Spanish." She argued that the ideological work of these phrases involved a particular confluence of direct and indirect indexicality. That is, these phrases simultaneously communicate characterizations of the speaker and of the people being imitated by the speaker in ways that reinforce ethnic and social hierarchies.

https://doi.org/10.5876/9781646424276.c003

In a given conversation, the English-speaking user of mock Spanish directly indexes positive elements of their own personality, such as being laid back and cosmopolitan. This level of indexicality would be innocuous enough if the code-switching did not involve a historically stigmatized language. But, as Hill argued, what are seen as positive characteristics in an English speaker that self-consciously uses mock Spanish are seen as negative characteristics of the presumably backward and immoral people who use Spanish as their primary form of speech (Hill 1993, 1998).

Something that will be a recurring theme in this chapter is a particular repertoire of "Mock Spanish" that is common among many archaeologists and anthropologists working in Latin America and that seems to have its roots in nineteenth-century travel writing. It is not simply a literary trope that is reproduced in narrative representations of life in the region, but it also plays an important role in the sociality of English-speaking academics who work and learn in Spanish- (and Maya-)speaking spaces. Later, I will discuss how Morley's tendency to revel in this sort of linguistic play, and Redfield's far more circumspect relationship to it, embodies changes in the social and intellectual contexts of anthropology that were taking place in the 1930s. But first, I will open with an anecdote regarding my own experience of this mock Spanish.

HOW MOCK SPANISH TURNED ME INTO A GRINGO

In many respects, my own fieldwork encounter with anthropological mock Spanish was consistent with the rites of passage that are traditionally celebrated in anthropology, albeit tinted through my own experience as a US Latino. I am a native Spanish–speaking Puerto Rican who was raised in the United States from the age of four. Early on in my academic career, I chose to resist the institutional pressures that lead many people from ethnic minorities to become native ethnographers and entered the field of Maya studies. But, even though I never took courses that focused on US Latinx studies, I began college with an experiential knowledge of the linguistic performances that Hill dubbed "mock Spanish." I grew up in the 1980s and 1990s, when Bart Simpson's "ay carumba" and the Terminator's "hasta la vista, baby" were pervasive in popular culture. This was also a time when my family's public conversations in New Jersey and Philadelphia were sometimes interrupted by strangers' hostile demand that we "talk English." Not surprisingly, I was subjected to frequent bullying with mock Spanish in the predominantly white public schools that I attended. Given that my sister and I were light skinned enough to pass for Italian American among people who did not know our actual ethnicity, these linguistic incidents were the primary moments that "outed" us as nonwhite to potentially hostile peers and neighbors.

In my late teens, I participated in archaeological and ethnographic field schools with primarily Anglophone American students. After a week or so in Belize, my fellow students and I had taken to referring to hangovers with the common local term *goma* in our English language conversation. A year later, I attended an ethnographic field school in Mexico that involved a more extensive interaction with a community that was bilingual in Spanish and Yukatek Maya. In this case, it became common for my fellow students and me to characterize places and people as *tranquilos* or *pesados* depending on our experience there. Questions about local politics or the exact meaning of certain phrases in Yukatek led some of us to answer with "¿quién sabe?" We sprinkled the few Maya phrases we knew into our English as well.

There were several reasons why the other students' use of *quién sabe* and *tranquilo* didn't inspire the anger that it would have earlier in my teens. First, the particular words that were being code-switched were not exactly the same stereotypical repertoire of mock Spanish that I had encountered in New Jersey. Second, I knew that the white students on those programs were in most ways respectful and even deferential to members of the local community. But perhaps most significant, my own desires to become an anthropologist primed me to accept forms of linguistic play that bonded me to my English-speaking peers and instructors.

The memory of this style of youthful sociality would come to trouble me by my midtwenties. I sometimes winced when I recalled my complicity with a form of mock Spanish, notwithstanding the differences in context. As I processed this experience, I also learned a valuable lesson about the nature of academic sociality and its often-ambivalent relationship to ideologies of language and race. "Calling out" potentially harmful linguistic practices is important for creating spaces of work and learning that respect the dignity of all participants. But in and of itself, that corrective gesture doesn't answer the question of *why* these kinds of linguistic play answer to certain social and emotional needs of anthropologists "in the field." My discussion of Morley and Redfield in this chapter is an attempt at a broader theoretical and historical reckoning with ways of performing identity that figure in the intimate experience of most US-trained scholars conducting fieldwork in Latin America. I will refer to this particular set of behaviors, which often includes some form of mock Spanish, as different means of performing gringohood.

Placed within its larger historical context, the most obvious subtext of performative gringohood is US territorial expansion and its various racial corollaries. These linkages range from the "archaeological Monroism" of John Lloyd Stephens (Ortega y Medina 1953) that Fallaw and I noted in the introduction to this volume to the confluence of twentieth-century imperialism and eugenics that will figure in some of the episodes that I discuss from the careers of Sylvanus Morley and Robert Redfield. For generations of travelers, playful uses of what Hill referred to as "mock

Spanish" took on the paradoxical role of turning linguistic incompetence into an expression of national prestige.

In the cases that I will focus on here, the interlinguistic constitution of "gringo-hood" is also central to the performance of a particular masculinity. Although a number of women, particularly Margaret Park Redfield, will figure in this narrative, my focus will be on the subjectivity of the male characters. This is, in part, an attempt to complement the existing gender analysis of feminist scholars such as the Mayanist anthropologist Diane Nelson, who made "*gringa* positioning" a central part of her reflections on fieldwork and activism in Guatemala (1999, 41–50). My focus on men also reflects the fact that this inquiry began through personal experience. Despite the fact that my ethnic background made my negotiation of certain gringo discourses highly ambivalent, I experienced that ambivalence from the relative privilege of inhabiting a cis-male body in what developed historically as a discipline for "manly" adventurers.

As I will argue in the sections that follow, particular styles of appropriating or negotiating languages are central to these two components of performative gringo-hood. Morley and Redfield engaged in these performances in quite different ways, reflecting differences in their generational and individual experiences. I will discuss each scholar in two sections, first providing relevant biographical context that highlights the personal and political factors that brought them to the field of Maya studies. Afterward, I will examine stylistic choices that marked their use of Spanish and Maya in English-language prose and what this implies about their relative positionality in relation to performances of gringohood.

SYLVANUS MORLEY: MAYA ARCHAEOLOGY'S RACIST GRANDPA

In 1906, Sylvanus Morley was a scrawny, nearsighted twenty-three-year-old Harvard student with a love of Rudyard Kipling and a penchant for late night "jonesing." Despite his middling grades and frequent ill health, he was determined to join an archaeological expedition to Yucatán. This request was vetoed by his mentors George Putnam and Alfred Tozzer, who thought that he would "surely croak" in the tropical heat and malarial atmosphere of the peninsula.[1] A little over a year later, however, Morley got his wish. His willingness to subject himself to the rigors of long expeditions in poorly mapped regions of southern Mexico, Belize, and Northern Guatemala inspired the respect of his peers. Given the timing of his years at Harvard, it's easy to imagine that he saw a bit of himself in then-president Theodore Roosevelt, another sickly and nearsighted boy who would leave Harvard to invade and explore Latin America, becoming a renowned explorer, outdoorsman, soldier, and all-around paragon of Anglo-Saxon masculinity.

Not only did Morley not "croak" in the Yucatecan sun, but he also produced a collection of drawings, photographs, and readings of Classic Period calendrical inscriptions that would be important in the development of Mayan epigraphy and archaeology. Beginning in the mid-1920s, he served as the director of the Carnegie Institution of Washington (CIW) project at Chichén Itzá. From their inception until the 1950s, CIW projects in Mexico and Central America were a dominant force in the development of Mayanist archaeology and ethnography. As the director of the flagship project at Chichén Itzá, Morley became a highly influential figure in the career of dozens of scholars and played an important role in cultural diplomacy that facilitated the presence of American researchers in postrevolutionary Mexico.

Despite his prominence in the field, Morley's reputation in anthropology is controversial. During the First World War, he used his work as an archaeologist as cover for spying as a paid agent of the US naval intelligence. His activities, along with those of several other American anthropologists, were famously criticized by the patriarch of US anthropology Franz Boas (see Harris and Sadler 200, 284–89).

The sometimes shocking racism of some of Morley's private writings has added another wrinkle to his legacy among contemporary scholars (see Brunhouse 1971). Some of his recent biographers have sought to frame him as a product of his time, who deserves a generous reading (Harris and Sadler 2009). But, by any reasonable assessment, Morley's diary presents the contemporary reader with an unflattering portrait of Anglo-American racial perspectives in the early twentieth century. His discussion of his various travels is peppered with casually dropped racial slurs. The Afro-Cuban women that he saw in his early twenties are "coons,"[2] and the Chinese proprietor of a restaurant that he frequented in coastal Honduras during the Great War is only ever referred to as "the chink."[3] Comments that Morley makes about some of his Jewish colleagues and acquaintances, including an apparent lover from the early 1920s, hint at a thinly veiled anti-Semitism.[4] Mock Spanish phrases figure prominently in some of the more unpleasant passages. Referring to a mixed-race worker he hired in Holmul, Guatemala, he noted that "A Latin-Negro mixture is the worst possible, and though he does not show his Latin blood—his mother came from Chachacluum and he is black [*sic*] as the ace of spades—but it is there and he is *no bueno* like the rest of that breed."[5]

Interestingly, it was a group of Europeans who invoked some of Morley's most shocking statements. During his years of spy service, he would go so far as to write that an entire generation of Germans who had supported Kaiser Wilhelm's war effort was beyond redemption and deserved extermination for the sake of a larger humanity (MD: October 7, 2018). This characterization of Germany, like his frequently expressed racial disdain for Latin Americans, coalesced into a more-or-less consistent "internationalist" doctrine that he would express throughout the 1920s and 1930s. One incident in 1916 seems to have been a particular turning point in forming this vision. That year, Moise Lafleur, a United Fruit Company physician who accompanied him into the Petén, was shot and killed when Guatemalan troops mistook the party for members of a filibustering expedition that had been mounted by Mexican revolutionaries. Morley's biographers observe that the death of a fellow American scholar in a feud between Latin nations would haunt him personally and shape his political vision for much of his life (see Brunhouse 1971, 106–11).

In August 1917, Morley reflected on an unpleasant encounter that he had with a pair of Guatemalan political exiles who railed against President José Manuel Estrada Cabrera, who by then had been in power for nearly twenty years. Estrada Cabrera had first invited the United Fruit Company into Guatemala, and the exiles considered him to be a US puppet. Reflecting on that conversation, and the vitriol expressed against the employers of the dead Lafleur, Morley lamented the tendency of Latin Americans to "raise hell" in their own nations and view "any interference in their affairs as a moral insult to their national pride and sovereign dignity." Suggesting that the current global order had evolved beyond the unequivocal sovereignty of individual nations, he noted that

> the time has gone by when [Latin American Nations] can bubble over in seething revolutions destroying foreign life and property. If they cannot or will not maintain order and decency within their several selves by themselves, we and other nations will have to do it for them by force of arms if necessary.[6]

Morley's writings about the appropriate limits of national sovereignty in 1917 are consistent with an emergent ideology shared by American social scientists who were engaged in foreign policy in the first half of the twentieth century. In a 2003 biography of the geographer Isaiah Bowman, Neil Smith notes that the original, expansionist project of US imperialism essentially ended with the territorial acquisitions of 1898. By the dawn of the twentieth century, the United States would articulate its imperial ideal less in terms of the expansion of physical territory, emphasizing instead the creation of a stable global order for the expansion of an increasingly internationalized industrial and financial complex. Theodore Roosevelt famously distinguished this form of "expansion"—based on the shared economic progress that could be wrought by American capital—from the older and less noble goals of "imperialism" (McCullough 1977, 255).

I mention Isaiah Bowman, one of the intellectual architects of this "expansionist" vision, because of some important parallels between his trajectory and Morley's. Along with archaeologists Alfred Kidder and Herbert Spinden, Bowman and Morley overlapped as undergraduate students at Harvard during the Roosevelt presidency (Givens 1992). Like many of their fellow "Harvard men," they developed an early suspicion of "reds," "Bolsheviks," and "revolutionists" who threatened to derail international prosperity by seizing upon the discontent of politically disenfranchised and culturally "backwards" elements of their societies. In essence, they were part of a cohort of intellectual elites who shared a vision of global politics in which political stability hinged on the expansion of US power and capital to "backwards" parts of the hemisphere.

Elements of this "expansionist" global doctrine would continue to emerge in Morley's diaries through the 1920s and 1930s, as did references to his personal trauma around the death of Dr. Lafleur. However, when compared to entries from his years as a spy, later entries show a surprising degree of pragmatism regarding "reds" and "revolutionists." This shift, in part, reflects the change in Morley's academic role from that of an explorer documenting sites and hieroglyphic inscriptions throughout the Maya lowlands to being the director of the project of excavation and restoration at Chichén Itzá. Part of Carnegie's success in Mexico was due to its policy of leaving all antiquities that were uncovered in the host country, a tendency that rankled older institutions such as the Peabody Museum and American Museum of Natural History. Nationalistic laws that limited forms of collecting considered legitimate by prestigious American institutions ran counter to Morley's earlier thoughts about the limits of the sovereignty of "unsettled" nations. But he seems to have embraced the Carnegie policy to a degree that some of his North American colleagues considered to be sanctimonious. In a 1928 letter, Kidder commented to CIW director Merriam that Morley's repeated praise of the institute's no-collection policy in Mexico had created unnecessary friction with Harvard and related institutions, who feared that they would be cut out of any research in the country.[7]

Beyond the work of excavation and restoration, Morley's job as director of the Chichén Itzá project involved entertaining nearly constant visits from Mexican and foreign dignitaries, as well as delicate negotiations with the "revolutionists" who were then in charge of the Mexican government. The most central of these relationships was with the Socialist governor Felipe Carrillo Puerto. Referring to their first meeting in 1923, Morley noted that the governor was "very Red. Socialistic, if not to say Bolshevistic."[8] A week later, however, he was charmed by a "perfectly splendid" speech in Yukatek Maya that Carrillo Puerto gave at a dinner held for Mexican archaeologists and representatives of the CIW.[9] After his return to the vicinity of Chichén Itzá, Morley would send telegrams to the governor in which he playfully addressed Carrillo Puerto as the "Halach Uinic of Yucatán."[10] That March, Morley gave a talk to a large audience in Mérida in which he brought down the house by writing the birthdays of the governor and several other local notables in Maya glyphs. Afterward he recalled: "Don Felipe Carrillo came behind and gave me a real Yucateco *double abrazar*" (two-armed hug), and said it was "magnifico."[11]

This fast friendship with Carrillo Puerto may reflect a softening of Morley's feelings towards "revolutionists" in the years after the Great War, or the simple fact that the CIW required the governor's goodwill to gain the necessary support for their project at Chichén Itzá. But the tone of entries in Morley's diary suggests that his feelings toward the governor were sincere. By March 1923, he refers to him as "Felipe" in the diary and writes of their "jaunts" in the governor's car and shared love of oranges.[12] By that summer, he wrote about his eagerness to accept an invitation to stay at the governor's house and be the guest of honor at a formal dinner party upon his return to the state.[13]

This bromance would be short-lived, as Carrillo Puerto was arrested and assassinated during the De La Huerta rebellion, less than a year after his first formal meeting with Morley. Still, the memory of the unlikely friendship, and its impacts on the work of the CIW, crop up in Morley's later correspondence. In March 1930, he wrote to Merriam to describe a series of talks in the Socialist Party headquarters known as the Casa del Pueblo. He noted the martyr's cult that had developed around Carrillo Puerto just a few years after his assassination and that a number of "old friends" from his administration had found positions in the new gubernatorial administration after several years of having been sidelined from regional politics. He noted that "there can be no doubt that his friendship for us and our work here has helped ever since this new administration has come in, and will probably continue to do so during its incumbency."[14] Morley was correct in this regard, and his own personality as the CIW's representative in Yucatán would make him a popular figure among the state's urban elites. Among the various honors he received, he was inducted into the politically eclectic Liga de Acción Social, an invitation that he accepted after convincing his superiors that this was not a "red" organization, notwithstanding the reference to "social action" in its name and charter.[15]

By the time that he turned forty, Morley's archaeological career had two established dimensions. First, he was a scholar who published his extensive experience in Mexico and Central America for American academic audiences. Second, he was a successful and very popular representative of the United States in academic and political circles in Yucatán. Each of these two dimensions involved a distinct register of mixed Spanish and English. These different discursive tendencies, and their implications for Morley's perception of his own social roles, will be the focus of the next section.

ON MORLEY'S AWFUL SPANISH, AND EVEN WORSE YUKATEK

Morley's youthful endorsement of "Big Stick" diplomacy was not the only factor that made his popularity in postrevolutionary Yucatán surprising. There is also an issue of communication. By all accounts, Morley's Spanish was barely intelligible, improving only slightly over the course of the 1920s and 1930s. He was helped by the fact that many of his interlocutors were elite Yucatecans with some level of fluency in English. Nevertheless, Morley seems to have capitalized on the image that he projected of an affable gringo who charmed his listeners with nigh-incomprehensible expressions of affection and solidarity. Redfield referred to the success of Morley's speeches in "fluent, awful Spanish" in letters to his wife,[16] suggesting that the archaeologist's peers recognized a degree of method behind his performances of linguistic ineptitude. This is supported in some of Morley's own statements.

It's clear from Morley's diary that his knowledge of Spanish was rooted in the technical practicalities of his fieldwork rather than on systematic study. For example, like many beginning language learners, he pays little attention to assigning the correct gender articles to many nouns and confuses different iterations of the "to be" verbs. His use of many words seems to be based on interpretations of the context in which he learned them. For example, I remember being confused by a series of diary passages from 1914 that refer to inconveniences and misfortunes that occurred during that week as *bromas*, a word that means joke. I eventually surmised that Morley derived a contextual understanding of a common expression of frustration, parece broma, or "it seems like a joke," as a literal statement about the presence of misfortune.[17]

Like the instances of mock Spanish discussed by Hill, Morley's use of Spanish words and phrases in his English prose tended to carry a distinct moral commentary on the people that he encountered. The most common instances of Spanish words in entries from Morley's days trekking through the lowlands are in contexts that express frustration about the difficulty of sourcing supplies. Writing of one of his first expeditions in Yucatán, when he was twenty-four, he noted that he

> did some shopping but ran across my four old acquaintances—"no hay," "quien sabe," "manana," [*sic*] and "ahorita"—so that I could accomplish nothing.[18]

This type of sentence remained fairly consistent during the decades that he conducted research in Mexico and Guatemala. In 1914, he wrote from Guatemala that "we are going to cook our own supper, as none in the village will prepare a meal"— "no hay frijoles"—"no hay carne"—"no hay arroz"—"no hay nada."[19]

This use of "no hay" has deep roots in the writing of Anglo-American travelers, from at least the time of John Lloyd Stephens (1836–41). Like Morley, Stephens seems to have spoken a quite rudimentary Spanish. Stephens's tendency to use Italian cognates to Spanish words in his books led his contemporary and fellow travel writer Fanny Calderón de la Barca to comment that he should at least learn how to spell Spanish if he was to write about Mexico (see von Hagen 1947, 200). Also, like Morley, Stephens used Spanish phrases as an expression of frustration toward the people that he encountered on his travels. Throughout his texts, he made frequent references to the "mortifying answer [of] *no hay*" that often accompanied his requests for basic supplies in rural areas ([1841] 1963, 239). In this sense, Morley's relationship to certain lexical "old acquaintances" was anticipated by a trope in Anglo-American travel writing that he would have encountered years before entering the field.

Over the years, Morley's repertoire of stereotyped Spanish phrases expanded beyond the basic toolkit that he acquired from reading nineteenth-century travelers. After the mid-1920s, when he took the reins of the CIW project at Chichén Itzá, his Hispanicized statements of frustration tended to focus more on developments in local politics than on the difficulties of provisioning excursions into the bush. This type of phrasing became common in his letters to CIW director John Merriam. Mirroring the more formally educated language of his elite interlocutors in 1930s Mérida, he referred to the difficulty of conducting work in the weeks after an election with the phrase "todo está paralizado."[20] A 1935 historical congress in which discussion was usurped by left wing students and agitators as a "fracaso completo."[21]

To summarize, the stereotypical Spanish phrases that dot Morley's informal writing evolve along with his role in the field, but they remain fairly consistent with the same established pattern. As a form of mock Spanish, it invoked stereotypes of impoverished and unreliable Latin Americans to generate solidarity among Anglo peers who saw themselves as "old hands" at working in that region of the world. But Morley also seems to have mastered another register of hybrid Spanish/English discourse. Performances of what Redfield referred to as his "fluent awful Spanish" to Mexican audiences played a complementary role in generating a different kind of solidarity with "natives." Referring to a talk that he gave to a large and socioeconomically diverse crowd at the Casa del Pueblo, he wryly observed that "I suspect that my Spanish contributed as much to their entertainment as the slides." Well aware that many Yucatecans found his fumbling gringo act disarming, he went to considerable lengths to place his well-intentioned linguistic incompetence on display.

These performances weren't limited to awful Spanish. There was some truly atrocious Yukatek Maya as well. In March 1923, when Morley was preparing for a second lecture on the project at Chichén Itzá, he remembered the fine speech that Carrillo Puerto had delivered in Maya during their first public meeting. He asked the governor to provide him with a simple Maya closing. Below is Morley's written text of the governor's words, which he delivered to the audience. It is followed by my best attempt to decipher his transcription, and a translation into English.

Itial in socal in cichpan, non nanex yetel in uechebelex in kat in sates in yacunail tumen Talerx a u yox in kaite, to lacal le balcak, umen te maob. Le uch ben vinicob vay Yucatáne, to loomil kutz, u lookil cek soc belo.[22]

*

Tial in ts'o'okol [in t'aan], in ki'ichpam xunane'ex yetel in weetxiibile'ex, in k'at in ts'aike'ex in yakunail tumen a taale'ex a wu'uyike'ex in k'aite, tu laajkal le ba'al[o'ob] tu mentaj le Mayao'ob, le uchben winiko'ob way Yucatáne, tu luumil kutz, u luumil kej. Ts'o'ok beyo.

In closing, my beautiful ladies and fellow gentlemen, I want to give you my love because you came to listen to me sing about all of the things that the Maya made, the ancient people of Yucatán, in the land of the pheasant and the deer. I am done now.

I provide a full transcription for two reasons. First, I want to underscore the lack of any attempt on Morley's part to record the words offered to him by the governor with any consistency or accuracy. The orthography that he used is a purely improvised one, that makes little use of graphic conventions that were well established in colonial period texts and that had been adapted by Anglo-American scholars since at least the work of Daniel Brinton in the 1890s (Brinton 1882). Second, the context of this narrative highlights the purely performative, rather than denotative, context of Morley's speech. It's tempting to think that Morley and Carrillo Puerto both assumed that there was little point in trying to compose a message with more substance, due to the former's limited linguistic ability. Given how much phonetic information seems to have been lost between Carrillo Puerto's utterance and Morley's improvised transcription—which included the omission of entire syllables as well as the misrepresentation of key glottalized consonants and rearticulated vowels—it is unlikely that Morley could have repeated this speech in a way that would have been intelligible to the Maya speakers in the audience. In essence, this closing serves no real purpose other than to stage a moment in which Morley publicly attempts to speak Maya for the entertainment of his listeners.

Morley's characterization of his own performances for Yucatecan audiences seem to confirm this strategy. Referring to one of his speeches that he delivered to Carrillo Puerto's court, he noted that

> just before the speeches were over I rose, and as a fellow Yucateco proposed a toast to the visiting strangers from the north of our country of Yucatán and wished them welcome down here. The idea seemed to tickle everyone's fancy, calling myself a fellow-Yucateco, and I really got the largest round of applause of all. People are the same all over the world. They would rather be amused than instructed, and will pay higher for a good laugh than for a serious valuable thought.[23]

Like the stylistic choices that he made when incorporating Spanish terms in his informal English prose, speeches performed in "fluent awful Spanish" made a strategic use of humor (see Brunhouse 1971, 319). Building upon Hill, Jennifer Roth-Gordon has suggested that these joking registers reflect the vulnerability and permeability of whiteness as much as they do a more-or-less stable racial hierarchy. She notes that for many English monolinguals, their own knowledge of certain Spanish words and phrases embodies an uncomfortable social proximity to the Spanish-speaking underclass that they wish to differentiate themselves from. The "mock" component of their humorous performances of Spanish achieve this by placing the speakers' uncomfortable knowledge of the language into its hierarchically correct place (Roth-Gordon 2011).

The archival record of Morley's informal writing suggests that his mixing of "proper" and "improper" language worked in two self-conscious and distinct registers. First, in his diary entries and letters to Merriam and Kidder, choosing lexical "old acquaintances" to express logistical frustration and superficial contentment allowed him to draw a line between the Mexicans with whom he collaborated by necessity and the WASP intellectuals he saw as his true national and professional peers. Second, his performances of "fluent awful Spanish" in Mérida demonstrated that, notwithstanding humorous claims to be a "fellow Yucatecan," he was indisputably a gringo. While the first of these registers served to articulate solidarity with those he considered serious scholars, the second was useful for inspiring affection in people who preferred "a good laugh" to "serious, valuable thought."

REDFIELD: A MIDWESTERN FAMILY MAN IN MORLEY'S YUCATÁN

If Morley's national and ethnic identity seems to map neatly onto his social solidarities, Robert Redfield's private writings reveal someone with a far more circumspect attitude toward the political and professional aspects of gringohood. In many passages, he shows an almost aloof attitude to many of the contexts in which Morley seemed to have relished the performance of gringohood. This applies to both his encounters with elite and middle-class Yucatecans, and to his working dynamic with his fellow CIW scholars. As I will argue, this expression reflects generational and geographical differences as much as it does Redfield's own personality.

My perspective on how Redfield viewed his place in Mexico is skewed by the fact that one of the richest sources for this analysis are letters he wrote home to his wife, Margaret "Greta" Park. These are marked by an affect that is very different from the homosocial bonds that characterized Morley's diary entries and his exchanges with Kidder and Merriam. Nevertheless, the dynamic embodied in these letters is consistent with a larger set of generational and theoretical as well as personal differences that made Redfield's consciousness of his own gringohood substantially different from Morley's.

By the mid-1930s, Redfield had established himself as a theorist of folk culture, hinting at a taste for conceptual abstraction that would define modern anthropological theory but that had almost no place in Morley's intellectual realm. Redfield's own writing hints at how these different predilections shaped the way that each author processed their personal encounters with Maya people. In *The Little Community*, which he published five years after his last major foray in Maya studies, Redfield reflected on how standardized psychological tests had transformed studies of personality or "character" in the decades since his Carnegie days. He noted, for example, that CIW eugenicist Morris Steggerda's attempt to apply controlled psychological tests in the 1930s was unconvincing, without the benefit of Rorschach and other tests that emerged later in the 1930s. Redfield seems to ascribe a similar lack of academic relevance to the highly personal anecdotal evidence that marked the writing of his old collaborators. Including his own early impressions in this critique, he noted that

> I know that Dr. Morley enjoyed and liked the Maya Indians even more than I did, and although much of what he tells me to be true about Maya personality agrees with my own impression, such assent as I give to it rests on Dr. Morley's impressions and their coincidence with my own . . . Both of us, saying what we could about Maya personality, were swayed by I do not know what uncontrolled personal experiences (1960, 70–71)

"Uncontrolled" in this context doesn't refer to an excess of sentiment, but to the fact that the intimate interpersonal experiences that mark ethnographic fieldwork lack the experimental "controls" of a lab-based study. This rejection of subjective ethnographic impressions is consistent with tendencies that placed Redfield on the margins of US anthropology from the beginning of his career. Even before he joined the Carnegie project, Redfield proclaimed a "sociological" emphasis that reflected the influence of his mentor and father-in-law, the sociologist Robert Park, and often drew from nineteenth-century figures such as Ferdinand Tönnies and Henry Maine. The influence of these evolutionist figures posed a stark contrast to Franz Boas's students, whose focus on cultural relativism was leading them to a series of psychologistic theories that sought to explain the emergence of distinct collective personalities or "national characters" in different human populations. This theoretical contrast was even starker with the Carnegie crowd, whose focus on descriptive culture history left little room for comparative analysis or abstract generalizations of any sort.

If Redfield "enjoyed and liked" Yukatek Maya people a bit less than Morley did, it might also be because Morley was more fully integrated into the larger sphere of sociality that had brought this particular group of gringo researchers to the peninsula. This provided the context for social interactions with Yucatecan "locals" that ranged from the visits by the Mérida Rotary Club to Chichén Itzá to dances and parties that Morley sponsored for residents of Pisté and other Maya-speaking communities that surrounded the site.

Redfield's awkward fit into the social "scene" of the CIW reflects a range of geographical and generational factors that set him apart from the somewhat older "Harvard Men." Morley had participated in the Great War as a thirty-something spy in a region where he had already conducted close to a decade of research. His initial suspicion of "revolutionists" reflected the fact that he had begun his research as a young adventurer during the final few years of the relatively xenophilic Porfiriato. He shared these experiences and perspectives with fellow "Harvard Men" such as Kidder, Tozzer, and Karl Ruppert. In contrast, the Midwestern Redfield's war experience was as a twenty-year-old volunteer ambulance driver on the Western Front. He returned home to Chicago to earn a law degree, practice for several years, and marry Greta Park, before exploring a career in academia under the mentorship of her father, Robert. By the time that he and Greta first visited Mexico in the mid-1920s, he was a family man in his early thirties (Wilcox 2004). For the Redfields, the nationalistic revolutionary state was a pervasive fact of life, and no longer an unfortunate turn of events that had led to Tozzer's temporary expulsion from the country in 1914 (Ruiz 2003) and frustrated the early projects of the older Harvard Men.

Earlier in this chapter, in the section on Sylvanus Morley, I mentioned parallels between the intellectual and career trajectories of Morley and the geographer Isaiah Bowman. Tensions between Bowman and the social theorists of Redfield's generation are just as telling. Neil Smith describes a 1930 conference of the recently founded Social Science Research Council (SSRC) in which Bowman presented a version of his "pioneer fringe" theory to argue for the role of geography as a social science. As I noted earlier, this theory can be read as a broad legitimation of both western expansion and turn-of-the century imperialism, which accounted for its popularity during the era of colonial administration and "Big Stick" diplomacy. Decades later, Bob Redfield wrote to Greta from the SSRC conference. He described Bowman's perspective as "claptrap" that was widely panned by the younger sociologists who were present (Smith 2004, 219–220). When he joined the CIW effort in Yucatán in 1930, he must have been aware that the older scholars on the project shared an intellectual trajectory with Bowman, as well as visions of universal history that he and his cohort were working to transcend.

In this sense, Redfield's identity as an Anglo-American ethnographer in Mexico seems to have been shaped by a simultaneous sense of ethnic difference from his native interlocutors and of intellectual difference from his gringo peers. If the latter difference threatened his long-term employment by the project, the former had immediate impacts on his ability to conduct research. Unlike Morley and the other archaeologists, Redfield was expected to successfully communicate with rural Yucatecans who were far more fluent in the Maya language than they were in Spanish. This is evident from the very different role that languages play in Redfield's letters to Greta than they do in Morley's private writings.

MUGGERT AND BUGGERT

In many of Redfield's letters home, Greta is addressed with the pet name "Muggert," and Robert signed as "Buggert." But underneath this uxorial sentimentality, the letters are detailed about both life in Yucatán and theoretical debates and political conflicts within anthropology. This content reflects the fact that Greta was not simply the daughter of Redfield's mentor but also a partner in his research since his first field seasons in Tepoztlan. She conducted her own research on folklore in Dzitás, which was published in 1935 as *The Folk Literature of a Yucatecan Town* (Redfield 1935). Through this intimate relationship with an intellectual peer, Redfield confided a series of doubts regarding his place in the Carnegie project and, more broadly, as a fieldworker.

Bob wrote to Greta after the first day of the 1930 conference at Chichén Itzá in which he first laid out his research proposal to Kidder, Morley, and the other Carnegie archaeologists. From the beginning, his proposal of a theoretically informed study of modernization in the region was a difficult sell. He confessed that he was fairly sure of having "talked his way out of a job," though he claimed that he preferred to search for a new field site over spending time documenting "how Maya play cat's cradle"[24]

This and other letters also suggest that his reservations about the Carnegie project had as much to do with the political constraints imposed by the institute's unique position in Yucatán, and the personalities involved. He referred to Morley as "The Earl of Chichen," suggesting that he spent more time entertaining Mexican and foreign dignitaries from his archaeological fiefdom than conducting serious academic work. Redfield would later tell Greta that Merriam and Kidder were pushing an expanded program in ethnography and linguistics on the Chichen project in order to justify the immense cost that had been incurred setting up headquarters at the site, much to the annoyance of Morley, Karl Ruppert, and the other Harvard archaeologists.[25]

Other tensions reflect the fact that Redfield was a disinterested latecomer to political negotiations that Morley, Kidder, and Merriam had been working through for close to a decade. After his second meeting with Kidder and Morley, he noted their continued reticence about his proposal to do a general ethnographic study of contemporary Yucatecan life. As he wrote to Greta, "They were very afraid of this, because their position with the Yucatecans is pretty delicate anyway, and they want no sensitive spots touched."[26] These concerns would continue throughout his relationship with the Carnegie. Two years after beginning his research, he noted that he sent the initial manuscript of what would be the monograph *Chan Kom* to Kidder so that the latter could confirm that it included no material that would be "offensive to the Yucatecans."[27]

In Redfield's letters home, "the Yucatecans" refers not to the Maya-speaking agriculturalists who were to be his research subjects but to people of Hispanic social identity from the predominantly urban middle and upper classes. These are individuals with whom Morley seems to have thoroughly enjoyed socializing, from the bromance with Governor Carrillo Puerto, to a dalliance with the Mérida socialite Margarita Sauri, to the various visitors that he entertained at Chichén Itzá. Bob Redfield, however, showed a marked reserve toward this group in his letters to Greta. His first impression is telling. Writing home in January 1930, he noted that "it is certainly odd to see their facial contour repeated over and over again . . . like a crazy cartoon where everyone looks like Andy Gump."[28]

On the surface, Redfield's comparing the "facial contour" of Yucatecans to the popular Midwestern comic character is consistent with a pejorative stereotype that is common in central Mexico, where residents of the state are still referred to as *cabezones y narizones* (big-headed and big-nosed). But there is also a moral commentary behind the association that seems consistent with other descriptions that he provides of Hispanic Yucatecans. The comic strip *The Gumps* was conceptualized by publisher Joseph Patterson as focusing on an essentially ordinary American family. "Gump" was a term that Patterson used to refer to boorish and opinionated members of the general public, qualities embodied by the grandiose but always lazy and incompetent character of Andy (Welky 2008, 68–70). There is a notable "gumpishness" in many of Redfield's characterizations of urbanized Hispanic Yucatecans. He related to Greta how members of a Merida Rotary Club swarmed into Chichén Itzá, where they were feted by Morley with beer, tacos, and a speech in his characteristic Spanish. He noted that many of them had taken American nicknames such as "Deek" and "Arry" (Dick and Harry) and drunkenly bestowed the Rotarian nickname of "Chichen" onto Morley.[29]

Similar disdain is evident in the description that Redfield gave of a tour of the vicinity of Tizimin, where he was taken by the Yucatecan educator and CIW collaborator Pedro Castillo. He wrote disapprovingly about the "commercialization" of the town's fiesta, which today brings millions of pesos to the town as one of the largest regional expos in Mexico. Castillo introduced him to an individual that he refers to only as "Don Pepe," who is likely a local politician named José María Arce.[30] Don Pepe took him on a tour of surrounding villages. Redfield described to Greta how this "tedious companion" spoke almost nonstop about his popularity in the town, various political intrigues, and any political opinion that came to his mind. They stopped at the village of Pambiha, which Don Pepe said would be of interest to the ethnographer. Redfield soon realized that the choice of that village was so that they could have a meal at the house of Don Pepe's married mistress while her husband was in the milpa. As they rested in their respective hammocks, Redfield's guide offered him unsolicited details of the affair in Spanish, including the fact that he was the father of one of the hostesses' sons. Perhaps sensing the disapproval of this gringo ward, Don Pepe eventually ignored Redfield to engage in a Maya-language conversation with the woman.[31] At the conclusion of the tour, Redfield wrote to Greta that the behavior of the "townsmen" of Tizimin made him "ashamed of the race."[32]

The characterization of Don Pepe and other Hispanic Yucatecans as "townsmen" hints at some of the early reactions that may have shaped Redfield's mature theory of modernization, which focused on the diffusion of cultural traits that assimilated "folk" cultures into more westernized ones. In his letters, the Rotarians "Dick" and "Harry" are provincial but aspiring copies of their gringo fellow club members. Where Morley drew on old stereotypes of Hispanic backwardness, Redfield saw a society transforming into a tropical simulacrum of the quintessential Midwestern blowhard Andy Gump.

Where Redfield's frequent frustrations about Mexico stemmed from the country being "too" Latin, Redfield's "gumpish" characterization of Hispanic Yucatecans seems to hinge on the ways that they were assimilating the "worst" components of American modernity. This different emphasis may account for language choices of Robert Redfield's letters to Greta, which tended to make sparse use of stereotypical expressions of frustration like Morley's "old acquaintances." Even in the handwritten letters, Redfield tended to underline Spanish words, as if to italicize them for a formal academic publication. The only Spanish terms that he used in his account of his time with "Don Pepe" included one reference to his host as one of the *vecinos principales* (prominent citizens) of town, and one use of the term *blanco* to refer to his light skin. Redfield quotes Don Pepe as complaining about the state of *las cosas* ("things"), as referring to his traditionally garbed mistress as *mestiza*, as referring to his legitimate son as *de casa* (from my house), and as characterizing himself as a devoted friend to *gente baja* (poor people). Beyond these, the Spanish words in those passages are references to carts, benches, geographical features, and other household items. Notably missing are stereotypical phrases like *no bueno* that often accompanied Morley's description of characters that he found unsavory.

References to his and Greta's shared experience of Mexico also constitute a different cultural and professional landscape from Morley's diary. Morley's letter to Kidder and Merriam, like the diary entries composed for his own amusement, situated Spanish within the homosociality of self-identified gringos undertaking arduous adventures in "the bush," men who bonded through experiences of the Latin American "other" that they also shared with bygone figures such as John Lloyd Stephens. When "Buggert" wrote to "Muggert," gringohood was inflected through the different sentimentality of two people who had experienced Mexico as a married couple, bringing their children to extended field visits in Tepoztlan and later Dzitás. In January 1930, as he waited to hear if he had convinced Kidder and Morley to bring him on as the CIW's ethnographer, he confessed to Greta that he could not take the position "as seriously" as other men, since he viewed ethnography less as his personal occupation than as "part of our life together" since their first visits to Mexico as a married couple.[33]

This association of his experience of Mexico with the affective relationship of family life is evident in passages that express a kind of sentimentality that is rare in Morley's diary. Bob communicated his first impression of the people of Chan Kom to Greta in late January 1930:

[I] know that you would like the people. They are delightful, gentle, kindly, and timorous, they appear. Shaking hands they do with a slight touch of embarrassment, but they always do it. And smile beautifully. The children are exceedingly attractive. You remember in Tepoztlan they mostly had short thick stolid ones. Here, they are slimmer, livelier, more alert. They remind me of Japanese children. I saw several today [that] I wanted to hug.[34]

The vignette composed by this passage also brings us to another telling difference between Redfield's textual characterizations of his relationship to rural Maya speakers versus "the Yucatecans." Where he was able to provide Greta with the unsavory details of Don Pepe's story in Tizimin, his more favorable description of people from Chan Kom is based on physical appearance, expressions, and nonverbal behaviors and gestures. Even if he had wanted to include more details of conversations in Chan Kom, the words of Maya-monolingual rural people were inaccessible to him. Although colleagues such as the philologist Ralph Roys occasionally wrote to him to clarify points of Maya vocabulary,[35] there is little evidence that Redfield was truly conversational in the language.

Redfield's descriptions of his first encounters with the Yukatek language underscore how different fieldwork was before the wide availability of the textbooks, audiocassette series, and formal language courses with which anthropologists prepare for fieldwork today. He had never heard the language spoken before he arrived in the peninsula in 1930 and described it to Greta as sounding like "a series of stifled sneezes."[36] He even misspelled the name of his new field site as "Chan Com." It wasn't until early February, several weeks into his first field visit, that he realized that the "K" of the second syllable represented a glottalized consonant that he had only just learned how to pronounce.[37]

This lack of knowledge created the necessity for a series of translators that play a far greater role in Redfield's letters home and personal notes than they do in his published work. His first attempt to find a steady informant and translator was to hire a teenage boy from the Tamay family of Chan Kom, who had been recommended by a CIW colleague who visited the village. Redfield ultimately found him "dumb, but willing," and did his best to record the boy's genealogy before seeking out more successful translators.[38] Later on that trip, he met Alfonso Villa Rojas, who would be his most frequent collaborator. The two were often accompanied and assisted by their chief informant from Chan Kom, the political leader Eustaquio Cimé. Between 1930 and 1935, Redfield also reported to Greta about other excursions in which he was assisted by a teacher in Pisté named Castro.[39]

Where Morley was fond of making sweeping statements about the character and motivations of his Mayan and Hispanic interlocutors, Redfield made several confessions about the limitations of this approach in his letters to Greta. He described his disappointment with the results of his attempt to generate data on childbirth practices, which involved interviewing elderly midwives about intimate details of their work. He described the awkward scene of:

> three men descending upon a little old *viejecita*. I put the question in Spanish, the maestro [Villa Rojas] occasionally elaborated on my question for Eustachio [*sic*] [Cime], who then put the question in Maya, and returned what he could of the answer. I am more than ever convinced of the value of the intimate, friend-to-friend method of ethnological investigation.[40]

In passages like this, Redfield describes something that was a sort of open secret among anthropologists of his generation. Unlike earlier generations of missionaries and philologists who spent years mastering native languages, twentieth-century anthropologists worked with a paradigm of fieldwork that involved techniques for "working with" languages that they often had a pretty limited grasp of (see Borchgrevnik 2003). The pragmatic realities of "working with" Yukatek are less evident in the text of *Chan Kom* and Redfield's other published works, but his letters show that he recognized this as a limitation of his fieldwork. His reticence to comment about the subtleties of "personality" in *The Little Community* is consistent with the methodological concerns that he had communicated to Greta twenty years earlier.

Read alongside the particular style of Spanish code-switching that I discussed earlier in this chapter, Redfield's self-conscious admissions about the limits of his Yukatek present an important counterpoint to Morley's playful uses of language. Morley was an archaeologist, for whom languages other than English were incidental tools for social networking and managing laborers. If he used mock Spanish to bond with his Harvard peers, and fluent awful Spanish to amuse Yucatecans, it did nothing to detract from the seriousness of his real archaeological labor. For Redfield, Spanish and Yukatek played a more important role in generating scholarly data. "Friend-to-friend" interactions were not auxiliary to research. He characterized them specifically as a "method," highlighting their role at the heart of his intellectual endeavor.

By the time that he wrote *The Little Community*, Redfield was aware of the larger scholarly consequences of his linguistic limitations, which constricted his access to certain aspects of the Mayan peoples' "character" to "uncontrolled" impressions. Insofar as he was able to develop a "friend-to-friend" method of interviewing, it involved focusing his data collection on the subset of the community of Chan Kom that had a fair command of the Spanish language. A passage from a letter to Greta, written from Pisté sometime between 1935 and 1941,[41] shows just how much his research tended to hinge on this relatively small group of individuals. Redfield noted that he was "delighted" to see Eustaquio Cimé (Don Eus) for the first time in several years, noting that "it was like meeting a real friend." But when he learned that Don Eus and his companions were headed to Mérida to attend some agrarian committee business, he decided that it was not worthwhile to visit Chan Kom without them, and he headed to Dzitás to await word of their return.[42]

As Redfield's critics from the 1950s and 1960s noted, this reliance tended to narrow his perspective on the local political and economic realities of Chan Kom and to conceal factional conflict and class hierarchies within the community (Goldkind 1966, see also Armstrong-Fumero 2013, 38–43; 2018). Although Redfield died before much of this revisionist literature was published, he did live to engage in an initial defense of his work from critiques by Oscar Lewis (Stocking and Redfield 1989). Insofar as his inability to see certain forms of intracommunity conflict and hierarchy are a result of his reliance on particular bilingual informants, Redfield faced intellectual consequences for his linguistic limitations that Sylvanus Morley never did.

To summarize, Redfield's avoidance of the kinds of mock Spanish that pepper Morley's private writing reflects disciplinary and generational differences that are as significant as the differences in their personalities. An outsider to the Harvard crowd that formed the core of the CIW's Yucatán mission, Redfield may have been less inclined to invoke the well-worn ethnic tropes inherited from nineteenth-century travel writing. And where Morley seems to have reveled in his own linguistic incompetence, the very nature of fieldwork in Yukatek-speaking communities turned this into a source of anxiety for the ethnographer. Thus, while certain kinds of mock-Spanish performance would still be alive and well when I was initiated into fieldwork at the end of the 1990s, Redfield's experience hints at the emergence of new forms of linguistic and cultural self-consciousness in other spaces within the discipline.

CONCLUSION

As evolving standards of public behavior make certain forms of linguistic play less acceptable in professional and educational settings, it is important to place anthropologists' mock Spanish in historical context. In contrasting uses of stereotyped Spanish phrases by Morley and Redfield, I have tried to highlight a generational and experiential component. That is, part of Morley's proclivity to use this sort of linguistic play reflects his own experiences as part of a generation that tended to take the legitimacy of Anglo-Saxon imperialism and ethnic supremacy as more of a given than those educated after the First World War. Second, Redfield's linguistic anxieties reflected his very different fieldwork experience as an ethnographer. Intersections between this imperialist heritage and the more complex experiences developed through engagement with local communities are still a persistent part of the experience of anthropologists today. By extension, forms of sociality between scholars and students remain an important site for reflecting on the ethics of research and scholarship.

Morley's informal writing offers a seemingly incongruous mixture of narrow-minded bigotry and expansive conviviality. Apparent certainty in his own intellectual authority coincides with a willingness to play the clown for different audiences. While some aspects of this are idiosyncratic, others are consistent with his integration into elite social networks that constituted him as an American presence in Mexico and Central America from his early expeditions in search of inscriptions to his spy work, to his ascendancy as the "Earl of Chichen." His attitude toward "Bolsheviks" such as Carrillo Puerto may have evolved over time, but a style of gringohood that he developed in the age of Roosevelt remained central to his public persona in revolutionary Mexico.

Read against Morley, it's hard not to perceive a series of anxieties in Redfield's reflections on life in the field, anxieties that are reflected in a far more staid and "academic" invocation of Spanish in his letters to Greta. Whereas Morley used Spanish and Yukatek Maya to entertain local publics that were only tangentially related to his "real" work, Redfield was well aware that his own intellectual legacy hinged on the ability of successful communication across languages and cultures. Working on the margins of a project dominated by the Harvard-trained archaeologists, he had little motivation to engage in this register of joking just for fun. Along with the fact he experienced a "field" very different from the late Porfirian Mexico where Morley began his work, it is possible that he saw fewer parallels between his own experiences and the *no hay*'s that had been narrated by John Lloyd Stephens.

Just as Redfield qualifies his own assessment of the character of Maya people as the product of "uncontrolled personal experience," my own interpretation of his writing and Morley's is inextricably linked to gut feelings about what different phrases mean to their author. Those uncontrolled impressions tell me that mock Spanish play correlates to the degree that a given researcher is integrated into a network of "fellow gringos" in the field. It doesn't seem like a coincidence that my own temporary acceptance of mock Spanish coincided with a period when I was taking part in field schools that functioned as small, ephemeral communities within local towns and villages, much as the CIW enclave at Chichén Itzá had functioned for several decades. Just as it proved comforting to a group of young college students spending weeks in unfamiliar social and cultural contexts, this kind of play helped Morley and his fellow "Harvard Men" remind themselves of their collective priorities even as they were drawn into close and complex relationships with different groups of Yucatecans.

Although the colonial underpinnings of the "lone ethnographer" paradigm have been a focus of critical anthropologists since the late 1980s (see Rosaldo 1989), Redfield's experience is a useful reminder of how certain aspects of fieldwork have shaped different sensibilities in different subdisciplines of anthropology. Notwithstanding the very real social and national prejudices that are evident in his letters to Greta, Redfield's relative isolation in both Chan Kom and the larger CIW enclave probably contributed to a series of intellectually productive anxieties that are less evident in Morley's informal writing. In Redfield's letters, Spanish and Yukatek Maya were less objects of play and more tools for careful methodological reflection. Whether or not he "liked and enjoyed" Maya people as much as Morley did, he was forced to reckon with the vicissitudes of language in a way that his archaeologist colleagues weren't.

By extension, it could be argued that the impact of critical approaches to archaeology that emphasize multivocality (see Hodder 2003) and other forms of engagement with local stakeholders (McAnany 2016) has disrupted the enclave bubble that traditionally surrounded archaeologists in the field. The alternate—and rather disingenuous—public persona embodied through Morley's "fluent awful Spanish" is less tenable in a situation where larger publics are more than passive audiences for the presentation of archaeological knowledge. In this context, changing patterns of play and sociality among archaeologists are not simply a reflection of new standards of polite behavior but a reflection of more meaningful transformations in the social contexts of knowledge production.

NOTES

1. MD: February 14, 1906. NOTE: The abbreviation "MD" represents Morley's Diary. There are several copies of the diaries available in archives. The one that I consulted is at the American Philosophical Society of Philadelphia. The pagination is inconsistent within and between volumes, so all of the references in this chapter will be by date of entry.

2. MD: February 4, 1907.

3. MD: Multiple entries in fall 1917.

4. MD: February 19, 1906; September 28, 1917; July 1, 1923.

5. MD: April 25, 1922; italics mine.

6. MD: August 27, 1917.

7. CIW, Kidder Correspondence, NB VI Letter, February 9, 1928, Kidder to Merriam.

8. MD: February 7, 1923.

9. MD: February 15, 1923.

10. MD: February 22, 1923.

11. MD: March 1, 1923, see also Brunhouse (1971, 175–77).

12. MD: March 24, 1923.

13. MD: June 22, 1923.

14. CIW, HS Kidder Correspondence, March–July 1930, NB VII, Morley to Merriam, March 24, 1930.

15. CIW Archives, Kidder Correspondence, NB VII, copy of letter dated February 13, 1934, Pedro Rivas of the Loga de Acción Social to Merriam; copy of letter from March 4, 1934, from E. Gil Borges of Pan American Union to Merriam.

16. Robert Redfield to Margaret Redfield, February 14, 1930, Redfield Papers, box 1, folder 5.

17. MD: February 14, 1914.

18. MD: April 7, 1907.

19. MD: April 20, 1914.

20. CIW/ HS, Morley Correspondence, 1934–35, Morley to Merriam, January 7, 1934.

21. CIW/HS, Morley Correspondence, 1934–35, Morley to Merriam, December 9, 1935:

22. MD: March 22, 1923.

23. MD: February 15, 1923.

24. Redfield to Margaret, Redfield Papers, box 2, folder 6.

25. Redfield to Margaret, February 14, 1930, Redfield Papers, box 1, folder 5.

26. Redfield to Margaret, January 21, 1930, Redfield Papers, box 1, folder 5.

27. Redfield to Margaret, n.d., Margaret Redfield Papers, box 3.

28. Redfield to Margaret, January 11, 1930, Redfield Papers, box 1, folder 5.

29. February 14, 1930, Box 1, folder 5, Redfield Papers, box 1, folder 5.

30. Many thanks to Ben Fallaw for this tentative identification of "Don Pepe."

31. Redfield to Margaret, March 29, 1930, Redfield Papers, box 1, folder 5.

32. Redfield to Margaret, March 30? 1930, Redfield Papers, box 1, folder 5.

33. Redfield to Greta, January 22, 1930, Margaret Redfield Papers, box 2, folder 6.

34. Redfield to Greta, January 24, 1930, Redfield Papers, box 1, folder 5.

35. Roys to Redfield, December 9, 1931, Redfield Papers, box 44, folder 5.

36. Redfield to Margaret, January 12, 1930, Redfield Papers, box 1, folder 5.

37. Redfield to Margaret, February 3, 1930, Redfield Papers, box 1, folder 5.

38. Redfield to Margaret, January 25, 1930, box 1, folder 5.

39. Redfield Papers, box 44, folder 5.

40. Redfield to Margaret, January 28, 1930, box 1, folder 5.

41. The letter is dated to March 27 but has no year. It was written before the Publication of *The Folk Culture of Yucatán* (1940) but after the designation of Chan Kom as an independent municipality.

42. Redfield to Greta, March 27, Margaret Redfield Papers, box 2, folder 9.

REFERENCES CITED

Armstrong-Fumero, Fernando. 2013. *Elusive Unity: Factionalism and the Limits of Identity Politics in Yucatán, Mexico*. Boulder: University Press of Colorado.

Armstrong-Fumero, Fernando. 2018. "Felipe Carrillo Puerto and the Maya Heroes That Weren't." In *Faces of Resistance*. Tuscaloosa: Alabama University Press.

Borchgrevnik, Axel. 2003. "Silencing Language: Of Anthropologists and Interpreters." *Ethnography* 4 (1): 95–121.

Brinton, Daniel. 1882. *The Maya Chronicles*. Philadelphia: n.p.

Brunhouse, Robert. 1971 *Sylvanus G. Morley and the World of the Ancient Mayas*. Norman: University of Nebraska Press.

Calderon de la Barca, Frances. (1842) 1982. *Life in Mexico*. Berkeley: University of California Press.

Givens, Douglas R. 1992. *Alfred Kidder and the Development of Americanist Archaeology*. Albuquerque: University of New Mexico Press.

Goldkind, Victor. 1966. "Class Conflict and Cacique in Chan Kom." *Southwestern Journal of Anthropology* 22 (4): 325–43.

Harris, Charles, and Louis Saddler. 2009. *The Archaeologist Was a Spy! Sylvanus Morley and the Office of Naval Intelligence*. Albuquerque: University of New Mexico Press.

Hill, Jane. 1993. "Hasta La Vista, Baby: Anglo Spanish in the American Southwest." *Critique of Anthropology* 13 (2): 145–76.

Hill, Jane. 1998. "Language, Race and White Public Space." *American Anthropologist* 100 (3): 680–89.

Hodder, Ian 2003. "Sustainable Time Travel: Toward a Global Politics of the Past." In *Politics of Archaeology and Identity in a Global Context*, edited by S. Kane, 139–47. Boston: Archaeological Institute of America.

McAnany, Patricia. 2016. *Maya Cultural Heritage: How Archaeologists and Indigenous Communities Engage the Past*. Lanham, MD: Rowman and Littlefield.

McCullough, David. 1977. *The Path Between the Seas: The Creation of the Panama Canal, 1870–1914*. New York: Simon and Schuster.

Morley, Sylvanus. 1905–34. *Diaries*. American Philosophical Society.

Nelson, Diane. 1999. *A Finger in the Wound*. Berkeley: University of California Press.

Ortega y Medina, Juan Antonio. 1953. "Monroísmo arqueológico: Un intento de compensación de americanidad insuficiente." In *Ensayos: Tareas y estudios históricos*. edited by Juan Antonio Ortega y Medina ed., 37–86. Xalapa: Universidad Veracruzana.

Redfield, Margaret. 1935. *The Folk Literature of a Yucatecan Town*. Washington, DC: Carnegie Institution of Washington.

Redfield, Robert. 1920s–1950 *Robert Redfield Papers*. University of Chicago Libraries.

Redfield, Robert. 1960. *The Little Community*. Chicago: University of Chicago Press.

Rosaldo, Renato. 1989. *Culture and Truth*. New York: Beacon Press.

Roth-Gordon, Jennifer. 2011. "Discipline and Power in the Whiteness of Mock Spanish." *Linguistic Anthropology* 21 (2): 218–29.

Ruiz, Carmen. 2003. "Insiders and Outsiders in Mexican Archaeology (1890–1930)." PhD diss., University of Texas at Austin.

Smith, Neil. 2003. *American Empire: Roosevelt's Geographer and the Prelude to Globalization*. Berkeley: University of California Press.

Stephens, John Lloyd. (1841) 1963. *Incidents of Travel in Central America, Chiapas and Yucatán*. New York: Dover.

Stocking, George, and Robert Redfield. 1989. "Ideal Types and Aging Glands: Robert Redfield's Response to Oscar Lewis's Critique of Tepoztlan." *History of Anthropology Newsletter* 16 (1): 3–10.

Vaughan, Mary Kay. 2015. *Portrait of a Young Painter*. Durham, NC: Duke University Press.

von Hagen, Wolfgang. 1947. *Maya Explorer: John Lloyd Stephens and the Lost Cities of Central America and Yucatán*. Norman: University of Oklahoma Press.

Welky, David. 2008. *Everything Was Better in America: Print Culture in the Great Depression*. Champagne: University of Illinois Press.

Wilcox, Clifford. 2004. *Robert Redfield and the Development of American Anthropology*. Plymouth, MA: Lexington Books.

4

American Idols

Bartolomé García Correa, US Americans, and the Transnational Construction of Mayanism, 1925–1935

BEN FALLAW

This chapter explores how Yucatecan politician Bartolomé García Correa and his intellectual allies collaborated with US American researchers of the Carnegie Institution of Washington (CIW) to craft what I have termed elsewhere "Mayanism," a distinct regional variant of revolutionary Mexican Indigenism (Fallaw 1997, 555–56).[1] In this dialectical process, Yucatecan revolutionaries and North American scholars modified the national discourse of Mexican Indigenism to represent pre-Conquest Maya civilization as distinct from and in some ways superior to the rest of Mesoamerica's. Like revolutionary Mexican Indigenism, Mayanism exalted a carefully curated image of the Indigenous past while integrating contemporary Indigenous people into the Spanish-speaking, culturally western, ethnically mestizo Mexican mainstream. Unlike national Indigenism, Mayanism was profoundly shaped by US American archaeologists' interventions as well as Yucatán's emerging tourist economy.[2]

In chapter 3 in this volume, Fernando Armstrong-Fumero sheds light on the close relationship between Yucatecan governor Felipe Carrillo Puerto (1922–23) and the CIW's Sylvanus Morley. This chapter explores Mayanism's formative period in the subsequent decade. From 1925 to 1935 Yucatecan politics was dominated by Bartolomé García Correa. Although virtually unknown today, García Correa served as senator (1926–28, 1934–40) and governor (1930–33), and co-founded Mexico's long-ruling national party known eventually as the PRI. García Correa's power came largely from his status as the primary ethnic broker (Wolf

https://doi.org/10.5876/9781646424276.c004

2001) between Yucatán Maya-speaking countryside and Mexico City. His preeminent role as a mediator between Spanish- and English-speaking elites on one hand and Maya culture and Maya people on the other encompassed not just electoral politics but archaeology and archaeological tourism, key parts of Mayanism coproduced with the CIW.

Understanding García Correa's status as ethnic broker requires grappling with the question of his own ambiguous ethnicity. Opponents recoiled from García Correa's populist political style, his modest origins outside of Mérida, and his dark complexion hinting at Indigenous and some said African ancestry; foes derided him as *indio*—an insult never hurled at lighter-skinned revolutionary leaders such as his mentor, Governor Carrillo Puerto. His complex ethnicity was mocked by Yucatán's regional oligarchy and conservative journalists across Mexico (Fallaw 2020, 63–64) but often fascinated US Americans who found it novel and exotic. An admiring *Boston Globe* reported the "Governor of Yucatán Is a Maya" (May 11, 1930, A:63). The *Globe's* source was a US American archaeologist of the Maya, almost certainly one affiliated with the hometown Harvard Peabody Museum such as Sylvanus Morley.

To understand how García Correa's relationships with US Americans, above all the archaeologists and anthropologists of the CIW, solidified his hold on state politics, I begin by unpacking this joint US-Yucatecan creation of Mayanism. Special attention is paid to mutual advantages in collaboration, how the CIW's research agenda reflected political necessities, and why García Correa came to prefer archaeologists and other Maya enthusiasts to diplomats as US interlocutors.[3] Next, I turn to the 1928–30 period, during which García Correa patronized neo-Maya art as part of his gubernatorial campaign and inauguration, and why US Americans archaeologists, journalists, and a banker were intrigued by a neo-Maya operetta commissioned by García Correa. I conclude by analyzing the last three tumultuous years of García Correa's administration (1931–33), when he and the CIW sought to spur archaeological tourism during the depths of the Depression.

GARCÍA CORREA AND THE CIW: THE
RECIPROCAL CREATION OF MAYANISM

Yucatecan revolutionary politicians and North American researchers were both the authors and beneficiaries of Mayanism. Because so many archaeological finds were spirited away by foreigners such as US consul to Yucatán Edward Thompson before the Mexican Revolution (Albright 2015), the CIW's researchers bent over backward to reassure Mexicans of its goodwill. Since 1868, foreigners legally had had to secure the permission of the national Secretaría de Educación Pública (ministry of education; SEP) to conduct archaeological research (Bueno 2016, 48) meant the CIW had to be well attuned to Mexican politicians' sensibilities. The CIW's frequent comparisons of Chichén Itzá to Old World archaeological treasures such as Luxor and Athens made Mayanism an even more appealing ideology for the leadership of Yucatán's revolutionary party, the Partido Socialista del Sureste (PSS). Mayanism was thus an important source of political capital for García Correa in his dealings with Mexico City and North Americans (US diplomats excepted). Sylvanus Morley, field director of the CIW, promised the excavation of Chichén Itzá would "make [it] an enduring monument to the genius of the ancient Maya" (Weeks and Hill 2006, 90). The prospect so inspired socialist Governor Carrillo Puerto that he encouraged schoolchildren to visit Chichén Itzá, believing the sight of their ancestors architectural grandeur would wake them from their apathy to become agents of their own liberation (Joseph 1988, 188–222).

US American archaeologists had to be constantly on guard against offending their hosts. The CIW could not afford to alienate Yucatecan officials, whose cooperation was absolutely necessary for its work. For instance, Robert Redfield, head of the CIW anthropological research team, had to ask the Yucatecan Department of Education for permission to hire his indispensable Maya-speaking research assistant (and eventual collaborator), Alfonso Villa Rojas, because Villa Rojas was under contract as a state schoolteacher at the time.[4] CIW archives document its self-censorship to protect its hard-won contract with the Mexican and Yucatecan government. Morley and his supervisor, Alfred Kidder, director of CIW's Historical Research, blocked funding for sociologist Eyler Simpson's research because of its "political nature": Simpson's advocacy of agrarian reform (Simpson 1937, 116–17, 256n6,7) would have offended national and state officials, above all Governor García Correa.[5] The CIW boasted of sharing its research with Mexicans, but it ensured the scholarship it sponsored would not antagonize Mexican politicians.

Intentionally or not, Robert Redfield's ethnographic research team avoided topics that could antagonize García Correa. Consider Redfield's influential concept of the folk-urban continuum, based on fieldwork in a Maya hamlet (Tusik), village (Chan Kom), town (Dzitás), and the city of Mérida. Redfield argued that Chan Kom was in transition from the folk/rural pole represented by Tusik to the modern/urban one exemplified by Mérida. During this transition, a secular worldview replaced religion, biomedicine supplanted magic, holidays (and sports and films) displaced holy days, individualism eroded extended family and community, and identification based on social class superseded Indigeneity. Over time, the folk-urban continuum posited, Indigenous Yucatecans would become acculturated and absorbed into the dominant Hispanic national society (Redfield and Villa Rojas 1934, ix–x; Redfield 1941). Redfield's ethnographic survey largely overlooked Maya-speaking working people in Mérida and omitted the population on henequen haciendas, even though CIW scientist George Dee Williams had conducted research on several in 1927 (1931, iii, xiii–xiv).

To produce a sociological study of Mérida, Robert Redfield recruited Asael Hansen (Hansen's wife made many contributions as well). Hansen's unpublished manuscript greatly aided Redfield in analyzing Mérida as part of the folk-urban continuum. Hansen chose to do most of his fieldwork in the downtown, colonial-era neighborhood of Santa Ana (Weeks and Hill 2006, 289–92). Its partial gentrification reinforced Hansen's reliance on generally conservative informants from the middle and upper classes of Mérida and kept the poorest, most Indigenous part of Mérida outside of his scholarly gaze. Had Hansen (or other members of Redfield's team) researched the urban and semiurban Maya neighborhoods on Mérida's periphery, they would have been confronted with a wealth of data not easily reconcilable with the folk-urban continuum. These Maya-speaking, working-class, and peasant communities surrounding Mérida spatially occupied the urban, so-called modern end of the continuum, but culturally, linguistically, and even economically, their lives were not that different from the people of the designated village in the continuum, Chan Kom. At a few points, Hansen's research tested CIW's apolitical practice, though it was not published until decades after the end of the CIW's work in Yucatán. Hansen never mentioned Bartolomé García Correa or the PSS by name, but he suggested Mérida's politicians (all PSS) were motivated primarily by personal ambition, not revolutionary ideology, and that they obliged the poor to attend political demonstrations and vote (Hansen and Bastarrachea 1985, 57–58).

The Yucatecan henequen haciendas were nowhere to be found on Redfield's continuum. Consequently, 30,000 Indigenous Yucatecans residing on large henequen haciendas were left out of the CIW's ethnographic project. Moreover, the henequen hacienda was almost impossible to place on Redfield's continuum. As Allen Wells and Gil Joseph have shown, the henequen hacienda was a hybrid institution. These plantations were technologically advanced (diesel-powered electricity, mobile narrow-gauge rail), highly capitalized open-air factories integrated into the global fiber market, at a time when many neighborhoods in Mérida lacked electricity. On the other hand, on many if not most haciendas, peons lived in what looked like a village, spoke Maya both at work and at home, and performed backbreaking manual labor for low wages; their children were often unschooled (Wells and Joseph 1996, 144–46). The one extant ethnographic work on haciendas in the 1930s was conducted outside the CIW's auspices by Siegfried Askinasy, a peripatetic dissident Soviet polymath. Askinasy found widespread survival of precontact Mesoamerican religious practices among peons. This was all the more remarkable because Askinasy conducted his fieldwork on Sacapuc, a model hacienda with a school, library, and brass band (Askinasy 1936). As a hybrid institution, then, the henequen hacienda simultaneously occupied both the urban/modern end and its Maya village/middle of the continuum.

By omitting the henequen hacienda and urban and semiurban Maya communities in and around Mérida, Redfield and his team avoided offending political authorities. CIW social science downplayed the desperate poverty that grew disproportionately in Indigenous communities ringing Mérida and on henequen haciendas during the Great Depression. García Correa's hold on regional power was threatened in 1931 by *marchas de hambre*, by thousands of poor hacienda residents on Mérida demanding food (*El Machete*, second half of April 1931, 2). And in the 1933 gubernatorial campaigns, foes of García Correa sought votes among the belt of poverty around Mérida (*El Yucatanista*, August 12, 1933; *Diario del Sureste*, July 16, 1933). A recent Mexican history of social anthropology in Yucatán recognizes the important role of the CIW and the University of Chicago academic researchers in spreading new methodologies in the fields of archaeology, anthropology, and linguistics but also faults Morley, Redfield, and in particular the biomedical research of George Shattuck of Harvard's Department of Tropical Medicine for attributing poverty and perceived lethargy among Maya peons of henequen haciendas to the persistence of Indigenous culture (Shattuck 1933; Guzmán Medina 2020, 79–80).

Intriguingly, Redfield's continuum mirrored Yucatecan revolutionary politicians' Mayanist claims to be modernizing the countryside but downplayed the role of the PSS in providing villages such as Chan Kom a path to modernity. The CIW social scientists never fully recognized the fact that Chan Kom's forward-thinking Maya leader Eustaquio Cimé and the village schoolteacher-turned-CIW collaborator Alfonso Villa Rojas worked from a template for "progress" that PSS leaders like Felipe Carrillo Puerto and Bartolomé García Correa had used for years in a host of small communities across Yucatán, though none achieved Chan Kom's transformations (Fallaw 2004, 165–69). Bartolomé García Correa's 1928 gubernatorial platform known as the Forty-Five Concrete Points shared a number of important assumptions about the means to modernize Maya communities with what Redfield identifies as transformative forces in Chan Kom (Bolio Ontiveros 1930, 38–41). In particular, point 11 promises to "stimulate the Indian (*el indio*) to have a better life, providing basic necessities like healthy homes, clothing, shoes and other domestic conveniences, instilling in him, moreover, sports and other diversions." Other points emphasize secularizing religious festivals, rural schooling, and showing motion pictures (38–41). Instead of Bartolista modernization, the CIW attributed Chan Kom's transformation to US researchers, Cimé, and Villa Rojas (Redfield 1950, 169). In private correspondence, Morley singled out the power that Villa Rojas enjoyed in Chan Kom, calling him the "advisor and unofficial dictator of the community."[6] In public, Redfield was careful to offer some credit to Yucatán's revolutionary government, quoting Felipe Carrillo Puerto's brother Benjamín's maxim that "it is the PSS [that] makes pueblos" (Redfield and Villa Rojas 1934, 27).

García Correa consistently supported the CIW's efforts in Yucatán but never had the close relationship with Morley as had Carrillo Puerto. Whether a genuine admirer of archaeology or not, García Correa certainly grasped its value as cultural capital and the economic potential of archaeological tourism. García Correa spent enough time visiting small pueblos in the "interior" (everything outside of Mérida) talking to his rural constituents during his long (1915–33) political career to understand what Redfield and his team of anthropologists were doing in Chan Kom. On a visit to the small towns in the far south of Yucatán, he told the *Diario de Yucatán*'s reporter that he was undertaking "a serious ethnographic study" (June 18, 1928, 6).

Despite his support for the CIW's researchers and contact with US American businessmen, he never won over US diplomats in Yucatán. In fact, State Department officials stationed in the Progreso Consulate disdained García Correa and were ignorant of (or simply ignored) García Correa's frequent interactions with the CIW and other North Americans. Perhaps the dislike was mutual. Like most revolutionary politicians, García Correa was wary of being too closely identified—at least in public—with the US government and US capital. As governor, he gave Communist organizer Antonio Betancourt Pérez—a man Morley despised—space in the Casa del Pueblo to blame Wall Street for the Great Depression (Brunhouse 1971, 259; Fallaw 2000, 3–5). García Correa also clashed with the US-owned Mérida electrical company, even briefly threatening to jail its owner (O'Brien 1996, 287–94).

Undoubtedly, US diplomats resented these actions, and they failed to understand that they were just populist posturing. This is not surprising given that there is little evidence US diplomats in Yucatán had contact with García Correa or others close to him. During this time, the US State Department required Progreso consuls to routinely submit information on religious restrictions, political violence, and henequen market conditions, but their reports do not suggest the Yankee diplomats monitoring peninsular affairs were talking to knowledgeable Yucatecan political observers. Instead, the Progreso consular reports seemed to be based entirely on information gleaned by reading Mexican newspapers and henequen trade journals, and talking to members of Mérida's upper class, a group that often spoke English and disdained García Correa.[7] Ironically, US consuls might well have been talking to some of the same Anglophone members of the Yucatecan oligarchy who hobnobbed with CIW's man in Mérida, Asael Hansen.

While obvious racism is absent from the language of diplomatic reports from Yucatán, the State Department's members stationed in Latin America and the Caribbean generally shared the racial and social biases of Latin America's upper class who served as their main informants. This perspective, in turn, shaped the

US State Department's view of populist politicos in Latin America (Roorda 1998). In early 1928, Tabascan consul Fayette J. Flexer explained the rise of authoritarian, populist governors in southeastern Mexico by citing the alleged docility of Indigenous population and region's legacy of revolutionary radicalism. In his words "Tabasco, it is recalled, shares with Yucatán the notoriety of having nursed Mexican radicalism into strength, its 85 per cent of pure or predominant Indian stock having been and being easily and blindly directed by forceful leaders."[8] Such attitudes do not seem to be outliers, and likely served as the lens through which US diplomats would view a dark-skinned populist leader such as García Correa.

US ambassadors to Mexico Dwight Morrow (1927–30) and Josephus Daniels (1933–40) embodied what would be known after 1933 as the US's Good Neighbor Diplomacy. The two ambassadors clashed with the much more probusiness, conservative State Department bureaucracy in Mexico (Cronon 1960, 11, 64, 65). Morrow, who considered García Correa a friend, criticized State Department professionals in Mexico as "cookie pushers with the milk of Groton still on their lips" (Milton 1993, 150). For its part, the CIW apparently usually detoured the Progreso Consulate and went straight to Ambassador Morrow, just like García Correa.[9] The mutual interest in archaeology, Mayanism, and Morley's diplomatic skills helped cement a relationship between the CIW and Yucatecan socialism at a time when professional diplomats residing in Yucatán showed little interest in being good neighbors with García Correa.

Little wonder, then, that US diplomats (Morrow aside) were oblivious to the fact that García Correa was by no means anti-US. Indeed, García Correa traveled frequently to the US, starting in May 1919, when he went to New York to negotiate wholesale purchases for Socialist consumer cooperatives. Before taking office as governor, he spent almost a month in late 1929 seeking investments in the US. He met with US bankers who were chartering a 2 million dollar company to look for oil in Yucatán, and he interviewed US manufacturers of textile machinery for use in industrializing the processing of henequen fiber (Comité 1930, 36–38, 219–21, 226–30). In late 1930 García Correa visited New York, but even help from former ambassador to Mexico and Wall Street banker, Morrow, could not help him achieve his likely goal: securing US credit for infrastructure, including a new road to Chichén Itzá.[10]

While García Correa's repeated efforts to lure US capital to Yucatán fell through, his real and lasting enthusiasm for US American technology never waned. García Correa was an early adapter: he owned the first bicycle in Umán, replaced Mérida's beloved electric trolleys with buses, bought a Sikorsky seaplane, and loved US-made automobiles. García Correa took time out from a political meeting in Motul to visit the local Ford distributor and try out the newest tractor model (*Diario de Yucatán*, July 29, 1927). His *pareja sentimental* Armantina Montero taught English, and he sent his first two sons by his first wife to private school in Canada, where they learned English and even converted to Anglicanism.[11] García Correa's frequent trips to the US and transnational links to North America likely helped him to grasp the advantages that came from welcoming US archaeologists and US tourists.

GARCÍA CORREA'S ASCENT AND NEO-MAYA ART

The stories of Bartolomé García Correa's political rise and the CIW's massive multidisciplinary research project both begin in 1925. The CIW had finally gained entrée to Chichén Itzá and begun its reconstruction in no small part because of help in Mexico City from Dr. Manuel Gamio, head of the Secretaría de Educación Pública's Dirección de Anthropología. Gamio, who completed his doctorate in cultural anthropology at Columbia University, overcame nationalist objections within the federal government that had long delayed the project. As Armstrong-Fumero shows in chapter 3, the CIW's dashing lead scientist Sylvanus Morley had forged a close relationship with Felipe Carrillo Puerto as well as a coterie of leftist Yucatecan intellectuals in his orbit. (Armstrong-Fumero in this volume; Morris 1931, 29–30). After Carrillo Puerto's death, both the PSS and the CIW needed each other more than ever. The PSS had been debilitated by over a year of infighting, and its future was unclear after Mexico City imposed a conservative, middle-class bureaucrat and diplomat with no support in the party, Dr. Alvaro Torre Díaz, as governor of Yucatán (February 1926 to February 1929). Although Torre Díaz marginalized some of the CIW's key contacts in the PSS, the CIW soon won the urbane bon vivant over. A ceremony on March 10, 1928, marking the CIW's return of the restored Temple of the Warriors at Chichén Itzá to the federal government attracted national Secretary of Education J. Manuel Puig Casauranc and CIW President Dr. John Merriam. Playing to Governor Torre Díaz's vanity, the CIW reminded the governor that his attendance was "was almost indispensable" because Chichén Itzá could teach so much about "the glorious race's past."[12]

The political utility of CIW and Mayanism for the PSS was on full display at the ceremony. The PSS's monthly magazine *Tierra* quoted Merriman's speech honoring the hard work and enthusiasm of the workers from the neighboring villages. The CIW's president pointed out that "the red race" and not genies built Chichén Itzá. *Tierra* went on to compare the triumphant resurrection of Chichén to Governor Torre Díaz's construction of a rural school (March 8, 1928). The modern Maya labored to build both and would (presumably) reap the benefits of both. Not for the last time, the Mayan past as remembered (or imagined) at Chichén

Itzá emphasized that the first Yucatecans had skills as peaceful, hardworking engineers and builders, not warriors. The state museum director Luis Rosado Vega, a key advisor to García Correa, endorsed educating Yucatecans about archaeology's scientific understanding of "our legendary antecedents." In praising Carrillo Puerto's love for the Maya, however, Rosado Vega elided any mention of Carrillo Puerto's tactical use of political violence and downplayed nineteenth-century ethnic violence of the "so-called Caste War."[13] Bianet Castellanos in chapter 8 discusses how tourist discourse in Cancún makes a contemporary erasure of warfare from Maya history.

Shortly after returning to Yucatán in December 1925, Torre Díaz announced his attention to spend half a million pesos to build a monumental new headquarters for the PSS, the Palacio Socialista (Torre Díaz 1930; Espadas Medina 1993). Construction began on May 1, 1926, with the presence of former president Alvaro Obregón, who would return exactly two years later as President Plutarco Elías Calles's personal representative for the inauguration. Torre Díaz tapped Bartolomé García Correa to pick the winning design. The new young president of the PSS had been plucked from the party's second tier in May 1925. García Correa quickly amassed considerable power in the Torre Díaz administration by taking over elections, labor relations, and the day-to-day operations of the administration. García Correa's committee chose Italian-Mexican architect Angel Bachini's proposal over two rivals with Maya names, Bu-Bulhá (Water bug) and Chac-Box (Red-black), though he changed the name of the project from the more aristocratic "Palace of Socialism" proposed by Torre Díaz to the more demotic "House of the People" or Casa del Pueblo (Espadas Medina 1993, 4–6). Bachini's design was basically European Baroque, but the many neo-Maya features on its facade reflected its political intent. The eye-catching serpent headed columns bore an unmistakable resemblance to those unveiled by the CIW at Chichén Itzá's principal pyramid, el Castillo, only three months earlier. Socialist Party intellectuals frequently referred to the CIW's archaeological project when they celebrated the Casa del Pueblo's inauguration. Edmundo Bolio, García Correa's preferred intellectual interlocutor, praised its "Maya Renaissance style." To Bolio this style represented the PSS's "civilizing force" that would "uplift" Mérida's working class (which was mostly of Indigenous descent) through discipline, organization, and education via the Casa's library, "Practical Night School for Workers, Popular Institute for Social Science." The Casa also offered Mérida's workers access to a free medical clinic and sporting fields.

Only a few months after the Casa del Pueblo's dedication, García Correa headed for Mexico City to serve in the national Senate. He did not leave Mayanism behind. To the contrary: it was in some ways even more important to his career in the nation's capital. In his new house on Veracruz Street in the fashionable Condesa neighborhood, the parlor became his Maya Room with archaeological pieces on exhibit to impress visitors (Comité 1930, 113). In dealings with national political elites, García Correa boasted of how the PSS centralized structure and his own profound understanding of Maya Yucatecans made him the only possible middleman between the national capital and Yucatán's countryside (Fallaw 2008, 564.) Making a pun in Spanish on his matronymic, he called himself the *correa de transmisión* (Nardelli 1928, 20–21), or transmission belt, between peasants on the peninsula and national authorities.

Mayanist spectacle reinforced this rhetoric. To launch his 1928–29 gubernatorial campaign, García Correa sponsored the Mexico City performance of a neo-Maya opera, *Payambé*, written by Luis Rosado Vega with music composed by Fausto Pinelo Río (Rosado Vega 1929; Ramírez 2009, 70). The melodramatic plot of doomed love and war set in Chichén Itzá and Tulum had no connection to Maya history before the conquest. Rosado Vega, head of the Yucatecan Museum and García Correa's inaugural committee, discreetly called it an "Evocation" of "the Maya" (Rosado 1929; *Diario de Yucatán*, February 1, 1930). While it was only performed once more (at García Correa's gubernatorial inauguration in Mérida in February 1930), it captured the imagination of both Mexico City and the US. The Mexican national government considered filming it for showing at the Expo Iberoamericana in Seville. Wells Fargo Bank's president Elmer R. Jones intended to have it performed in the Metropolitan Opera in April 1930. Pinelo Río and Rosado Vega sold the film rights to perform it in the US and Europe and signed a deal with Empire Film. There was even talk of making it the first in a planned Mayanista trilogy to be followed by *Florecimiento del imperio maya* and *Decadencia y desmembramiento y la Tercera Conquista* (Ramírez 2009). None of these plans came to fruition, but these responses point to the extremely positive reception for *Payambé*.

For our purposes, the most intriguing potential future of *Payambé* was the CIW's hope to have it performed in March 1930 in Chichén Itzá (probably on the ball court where Morley liked to play phonograph records) and to film a performance to show in the US (Ramírez 2009). Morley recognized the importance of promoting the CIW's work to the general public as well as for his institutional patron, and he was apparently something of a showman. Morley enjoyed attending musical theater (Armstrong-Fumero, personal information, 2021) and when he designed the Mayan costumes for a festival held at Chichén Itzá in 1931 (Brunhouse 1971, 214) they strongly resembled those from *Payambé*.

Morley's apparent attraction for *Payambé* underscores two larger points about the way that North American researchers and Yucatecan revolutionary politicians and intellectuals jointly constructed Mayanism. First, while the CIW promoted rigorous scientific inquiry as the only legitimate way to know the Mayan past, it still relied on highly fictionalized interpretations of preconquest Maya history with high production values such as *Payambé* to promote them. Science needed spectacle. Second, García Correa realized that *Payambé*'s political value to advance his gubernatorial ambitions in Mexico City was due in no small part to the validation that the CIW's North American researchers bestowed upon Yucatán's Maya past. García Correa's own political legitimacy as president of the PSS came from the party's claim to be the only voice of Yucatán's Maya majority, a claim bolstered by Mayanist art. Neo-Maya architecture such as the serpent columns on the Casa del Pueblo signified the party's Mayanist authority and authenticity derived in part from the CIW's research at Chichén Itzá, as well as the fact that this archaeological knowledge that was well publicized both in Mexico City and in the US. García Correa's gubernatorial campaign, it could be said, converted Mayanist cultural capital into political capital.

As part of this process, García Correa personally promoted *Payambé* in Los Angeles in January 1930.[14] It would be intriguing to imagine García Correa the tourist taking in a film at the recently opened (1927) Mayan theater (its lobby was called the Hall of the Feathered Serpent) or taking a taxi to look at one of Frank Lloyd Wright's four Maya Renaissance houses. We do know he met English-born, LA-based architect Robert Stacy-Judd in a hotel (perhaps the Aztec Hotel which Stacy-Judd designed in 1924). Stacy-Judd was so impressed by García Correa's "commanding . . . appearance," "democratic formality," and "ready smile, flashing eyes, courteous alertness and energy" that he claimed the governor elect was almost six feet tall (Stacy-Judd 1934, 36–37). García Correa convinced the architect and Maya enthusiast to come to his February 1, 1930, inauguration, where the Yucatecan politico warmly greeted his Angeleno admirer and asked to see his drawing. García Correa was in Stacy-Judd's words "vitally interested" in archaeology and asked if Stacy-Judd would support his work of "displaying to the world some of the wonders of his extraordinary country" (Stacy-Judd 1934, 37). (Perhaps his request worked too well because Stacy-Judd would go on to give lectures dressed as a Maya god.) A few days after the inauguration and Stacy-Judd's viewing of the second (and last ever) performance of *Payambé* in Mérida's Teatro Peón Contreras, Stacy-Judd and other visiting dignitaries—such as Luis de Otero, the Spanish novelist; US American journalist Emma Stevenson; and Yol-Izma (born Rebeca Viamonte Fernández [1904–1992]), the fair skinned, blue-eyed lead actress of *Payambé*—visited Chichén Itzá. Yol-Izma stayed on in Yucatán to learn more regional dances and became a dedicated exponent of *indigenista* dance across Mexico (*Diario de Yucatán*, February 7, 1930; Martínez and Villalvar 1997).

GARCÍA CORREA'S TROUBLED GOVERNORSHIP AND THE
RESILIENCE OF ARCHAEOLOGICAL TOURISM, 1931-1933

García Correa began his gubernatorial term with grand plans for modernizing Yucatán and boosting his own political future. Promoting archaeological tourism was crucial for both. His governorship was marked by frequent conflicts in Yucatán and Mexico City. Although he would return to serve in the Senate until 1940, he spent little time in Yucatán after 1934 and would move to Colima for good in the 1940s. The causes for García Correa's reverses are many, including the Great Depression, growing political opposition from the Left and Right, and a hostile Mexico City press (Fallaw 2020). These parts of García Correa's story, however, are beyond our scope here.

Despite the Depression, García Correa doubled down on archaeological tourism because it would promote economic diversification and escape dependence on the declining monocrop of henequen, spur development by getting federal help to improve infrastructure, and help him pursue a kind of regional diplomacy with important US Americans. The CIW's archaeological excavation in Chichén Itzá was already putting dollars into the pockets of Maya workers from Pisté and nearby pueblos such as Chan Kom; more gringo tourists would spread more wealth across Yucatán.

García Correa must have known that the national government had recently made tourism a priority (President Pascual Ortiz Rubio convened the first national tourist commission) and probably hoped that he could use the lure of Chichén Itzá for North Americans to tap federal funding for port and road improvements. Yucatán's archaeological heritage and contacts with the CIW amounted to valuable cultural capital that allowed García Correa to bypass the hostile US diplomats in the Progreso Consulate to deal directly with US Americans such as Robert Stacy-Judd. Another one of his acquaintances north of the border was Chauncey McCormick, an heir to the International Harvester fortune made in the henequen trade. McCormick invited García Correa to attend the Chicago opera with him in December 1930. Perhaps the two discussed the 1933 Chicago World's Fair that McCormick helped organize. Two years later, *Diario del Sureste* picked up a US wire service story that Mexico constructed a replica of the Nunnery of Uxmal for the fair (November 26, 1932). During this critical time for García Correa, he could count on the support of the CIW in promoting archaeological tourism. In his beautifully illustrated 1931 book *Temple of the Warriors*, archaeologist Earl Morris was quite candid in saying that that the CIW's project was intended not only to expand the field of human knowledge through science but also to spur Yucatán's nascent tourist industry (Morris 1931, 222–23).

Mounting political crises prevented García Correa from making long trips to the US or spending much time at Chichén Itzá for the rest of his term. We do not know if Morley, another CIW official, or Stacy-Judd lobbied Twentieth Century Fox, but the media giant dispatched a crew in February 1931 to film Movietone News features that would draw US tourists to the archaeological treasures of Chichén Itzá. They also produced a short newsreel of García Correa viewing the *jarana*, Yucatán's regional dance, performed by dozens of young women dressed as *mestizas* in dress huipil (*Diario de Yucatán*, February 10, 1931). La mestiza, something of a trope in Mayanism (Eiss 2008), popped up in the US as well. Morley's *National Geographic* article included a Maya woman in a huipil (July 1931, 109). On July 13, 1932, García Correa squeezed in a visit to Chichén Itzá to take in the new discoveries, then passed through Dzitás, where he inaugurated a new subdivision on the southwest side of town on the road to the ruins. Its growth was spurred by the Mérida-Chichén Itzá road's construction and the economic opportunities created by the CIW's nearby massive reconstruction project. Supporters in Dzitás greeted him with cheers and a triumphal arch with the slogan "Bartolo ve como te quieren y reciben los de tu raza" (Bartolo, see how the men of your race love and welcome you) (*Diario del Sureste*, July 14, 1932). On February 1, 1933, García Correa took time away from his prized Industrial and Agricultural Exposition, to make a quick trip to Hoctún to inaugurate another section of the road from Mérida to Chichén Itzá. At the ceremony, Luis Rosado Vega mentioned not only the state museum he directed but also Sylvanus Morley and the CIW by name (*Diario del Sureste*, February 2, 1933). The people of Kanasín, a village just south of Mérida, were so excited about jobs working on the road to Chichén Itzá during the depth of the Great Depression that they threw a *vaqueria* (rural-style barbeque and dance) in García Correa's honor (*Diario del Sureste*, September 21, 1932). Little wonder that García Correa saw the combination of archaeology, development, and Mayanism as a potent populist political formula.

Roadbuilding united all three of these elements. García Correa was determined to build a new, better road allowing for quicker travel from Mérida's hotels to Chichén Itzá directly by car or bus, shaving many miles off the existing trip by train, narrow-gauge trolley, and horseback (Stacy-Judd 1934, 38). The road was not just for tourism. Roadbuilding symbolically helped cement García Correa's status as a leader of the Maya. On February 24, 1930, the *Los Angeles Times* ran an article entitled "Mayans Yield to Civilization: Yucatán Will Construct Modern Highways." On October 12, 1932, García Correa dedicated the first segment of the road to Chichén Itzá by unveiling a granite cube marker topped with a Chacmool, the iconic statue from Chichén Itzá (Ferrer de Mendiolea 1947, 538; *Diario de Yucatán*, June 28, 1931, section 2, p. 2). The next month he claimed Mexico City had greenlighted his plans to hire the "powerful North American Company" of Michael Del Balso and John R. Sprague that built subways in New York City to build roads in Yucatán (including a Mérida-Umán road to promote tourism to Uxmal), as well as a new dock in Progreso. No funding from the national treasury was forthcoming (*Diario del Sureste*, September 14, 1932). Progress on the vital road to Chichén Itzá apparently slowed as state funds evaporated and the business community distanced itself from García Correa.

Infrastructure woes never diminished García Correa's enthusiasm for promoting CIW's research. Since its founding by García Correa on the Day of the Revolution, November 20, 1931, the PSS's newspaper *Diario del Sureste* frequently covered the CIW's Maya archaeological research, including Morley's early efforts to read date glyphs and CIW publications translated into Spanish by Alfonso Villa Rojas. These articles were a key part of the newspaper's social mission of diffusing scientific advances in a form readily accessible to the masses—and dovetailed with the CIW's own efforts to share its findings with the general public (*Diario del Sureste*, December 27, 1931). In at least one case, the *Diario del Sureste* picked up a *New York Times* wire service story about Maya archaeology (April 22, 1932). García Correa also revived the "Lunes Culturales" in the Casa del Pueblo founded by Carrillo Puerto to "give young people and members of the proletariat a break from work and study" and "elevate them to a superior level of culture" (*Diario del Sureste*, January 14, 1932). Not long after his elaborate inaugural celebration, Morley at García Correa's express invitation spoke at the "Lunes Culturales" before a packed house of at least 2,000.[15] The close association with the CIW likely boosted García Correa's standing at home (dealing with a largely hostile upper class), in Mexico City, and in the US.

By the early 1930s there was a new generation of PSS intellectuals who did not remember the Carrillo Puerto-Morley bromance and were sensitive to growing nationalism in Mexico spurred by the Depression and US expulsion of Mexicans and Mexican Americans. While not directly criticizing the close relationship between federal and Yucatecan officials and the CIW, these younger intellectuals celebrated the work of Yucatecan archaeologist Eduardo Martínez Cantón at Chichén Itzá (Morris 1931, 22; *Diario del Sureste*, June 17, 1932, September 29, 1932). After all, at the same time the Mexican press was canonizing Mexican pilots and boxers as heroes competing against foreign rivals. The CIW's scientific archaeology never diminished the interest of many Yucatecan Maya experts in the older theories produced by what could be called alternative or fantastic archaeology, which relied in part or entirely on untested if not outright false data (Williams 1991). After Yucatecan fieldwork in the 1870s and 1880s capped by the first unearthing of a Chacmool at Chichén Itzá, Augustus Le Plongeon went on to posit that the ancient Maya were in fact the source of Ancient Egyptian civilization via the peregrination of Queen Móo from Chichén Itzá to the Nile Valley. Augustus Le

Plongeon's unorthodox interpretations based on respectable fieldwork funded in part by the Worchester's American Antiquarian Society was posthumously promoted by his wife and collaborator, Alice Dixon Le Plongeon. Scorned by US scholars, it would later be eagerly embraced by students of Atlantis, scholars of the Land of Mu and theosophists (Desmond and Messenger 1988, 102, 123–31). Yucatecan Maya experts affiliated with the PSS continued to invoke Le Plongeon and other alternative archaeologists long after professional archaeology practiced by nationals and foreigners flourished in Mexico. Consider the review of Rafael Requena's *Vestigios de la Atlántida* in the *Diario del Sureste* (September 20, 1932). Motives for the enduring popularity of fantastic archaeologists such as the Le Plongeons among Yucatecan Mayanists are complex and require further research. I would suggest, however, that their enduring appeal could be read as an indirect, nationalist challenge to the North American CIW's scientific archeology.

Among those Yucatecan Maya experts influenced by the Le Plongeons' alternative archaeology was Ricardo Mimenza Castillo. Like many PSS intellectuals featured in the pages of the *Diario del Sureste*, he preferred poetry, not scientific archaeology, to explore the Mayan past (*Diario del Sureste*, April 5, 1932). Unlike his fellow Mayanist intellectuals, he was dark skinned, and sources euphemistically referred to humble origins. He almost certainly knew García Correa well, and the two shared provincial origins and outsider status among the Mérida intelligentsia. Mimenza Castillo earned a degree as a teacher from the Literary Institute five years before García Correa did, and the two helped found the PSS under a slightly different name in 1916 (*Diario del Sureste*, December 19, 1931; Tello Solís 1991). Like García Correa, Mimenza Castillo empathized with contemporary Maya people and frequently spoke for them yet sought to position himself as a non-Indigenous person. In his Mayanist essay "La Raza del Indio," Mimenza wrote one could go to Valladolid to see "long-suffering race" and lauded "the race whose nobility has always sustained our Party." In classic indigenista fashion, Mimenza Castillo boasted of how the "social revolution" had "mitigated" the "great pain" of "the red man" (*Diario del Sureste*, December 19, 1931). In many ways, Mimenza Castillo's Mayanism was compatible with the CIW's efforts, for instance, in making favorable comparisons with Classical Old World civilizations. His article "How the Maya Conceived of the Universe" made a relativist apology for human sacrifice in Mesoamerica, pointing out similar practices among Romans and Greeks (*Diario del Sureste*, November 26, 1931). Like García Correa and the CIW, Mimenza Castillo believed social sciences would help uplift the contemporary Maya peoples, speaking of the need to "Reincorporate the Indian to Civilization" via "the school of life" and the application of historical sociology (*Diario del Sureste*, December 4, 1931). As one of the leading Mayanist writers in the *Diario del Sureste*, Mimenza Castillo politely praised the work of the CIW for its "technical" and "scientific" excellence (1938, 73–77), but he continued to include Le Plongeon among the pantheon of the great Mayanists (*Diario del Sureste*, May 17, 1932; Mimenza Castillo 1938, 51). Just as Morley sought (unsuccessfully) to acquire the Le Plongeons' archive (Desmond and Messenger 1988, 126–27) and the CIW hoped to sponsor *Payambé*, so too did Mimenza Castillo continued to recognize Le Plongeon as a way of "evoking" the Maya, to borrow Rosado Vega's phrase.

The CIW was almost certainly sensitive to Mexicans' archaeological nationalism and interest in the Le Plongeons and other alternative archeologists among some Yucatecans. Its promotion of Mexican scholars' research was likely in part a response to it. The CIW highlighted the contributions of Yucatecan archaeologist Eduardo Martínez Cantón, director of pre-Hispanic monuments in the state, by sending him to Europe to speak about his own and Sylvanus Morley's discoveries (*Diario del Sureste*, July 17, 1932). However, Alfonso Villa Rojas was the Yucatecan face of the CIW, in no small part because he was an increasingly important member of the CIW team. Villa Rojas was apparently the only member of the CIW in Yucatán who published in Spanish, and he frequently wrote for the *Diario del Sureste*, another indication of García Correa's desire to promote the CIW's work (*Diario del Sureste*, November 18, 1932). He translated a two-part summary of Kidder's tract summarizing the archaeological research of what Villa Rojas entitled the "Instituto Carnegie de Yucatán" (*Diario del Sureste*, January 1, 1933). Similarly, Villa Rojas published a two-part summary translated into Spanish of Morris's *Temple of the Warriors* (*Diario del Sureste*, December 9, 16, 1932). Villa Rojas, like Morris and García Correa, grasped archaeology's role in drawing North American visitors, as he put forth in "Los turistas y nuestras ruinas" (*Diario del Sureste*, December 1, 1932).

Why did García Correa never embrace what some might call alternative archaeology? He probably understood that the CIW scientists would bridle at appearing to legitimize ideas such as the Land of Mu and Atlantis, even if they exoticized their research findings as part of popularizing them. García Correa certainly understood quite a bit about the US tourist market and the value of what we now call multiplatforming (Smith 2019): using several channels ranging from Fox Movietone Newsreels to Stacy-Judd's outreach to the possible Met performance of *Payambé* to maximize US consumption of images of the Mayan peoples to spur archaeological tourism.

The marketing of the Maya's past glories relied in part on the personalities of the archaeologists themselves as opposed to the sensational ideas associated with alternative archaeology. North American audiences were riveted by stories about the proto-Indiana Jones-like Sylvanus Morley and Earl Morris who combined science with adventure in "exotic" places. Only the CIW, for instance, could get a large, beautifully illustrated article placed in *National Geographic*. In the July 1931 edition,

Morley lauded the work at Chichén Itzá (Uaxactún received some mention) and did not stint on the superlatives that distinguished the Mayan peoples as the Americas' most advanced pre-Columbian culture, hailing them as "the Greeks of the New World" (Morley 1931, 109) and builders of "the first observatory in the Americas" (114). Morley was also working assiduously to win over Mexican federal officials, whose presence expanded in the eastern region, or Oriente, as the SEP took over education from the state of Yucatán in the early 1930s. Because the SEP was chronically underfunded, Morley offered to pay for the construction of Pisté's school in 1933 and encouraged local workers at Chichén Itzá to make individual donations (Armstrong-Fumero 2013, 89). On the 1933 vernal equinox (fortuitously the birthday of Benito Juárez), Morley gladly welcomed federal educators who staged *reunión social* for Maya schoolchildren from Chan Kom and other nearby pueblos such as Pisté to view the serpent shadows creeping down the balustrades at el Castillo. The federal school superintendent proudly noted the program was witnessed by "quite a lot of foreign tourists." The next month, Morley donated 200 pesos for the new school building in the Sisal barrio of Valladolid (*Diario del Sureste*, April 15, 1933).[16] As a US archaeologist working in Yucatán not long after the scandalous dredging of the Chichen Itzá cenote by US consul Edward H. Thompson and at a time of rising Mexican nationalism, Morley carefully cultivated his Mexican hosts.

In 1936, the genial, indefatigable Morley would welcome US ambassador to Mexico Josephus Daniels to Chichén Itzá. Daniels's trip was lavishly covered in the *American Foreign Service Journal* magazine complete with aerial photography (July 1936). Daniels, owner of North Carolina newspaper, exemplified Franklin Delano Roosevelt's Good Neighbor Policy. In Morley Daniels might well have recognized a fellow media-savvy amateur diplomat who did a much better job than US State Department professionals in fostering a more cordial US-Mexican relationship. García Correa, though no longer governor, had helped to contribute to this more amiable binational association by collaborating with Morley and other US American Maya specialists in fostering Mayanism. This mutual US-Yucatecan creation foregrounded certain kinds of knowledge production such as the archaeological research showcased for visitors to Chichén Itzá, while at the same time concealing contemporary Maya communities on henequen haciendas and in Mérida's poor neighborhoods from the gaze of US Americans and Mexicans alike.

CONCLUSION

By the time Chichén Itzá received cultural diplomatic recognition as it were by Daniels's visit, García Correa was self-exiled from Yucatán after the rocky end of his gubernatorial administration. Although no monument exists to him today,

García Correa's legacy is still present in Yucatán, perhaps most visibly in archaeological tourism. No other governor before or after promoted Yucatán in the United States as energetically. Even in the depths of the Depression, he continued to build infrastructure that would later sustain Yucatán's nascent tourist industry. An early advocate of air transportation, he likely ensured the airport that still welcomes thousands of US American tourists every year would be constructed on the road from Mérida to his hometown of Umán. Mayanism helped García Correa build the PSS into probably the strongest regional affiliate of what would be the Partido Revolucionario Institucional (PRI). Mayanism, crafted by Morley and his colleagues as much as by García Correa and his collaborators, provided a powerful ideological foundation for Yucatán's revolutionary party.

The Mayanism that García Correa inherited from Carrillo Puerto and developed between 1927 and 1933 owed much to the efforts of the CIW, whose researchers eagerly sought the support of revolutionary administrations. The silences in the CIW's research agenda—some of them clearly intentional—when it came to poverty on henequen haciendas and Mérida's Indigenous neighborhoods aided the PSS. The program of town building in small rural communities such as Chan Kom pursued by revolutionary politicos such as Carrillo Puerto and García Correa provided a largely unacknowledged model for Redfield's continuum. Perhaps most important, the Mayanism crafted by Yucatecan politicians and intellectuals as much as by North American scientists and promotors such as Stacy-Judd was a crucial part of archaeological tourism initiated in the early twentieth century. For decades, tourism in Yucatán has marketed the idea of "the Maya" to a wide variety of foreign audiences as Castellanos and Córdoba Azcárate productively explore in chapters 8 and 9 in this volume. Mayanism's origins can be traced back to the administration of Felipe Carrillo Puerto, whose memory is kept alive by a hero cult and continues to inspire commemoration and historical research. It was Bartolomé García Correa, almost completely forgotten in popular and academic history, who proved to be the key Yucatecan collaborator with US Americans in creating Mayanism.

NOTES

1. I would like to gratefully acknowledge National Endowment for the Humanities grant (FT-61649-14), which made research for this chapter possible. Comments from Matilde Azcarra Córdoba, Fernando Armstrong-Fumero, and two anonymous readers made it better. Any remaining errors are my own.

2. US anthropologists—above all Franz Boas—were crucial role in training Mexican archaeologists in the rest of Mexico before 1915. See Rutsch (2007). See also Castañeda (1996, 268).

3. On the need to broaden our understanding of US-Latin American relations by taking into account previously ignored sites of encounter such as those described in this chapter and the entire volume, see Joseph (1998).

4. February 25, 1930, Morley to Merriam, ACIW, Merriam Cor., March–July 1930.

5. February 25, 1930, Morley to Merriam, ACIW, Merriam Cor., March–July 1930.

6. February 25, 1930, Morley to Merriam, ACIW, Merriam Cor., March–July 1930.

7. See reports filed from the Progreso consulate, RDSRIAM, 1930–39, roll 22.

8. February 15, 1928, Consul Fayette J. Flexer, "Political Summary for the State of Tabasco for the Year 1927," RDSRIAM, 1910–29, roll 96.

9. March 25, 30, Morley to Merriam, ACIW, Merriam Cor., March–July 1930.

10. February 12, 1930, Plutarco Elías Calles to Dwight Morrow, FAPECyFT, APEC Gav. MORROW, Dwight M. Gavila 54, exp. 107, inv. 3889, leg. 1 of 1; November 22, 1930, Calles to Morrow, http://www.biblioteca.tv/artman2/publish/1930_235/Comunicaci_oacute_n _de_Plutarco_El_iacute_as_Calles_a_Dwight_Morrow_en_relaci_oacute_n_a_Bartolom _eacute_Garc_iacute_a_Correa_gobernador_del_estado_de_Yucat_aacute_n.shtml.

11. Interview of Rosa García Montero by author, June 17, 2016. *México censo nacional,* 1930, database with images, *FamilySearch* accessed 10 November 2015, https://familysearch .org/ark:/61903/1:1:MK3C-QQT; Bartolomé Garcia, Quintana Roo, Mérida, Yucatán, Mexico, citing p. 448, AGN, FHL microfilm 1,520,522.

12. February 18, 1928, Sylvanus Morley to Alvaro Torre Díaz, AGEY, caja 865 Poder Ejecutivo, Sección de Gobierno 2. Translation by the author.

13. November 14, 1924, Luis Rosado Vega to José María Iturralde, AGEY, Poder Ejecutivo, caja 794, Sección de Gobierno 1.

14. Ancestry.com downloaded November 16, 2019. *Border Crossings: From Mexico to U.S., 1895–1964,* online database, Provo, UT. NARA, *Temporary and Nonstatistical Manifests of Aliens Arriving at Eagle Pass, Texas, July 1928–June 1953*; NAI: *2843448*; record group title: *Records of the Immigration and Naturalization Service, 1787–2004,* record group number 85, microfilm roll number 03.

15. February 25, 1930, Morley to Merriam, ACIW, Merriam Cor., March–July 1930.

16. Juan I. Flores, "Informe marzo de 1933," AHSEP 1671 IG/1343, expediente Juan I. Flores.

REFERENCES CITED

ARCHIVOS

ACIW: Archive of the Carnegie Institution of Washington. Washington, DC

AGEY: Archivo General del Estado de Yucatán. Mérida, Mexico

AGN: Archivo General de la Nación. Mexico City

AHSEP: Archivo Histórico de la Secretaría de la Educación Pública. Mexico City, Mexico

APEC: Archivo Plutarco Elías Calles. FAPECyFT. Fideicomiso Archivo Plutarco Elías Calles y Fernando Torreblanca. Mexico City, Mexico

FHL: Family Historical Library

NARA: The National Archives and Records Administration. Washington, DC

RDSRIAM: Records of the Department of State Internal Affairs of Mexico, Microfilm

Albright, Evan. 2015. *The Man Who Owned a Wonder of the World: The Gringo History of Mexico's Chichén Itzá*. Bourne, MA: Pickwick Books, an imprint of Bohlin Carr Inc.

Armstrong-Fumero, Fernando. 2013. *Factionalism and the Limits of Identity Politics in Yucatán, Mexico*. Boulder: University of Press Colorado.

Askinasy, Siegfried. 1936. *El problema agrario de Yucatán*. 2nd ed. Mexico City: Ediciones Botas.

Bolio Ontiveros, Edmundo. 1930. *Memoria documentada de la campaña electoral cuyo resultado fue elevar a la primera magistratura de estado al compañero Prof. Bartolomé García Correa*. Mérida: Pluma y Lápiz.

Brunhouse, Robert L. 1971. *Sylvanus G. Morley and the World of the Ancient Mayas*. Norman: University of Oklahoma Press.

Bueno, Christina. 2016. *The Pursuit of Ruins: Archaeology, History, and the Making of Modern Mexico*. Albuquerque: University of New Mexico Press.

Castañeda, Quetzil. 1996. *In the Museum of Maya Culture: Touring Chichén Itzá*. Minneapolis: University of Minnesota Press.

Comité Central de Propaganda Pro-Ortiz Rubio-García Correa (México). 1930. *Bartolomé García Correa, Como se hizo su campaña política: Recopilación de informaciones, comentarios, editoriales y artículos publicados por la prensa de la capital en los meses de junio, julio, agosto, septiembre, octubre y principios de noviembre, de 1929, en torno a la campaña electoral y personalidad del Presidente del Partido Socialista del Sureste*. Mérida: Imprenta Gamboa Guzmán.

Cronon, E. David. 1960. *Josephus Daniels in Mexico*. Madison: University of Wisconsin Press.

Daniels, Josephus. 1936. "Chichén Itzá and Uxmal." *American Foreign Service Journal* 12, no. 7 (July): 373–75, 415–19.

Desmond, Lawrence, and Phyllis Messenger. 1988. *A Dream of Maya: Augustus and Alice Le Plongeon in Nineteenth-Century Yucatán*. Albuquerque: University of New Mexico Press.

Eiss, Paul. 2008. "El Pueblo Mestizo: Modernity, Tradition, and Statecraft in Yucatán, 1870–1907." *Ethnohistory* 55, no. 4 (Fall): 525–52.

Espadas Medina, Aercel. 1993. "El Palacio Socialista / Casa del Pueblo." *Por Esto!* 3 (11) Part I: 3–9.

Fallaw, Ben. 1997. "Cárdenas and the Caste War That Wasn't: State Power and Indigenismo in Post-revolutionary Yucatán." *Americas* 53 (4): 551–77.

Fallaw, Ben. 2000. "Antonio Betancourt Pérez, la educación y la izquierda en Yucatán, 1931–1937," Part I, *Unicornio* #459 (February 13): 3–9.

Fallaw, Ben. 2004. "Rethinking Mayan Resistance: Changing Relations between Federal Teachers and Mayan Communities in Eastern Yucatán, 1929–1935," *Journal of Latin American Anthropology* 9, no. 1 (Spring): 151–78.

Fallaw, Ben. 2008. "Bartolomé García Correa and the Politics of Maya Identity in Postrevolutionary Yucatán, 1915–1935." *Ethnohistory* 55, no. 4 (Fall): 553–78.

Fallaw, Ben. 2020. "The Limits of the Independent Press and Civil Society in the Maximato: The Closing of the Diario de Yucatán, 1931–33." *Estudios Mexicanos / Mexican Studies* 36, nos. 1–2 (Winter/Summer): 43–67.

Ferrer de Mendiolea, Gabriel. 1947. "Historia de las comunicaciones." In *Enciclopedia yucatanense*. Vol. 3, 507–626. Mérida: Gobierno de Yucatán.

Gillingham, Paul. 2011. *Cuauhtemoc's Bones: Forging National Identity in Modern Mexico.* Albuquerque: University of New Mexico Press.

Guzmán Medina, María Guadalupe. 2020. *La antropología social en Yucatán: Panorama histórico y perspectivas desde el sur.* Mérida: Universidad Autónoma de Yucatán.

Hansen, Asael, and Juan Bastarrachea. 1985. *Mérida: Su transformación de capital colonial a naciente metrópoli en 1935.* Mexico City: Instituto Nacional de Antropología e Historia.

Joseph, Gilbert. 1988. *Revolution from Without: Yucatán, Mexico, and the United States, 1880–1924.* 2nd ed. Durham, NC: Duke University Press.

Joseph, Gilbert. 1998. "Close Encounters: Toward a New Cultural History of U.S.–Latin American Relations." In *Close Encounters of Empire: Writing the Cultural History of US-Latin American Relations.* edited by Gilbert Joseph, Catherine Legrand, and Ricardo Salvatore, 3–46. Durham, NC: Duke University Press.

Martínez, César Delgado, and Julio C. Villalvar Jiménez. 1997. *Yol-Izma: La danzarina de las leyenda.* Mexico City: Escenología AC.

Milton, Joyce. 1993. *Loss of Eden: A Biography of Charles and Anne Morrow Lindbergh.* New York: HarperCollins.

Mimenza Castillo, Ricardo. 1938. *Los templos redondos de Kukulcán.* Mexico City: Ediciones Botas.

Morley, Sylvanus. 1931. "Unearthing America's Ancient History," *National Geographic* 61, no. 1 (July): 99–126, 107, 109, 114.

Morris, Earl. 1931. *The Temple of the Warriors*. New York: Charles Scribner's Sons.

Nardelli, Albert. 1928. *Un hombre representativo: Bartolomé García Correa. Sus ideas y sus acciones en pro de los anhelos populares de Yucatán*. Mérida: Basso.

O'Brien, Thomas. 1996. *The Revolutionary Mission: American Enterprise in Latin America, 1900–1945*. New York: Cambridge University Press.

Ramírez, Gabriel. 2009. *Personajes de Yucatán: De la tierra salen voces que les hablan*. Mérida: Gobierno del Estado de Yucatán and Biblioteca Básica de Yucatán.

Redfield, Robert, and Alfonso Villa Rojas. 1934. *Chan Kom: A Maya Village*. Chicago: University of Chicago Press.

Redfield, Robert. 1941. *The Folk Culture of Yucatán*. Chicago: University of Chicago Press.

Redfield, Robert. 1950. *A Village that Chose Progress: Chan Kom Revisited*. Chicago: University of Chicago Press.

Roorda, Eric. 1998. *The Dictator Next Door: The Good Neighbor Policy and the Trujillo Regime in the Dominican Republic, 1930–1945*. Durham, NC: Duke University Press.

Rosado Vega, Luis. 1929. *Payambé Evocación de la Tierra del Mayab en 4 escenarios*. Mexico City: Talleres Gráficos de la Nación.

Rutsch, Mechthild. 2007. *Entre el campo y el gabinete: Nacionales y extranjeros en la profesionalización de la antropología mexicana (1877–1920)*. Mexico City: Instituto Nacional de Antropología e Historia.

Shattuck, George Cheever. 1933. *The Peninsula of Yucatán: Medical, Biological, Meteorological and Sociological Studies*. Washington, DC: Carnegie Institution.

Simpson, Eyler. 1937. *The Ejido: Mexico's Way Out*. Chapel Hill: University of North Carolina Press.

Smith, Paul Julian. 2019. *Multiplatform Media in Mexico: Growth and Change since 2010*. New York: Palgrave Macmillan.

Stacy-Judd, Robert. 1934. *The Ancient Mayas: Adventures in the Jungles of Yucatán*. Los Angeles: Haskell-Travers.

Tello Solís, Eduardo. 1991. *Ricardo Mimenza Castillo: Un poeta yucateco de acento melancólico*. Mérida: Universidad Autónoma de Yucatán.

Torre Díaz, Álvaro. 1930. *Cuatro años en el gobierno de Yucatán, 1926–1930*. Mérida: Compañía Tipográfica Yucateca.

Weeks, John M., and Jane A. Hill, eds. 2006. *The Carnegie Maya: The Carnegie Institution of Washington Maya Research Program, 1913–1957*. Boulder: University Press of Colorado.

Wells, Allen, and Gilbert Joseph. 1996. *Summer of Discontent, Seasons of Upheaval: Elite Politics and Rural Insurgency in Yucatán, 1876–1915*. Stanford, CA: Stanford University Press.

Williams, George Dee. 1931. "Maya-Spanish Crosses in Yucatán." *Peabody Museum of American Archaeology and Ethnology Papers*. Vol. 13. Cambridge, MA.

Williams, Stephen. 1991. *Fantastic Archaeology: The Wild Side of North American Prehistory*. Philadelphia: University of Pennsylvania Press.

Wolf, Eric, and Sydel Silverman. 2001. *Pathways of Power: Building an Anthropology of the Modern World*. Berkeley: University of California Press.

5

Funding Values in Highland Chiapas

How Harvard Anthropology Naturalized the Mexican State

MATTHEW C. WATSON

In 1955, when Harvard anthropologist Evon Zartman Vogt Jr. sought to fund a new research project, he reached out to a familiar institution: the Rockefeller Foundation.[1] Vogt had spent his first seven years on Harvard's faculty working as one of two field directors for Clyde Kluckhohn's Comparative Study of Values in Five Cultures.[2] The Values Study, as it was called, had Rockefeller's strong financial support. Vogt's 1948 hire owed to the department's receipt of a $100,000 grant to support collaborative research into the value systems of five cultures in the area of Ramah, New Mexico, where Vogt had grown up on a sheep ranch (Vogt 1994, 46). In the late 1940s, as a University of Chicago graduate student, Vogt completed ethnographic fieldwork on the Navajo veterans of Ramah. His Values Study contributions expanded this work into an examination of the value systems of Ramah Navajos and Texas homesteaders; project collaborators also studied value systems of the Zuni, Spanish Americans, and Mormons.[3] After his tenure and promotion, Vogt would turn to a less familiar pasture: the highlands of Chiapas, Mexico, where he endeavored to study "culture change" among Indigenous speakers of Tzotzil and Tzeltal.

Vogt initiated the Harvard Chiapas Project (HCP) in 1957, and it continued until 1980. The project brought undergraduate as well as graduate students to Chiapas, growing into what may be the largest collaborative ethnographic endeavor completed to date.[4] Vogt's memoir sums up the HCP's influence: "I count that of the 142 students we had doing field research in Chiapas from 1957 through 1980, 47 are now practicing, professional anthropologists, and another 17 are in closely

https://doi.org/10.5876/9781646424276.c005

related fields such as sociology, cognitive psychology, development economics, etc." (Vogt 1994, 348). But, first, it had to be funded. This chapter shows how Vogt got the HCP off the ground. The project formed through collaborations between Harvard scholars and development administrators employed by Mexico's Instituto Nacional Indigenista (INI), a branch of the Mexican government founded in 1948 (Escalona Victoria 2018; Lewis 2018; Mentanko 2020). The INI anthropologist-administrators, or *indigenistas*, worked to cultivate Indigenous attachments to the Mexican nation and state.

Vogt needed to build good relations and trust—*confianza*—with the corps of indigenistas. To do so, as I argue here, Vogt first had to *naturalize the state*. Knowingly or not, he secured the trust of Mexican anthropologist-administrators by proposing a study that cast their acculturative regime as an *apolitical* "variable" that induced "culture change"—the equivalent of a natural event. For US funding agencies, as for indigenistas, Vogt cast the state as a force and form innocent of—indeed, beyond—power. This US American anthropologist seemed to perceive state control over the Indigenous highlands teleologically; state capture was inevitable (see also Escalona Victoria 2009). But attendant cultural changes, in the end, were not.

The indigenistas believed that Indigenous subjects' disidentifications with mestizo Mexico resulted in their marginality and poverty.[5] To remedy this poverty, the INI would have to put anthropology into *action* by altering Indigenous communities' material conditions, intensifying their economic exchanges with mestizo neighbors (Escalona Victoria 2018, 246).[6] Chiapas would be the pilot campaign. In 1951 the INI founded the Centro Coordinador Indigenista Tzeltal-Tzotzil in the colonial city of San Cristóbal de las Casas. From the San Cristóbal center, named La Cabaña, indigenistas coordinated four major areas of development action in Tzeltal- and Tzotzil-speaking communities: building and staffing bilingual schools, establishing clinics that administered western medicine, instituting new agricultural projects, and building roads. The Coordinating Center also set up so-called cooperative stores in Indigenous communities. Supported by the reining nationalist Partido Revolucionario Institucional (PRI), the INI endeavored to help "modernize" the postrevolutionary Mexican nation-state (Lewis 2018).

The INI and the HCP might seem like strange bedfellows. Whereas the INI enacted the acculturating mission of *mestizaje*, Vogt would ultimately construct Tzotzil communities, particularly Zinacantán, as noble, barely changed inheritors of precolonial Maya traditions (e.g., Vogt 1969).[7] But, by 1955, the INI's campaign was already struggling, particularly in Tzotzil communities.[8] So, the indigenistas were generally supportive of Vogt's plan to develop a longitudinal study in the same communities. They hoped the HCP would help them understand communities' resistance to development (Rus 2004; Lewis 2018, 128).

This chapter clarifies the terms of the working relationship developed between the HCP and the INI between 1955 and 1960. By the 1960s, Vogt and his Harvard collaborators would come to celebrate the municipality of Zinacantán as a community that revealed deep "Maya" cultural continuity. In the process, as José Luis Escalona Victoria (2018) has argued, they "encapsulated history." But how did Vogt build the authority to produce such felicitous and consequential representations of Indigenous highland Chiapas? He would first have to frame his research in terms legible and potentially useful to the indigenistas. Vogt did so by proposing a project to assess the effects of their institute's pilot campaign in "directed culture change."

But this raises other questions, namely, How did a newcomer to research in Mexico and to Maya studies secure and maintain the support of powerful indigenistas for such a project? Vogt's archive of correspondence reveals that he maintained a tenuous, partial control over exchanges with indigenistas. I suggest that Vogt melded the dehistoricizing tradition of Mesoamerican "community studies" with an image of the "ethically" applied anthropology developed in the southwestern research of Kluckhohn (who was also a distant cousin of Vogt). Kluckhohn had fashioned the anthropologist as a cultural "broker" or "interpreter" obligated to "translate native cultures to others, including those teachers, health personnel, government agents, and other administrators who have to 'deal with' minority populations" (Lamphere 2002, 115). Such "ethical" application of research seemed *urgent* to Kluckhohn. He constructed the Navajo encounter with "technological change" as a disruptive, acculturative force that comprised "the nation's foremost Indian problem" during the 1930s and 1940s (Lamphere 2002, 115).[9]

In *Toward an Anthropological Theory of Value*, anthropologist and prominent activist David Graeber reads Kluckhohn's Values Study as a struggle to boost US anthropology's waning theoretical fortunes. It offered a comparative, empirical construction of value orientations as "practical philosophies of life" (Graeber 2001, 2–5). But Graeber's reading is glum; the years before Kluckhohn's 1960 death, at age fifty-five, entailed futile theoretical grasping. The project failed to effect a values-centered conceptual synthesis. A values-oriented anthropology foundered despite the modernist confidence of "Kluckhohn's disciples." One disciple, philosopher Edith Albert, "continu[ed] to pour out essays gushing with scientific confidence in the late '50s and early '60s" (Graeber 2001, 4, 5) and expressed a surprising affection for this attention to values, wistfully concluding, "the project had no intellectual successors."

Here Graeber errs—led astray by dogged attention to the value concept. "Value orientations" inquiry hardly invigorated a Kluckhohnian philosophical anthropology. But the Ramah Study's intellectual successor is clear. Vogt extended Values Study frames to research on "directed culture change" in Chiapas. He further emulated Kluckhohn's "ethical" orientation to help generate trust with indigenistas who were attached intellectually to the community studies tradition but invested politically in developmentalist "action" anthropology.

By 1960, Vogt better understood how deeply the INI's acculturative project was in trouble. He discarded central attention to a depoliticized "induced culture change" in favor of community-bound inquiry into Maya worldview, belief, and cosmology. The effort to reframe the project yielded his hypostasis of Zinacantán: the paradigm of deep-historical cultural conservatism, the quintessential community. This transcendentalizing or sacralizing move would have profound consequences in Maya studies, and in anthropology broadly (Watson 2020). But, to sacralize the community, Vogt first had to naturalize the state. Despite his understanding of the Coordinating Center's uneven successes, he continued envisioning Maya communities as external to politics.

A pivotal effect of state power here is that Vogt, an elite US academic bringing material and symbolic capital to a struggling project of Mexican internal colonialism, had little idea how he saw what he saw (and neither did many of his students, though some—mainly Marxists—saw power and history more clearly by the 1970s). Vogt came to see an unchanging, apparently-unchangeable community. But he had learned to see it through the lens of a state that desired, with growing force, to break the community's perceived stasis, its antigovernmental obduracy, in order to teach Tzotziles that they, too, were mestizo Mexicans. By imagining the state as an independent variable, Vogt not only came to see like a state (see Scott 1998). He came, I argue, to see *as* the Mexican state. Among other things, the HCP was initially a vehicle for the Mexican state to deepen its sovereign and governmentalist control over the highlands of Chiapas. That Vogt saw *as* the state does not mean that he *knew* his vision was so filtered. To see as the state is to immerse into statist ideology.

During the 1960s, Vogt began to transmogrify US anthropological "values" into "cosmology." Attention to cosmology, buoyed by the rising tide of French structuralism, would secure continued anthropological interest (e.g., Vogt 1976). From Kluckhohn through Vogt, then, "values" would remain in the anthropological family.

HARVARD FROM NAYARIT TO CHIAPAS

Vogt's plan for research in Mexico did not lead immediately to Chiapas. His initial proposal for fieldwork involved bringing students to the state of Nayarit to research the Huicholes. The idea for this project emerged between 1950 and 1954. Vogt, during that stretch, made three trips to Mexico. The first was a vacation with his wife,

Catherine ("Nan") Vogt, in Mexico City; the second was a sabbatical with his family near Lake Chapala; and the third was a summer "reconnaissance of Huichol
country" (Vogt 1994, 63–67). The reconnaissance was framed by an initial visit with
archaeologist Alfonso Caso, director of the INI, followed by visits with the governors of Jalisco and Nayarit (64–65). Aided by his Harvard credentials and connections, Vogt quickly worked his way into the bureaucratic field of anthropological
and state power in Mexico, where the INI functioned as a major federal agency
(Caso reported directly to the Mexican president) (Lewis 2018, 6–7). But Vogt's
preliminary research trip proved difficult, even perilous. To reach the Huicholes of
Nayarit, with whom he hoped to work, Vogt had to travel by small plane. The alternative would have been a rugged pack trip through canyons and then on horseback.
While Vogt was a very experienced rider, few Harvard students would be. He had
also learned of the dangers of a small, deadly scorpion in this region of the Sierra
Madre Mountains. He slept in a mosquito net and carried a kit with the scorpion
venom's antidote and a syringe to self-administer it. Vogt's published discussion of
logistical difficulties and omnipresent scorpion risk concludes with his decision to
"reluctantly abandon" the prospect of bringing Harvard students to work among the
Huicholes of the Sierra Madre (1994, 67).

This narrative runs against the grain of the epistolary record documenting
Vogt's fundraising efforts. He reached out to Leland DeVinney, his Rockefeller
Foundation contact, months after completing the summer 1954 reconnaissance. In
April 1955, Vogt and DeVinney arranged a May meeting to discuss further fieldwork in Nayarit.[10] During this same period, Rockefeller renewed its support for the
Values Study through June 1956.[11] But in his reply to DeVinney's letter conveying
the grant extension, Vogt sought to turn his Rockefeller contact's attention from
the US Southwest back to Mexico. Vogt worked to impress DeVinney by conveying that his Nayarit project had the strong support of Alfonso Caso, and, hence, the
Mexican anthropological establishment: "[Caso] promises his fullest cooperation
with our proposed project, and he has personally invited me to participate in a two-
week Symposium in August to assess the work of his Instituto."[12]

The symposium entailed a week's conference in Mexico City on the effects of the
INI Coordinating Centers in Chiapas and Veracruz, followed by a trip to each of
the centers. Vogt made the trip in an INI vehicle, accompanied by Mexican scholars
including Manuel Gamio and Gonzalo Aguirre Beltrán (Vogt 1994, 68–71). Gamio,
who had trained with Franz Boas, was Mexican anthropology's "elder statesman" at
the time. Aguirre Beltrán was the first director of the San Cristóbal Coordinating
Center. The account in Vogt's research memoir, *Fieldwork among the Maya*, casts
the experience of encountering San Cristóbal and neighboring Tzeltal and Tzotzil
Maya communities as "love at first sight" (71). He continues:

I knew by the end of our brief visit that the Highlands of Chiapas were where I wanted to spend the rest of my anthropological field career. Not only was I tremendously excited by the project of engaging in field research in the Maya communities, but I found I was intrigued by the patterns of life of the Ladinos in this old colonial town. Further, the ecological niche, with an altitude of seven thousand feet in the cool highlands covered with pine trees, was similar to the one in which I was reared, the Vogt Ranch in New Mexico. (71)

This passage echoes a briefer account of Vogt's first trip to Chiapas included in his monograph on Zinacantán: "From the moment I first entered the highlands of Chiapas I knew that I had discovered the type of exciting field situation in which I wanted to work" (Vogt 1969, x). But neither the danger of Nayarit's scorpions nor the Chiapas highlands' familiar, but romantic, enticement of August 1955 immediately altered Vogt's fundraising efforts. In October, he sent DeVinney a preliminary draft of the Nayarit proposal.[13] They proceeded to discuss the draft, at least once in person, as Vogt navigated Harvard's internal channels for research approval.[14] But DeVinney wrote the next month to head off any further efforts on Vogt's part: "I am sorry to have to tell you that the conclusion is that we are not in a position, at least for the present, to encourage you to submit a formal application."[15]

The funding denial must have been a blow to Vogt, who was also corresponding, by November 1955, with the Social Science Research Council (and fellow scholars, including Yale anthropologist George Peter Murdock) to try to procure three-year fellowships for extended field research by graduate students in anthropology.[16] Vogt continued to reference prospective fieldwork among the Huicholes into January 1956, but by that time he had also provisionally accepted a residential fellowship at Stanford's Center for Advanced Study in the Behavioral Sciences for the 1956–57 academic year.[17] The fellowship would afford Vogt time to resolve outstanding work on Ramah, and to transition to substantive preparation for his next project—redesigning it for Chiapas.

In a late January 1956 letter to University of Chicago anthropologist Fred Eggan, Vogt outlined the rationale for his shift in field sites:

I have . . . decided to shift the scene of operations for my Mexican field work from Nayarit to Tzotzil-Tzeltal in Chiapas for a number of reasons (a) better place from transportation and logistics point of view to handle and train students (b) work can tie in directly with an established center of the Instituto Indigenista [INI] at San Cristobal de las Casas (c) range of problems (from prehistory to contemporary change) we are interested in here at Harvard will be explorable with tighter research design.[18]

Established archaeological work on precolonial history made research in Chiapas seem more anthropologically robust to Vogt, who collaborated closely with Harvard archaeologist Gordon Willey (see, e.g., Vogt and Leventhal 1983). But a more salient factor was the geographical proximity of the Indigenous communities of highland Chiapas to San Cristóbal:

> The reasons for this change of plans are many, but have mainly to do with the fact that the problems of cultural process and change from Indian to Mestizo will, I now believe, be sharper and more easily studied out of San Cristobal than out of Tepic where there is something of a hiatus between the urban center and the actual Indian settlements.[19]

In a February 8 letter to Isabel Kelly, the Mexico City–residing anthropologist who had warned him of Nayarit's scorpion situation, Vogt put a finer point on the assimilative pressures that he wished to examine:

> After giving some further thought to the problems of cultural change that I am interested in studying over the next several years, I've decided that Chiapas may be a more fruitful field situation than Nayarit. I would like a situation in which the Mestizo impact upon the Indian population is stronger and clearer than it is in the Huichol area at the present time, and I would also like to gear the work closely with the program of the I.N.I. which does not yet have its Huichol Centro established.[20]

On the same day, Vogt informed a coterie of other correspondents of the change in research plans, including Howard F. Cline of the Hispanic Foundation, Summer Institute of Linguistics (SIL) missionaries Joe Grimes and John B. McIntosh, Gonzalo Aguirre Beltrán, Manuel Gamio, and Alfonso Caso.[21] Across these items of correspondence, Vogt drops the question of logistics (let alone the dreaded scorpions), focusing instead on the comparative feasibility of "culture change" research in Nayarit and Chiapas. But his phrasing of the problem in the letter to Kelly (and the earlier note to Eggan) differs in one important way from letters to his three vital Mexican contacts: Aguirre Beltrán, Gamio, and Caso. In letters to the latter, Vogt does not identify the Coordinating Center's presence as a factor differentiating Chiapas from Nayarit.

This omission, I suggest, reflects an early anxiety attached to the emerging frame of Vogt's project. If Vogt's Chiapas inquiry were to share the *values* of its ancestors, Kluckhohn's two southwestern projects, it would not only center questions of cultural continuity and change. It would also position the project director—in Kluckhohn's image—as a cultural broker, interpreter, or translator who could—and urgently *should*—make sense of Indigenized others for state actors who sought to assimilate them. Had Vogt cast himself explicitly as such an intermediary before fully securing the elite state administrators' *confianza*, he may have imperiled the project. Such a self-fashioning could have read as presumptuous for a novice to the landscapes of Maya ethnography, mestizaje, and the Mexican state. And, worse, it would have positioned Vogt as a subject powerful enough to trouble the INI's major pilot development campaign. As Vogt would find out, it was in plenty of trouble already.

CULTURE CHANGE RESEARCH AS DEVELOPMENT STUDIES

So Vogt set out to design a study of Indigenous cultural change in an area where the Mexican state was working, quite systematically, to *induce* that very change. A now-conventional anthropological approach to understanding such transcultural trading zones is to treat them, in Anna Tsing's terms, as "zones of awkward engagement, where words mean something different across a divide even as people agree to speak" (Tsing 2005, xi).[22] Instituto Nacional Indigenista administrators and Harvard anthropologists would, across the next two decades, find themselves in regular encounters where they could and would collaborate, maintaining good—or at least passable—relations in a zone—at once a colonial contact zone and a scientific trading zone—predicated upon forms of partial epistemic and cultural translation.[23]

But this would have to be achieved. Vogt could not inaugurate field research among the Tzotzil and Tzeltal communities of Chiapas without the support of INI administrators overseeing development work in those same communities. He had to persuade administrators, particularly Caso and Aguirre Beltrán, that his field-work would aid their campaign (or, at least, not become a source of interference). At the same time, Vogt, recently spurned by Rockefeller, had to angle to secure substantive support from funding agencies that might expect him to propose research spurring the emergent theoretical metanarratives of US Cold War social science. When distinguished from "applied" or "action" anthropology, such theoretical contributions—work on questions that included changing values and beliefs—read as "basic research."

Vogt was in an awkward position. But his initial gambit was not to devise ways of speaking "where words mean something different" (Tsing 2005, xi) across the divide between US and Mexican anthropologists. Instead, he curtailed and chan-neled his speech, constructing the Harvard Chiapas Project in lightly distinct terms for Mexican anthropologist-administrators and for some US colleagues and funding agencies. Vogt, neither subtle nor unsubtle, would have to take care to keep these two worlds apart, continuously cutting and recutting the network (Strathern 1996; see also Hayden 2003). In so doing, he came to employ a capacious sense of "basic research," one that constructed Mexican development work itself as a natural force. To navigate his awkward position, Vogt composed basic research into Maya cultural change and continuity as a study of the *effects* of the INI's development campaign but *not a study of the campaign itself.*

In this light, consider Manuel Gamio's reply to Vogt's February 8 missive on his shift in research plans:

> Although it is undoubtable that many points of investigation remain in Chiapas, I believe that the situation of the Nayarit Huicholes, by virtue of being more separate and less studied, may offer a more virgin field of investigation. But, of course, it remains for you to decide. When we chat in person, we can exchange viewpoints on this matter.[24]

As Fernando Armstrong-Fumero (2010) points out in his translator's introduction to Gamio's *Forjando Patria*, Gamio balanced a Boasian relativism with nationalist political advocacy for assimilationist policies enacting the ideology of mestizaje. Gamio viewed anthropology as a science serving the state's nationalist ends, and he supported the INI's efforts to effect cultural change. His light advocacy here for Vogt's continued work in Nayarit follows from this nationalist construction of ethnography, including Vogt's ethnography, as a resource helping to establish or deepen state control over Indigenous populations (in terms, of course, that touch an omnipresent colonial/anthropological erotics).

By 1956, the Chiapas Coordinating Center had been operational for five years. Given the logistical difficulties that complicated travel to Huichol communities of the Sierra Madre, Gamio may have hoped that Harvard's presence in Nayarit would help facilitate an expansion of the roadbuilding INI's development regime. Despite his own instrumental use of the INI's campaign, Vogt rarely seemed to consider that such Mexican anthropologists and administrators sought to influence him for their ideological and real-political ends. Perhaps the political instrumentality of anthropology in Mexico was not quite legible to an academic so immersed in a midcentury, modernist fantasy of "basic" social science's political innocence. In this respect, Vogt, who—when not rubbing shoulders with Mexican governors—tended toward political naivety if not willful ignorance, differed from Kluckhohn. The latter, for example, worked with the Central Intelligence Agency while serving as the first director of Harvard's Russian Research Center (Price 2016, 84–87).[25]

If Vogt was discouraged by Gamio's reply, he would have been pleased by Caso's: "It makes me very happy that you have decided to work in the region of Chiapas, where our Center will be able to give you all the support and cooperation that is necessary."[26] Aguirre Beltrán, in turn, wrote to convey his satisfaction with the choice to shift research to Chiapas, indicating that he was sending linguistic materials on Tzotzil and Tzeltal under separate cover and advising that he had arranged for Vogt to receive the INI's publications for a year, including their journal of Mexican applied anthropology, *Acción Indigenista*.[27] Of his three powerful Mexican anthropologist correspondents, then, both of the INI functionaries—the director of the institute and the director of the Centro Coordinador Indigenista Tzeltal-Tzotzil—conveyed support for the idea of Harvard faculty and students working in their midst. The Harvard Chiapas Project, or at least the idea of a Harvard Chiapas Project, was on. By mid-April, Vogt was corresponding with his contact at the Ford Foundation to arrange a meeting to discuss his "revised Mexican culture change project," alongside continuing exchange regarding lines of grant funding for graduate students' intensive, multiyear ethnographic fieldwork.[28]

By April 20, 1956, Vogt had drafted a proposal for the Harvard Chiapas Project. He circulated copies to colleagues at Harvard and beyond.[29] Most of the cover letters shared a script, requesting comments and indicating that he was considering submissions to the Ford Foundation, the National Science Foundation, the Rockefeller Foundation, and the National Institutes of Health. He waited three days to write tailored letters to two colleagues who had stronger ties to the Mexican anthropological establishment: Howard F. Cline of the Hispanic Foundation, and Vogt's Mexico City contact Isabel Kelly.[30] The language in the letter to Cline, who had encouraged Vogt's turn to Chiapas, conveys the concerns that motivated tailoring:

> Please do not circulate this preliminary draft widely—since I want to be careful about my relationships with Summer Linguistic Institute [SIL] people and in the I.N.I. whose programs you will note are basic variables to be studied. I would prefer to discuss the situation with them personally when I go to Mexico next Christmas-time on another preliminary look at the field situation before I start my research in the summer of 1957.

Within a week, Vogt would make preliminary inquiries to Ford, NSF, NIH, and Rockefeller about their prospective interests in supporting the proposal.[31] He was not, apparently, concerned about the viability of a proposal for studying the effects of a Mexican state development campaign on cultural change in Tzotzil and Tzeltal communities. The project's sensitivity was limited to the audience of Mexican supporters.

Despite a tepid initial reply from Philip Sapir at the NIH, the institute would ultimately fund Vogt's proposal, titled "Mexican Cultural Change: Comparative Analysis of the Processes of Cultural Change in Tzotzil and Tzeltal Indian Communities in Chiapas, Mexico."[32] They first provided a small grant of $2,000 to support a summer 1957 research trip, with Vogt accompanied by graduate student Frank Miller (Vogt 1994, 88). Then they came through in mid-December 1957 with a major grant: $63,200 to support five years of fieldwork.[33] The grant was made through the National Institute of Mental Health (NIMH), a subinstitute of the NIH.

In *Fieldwork among the Maya*, Vogt quotes, at considerable length, the "essence of the five-year proposal," including sections on "Research Plan," "Method of Procedure," and "Significance of This Research" (Vogt 1994, 82–88). The proposal centers, rather than obscures, cultural changes effected by the state development campaign: "The aims of the project are to describe the changes currently occurring in the cultures of the Tzotzil and Tzeltal Indians in Chiapas, Mexico, as a result of the action program of the National Indian Institute [INI] of the Mexican government; and to utilize these data for an analysis of the determinants and processes of cultural change" (82). It sets these possible changes against the backdrop of Spanish colonial transformations of Tzotzil and Tzeltal economies. The colonization of the Chiapas highlands was a remarkably pacific structural transformation for a grant-seeking Vogt:

> A pattern of intercultural life was developed in which the large rural [Indigenous] population supplied the [Ladino] town with food supplies, cheap manual labor, wood for construction, and charcoal for fuel. In exchange, the Ladino town supplied the Indians with products and services for their religious ceremonies: fireworks, candles, incense, colored ribbons for their hats, Catholic priests to perform ceremonies in their churches, and aguardiente to drink on ritual occasions. (82)

This cultural and economic equilibrium in the contact zone meant that "much of the aboriginal culture remained unchanged" at the time that the INI inaugurated development work in 1951 (82–83; see also Lewis 2018). Unchanged aboriginal forms could, apparently, be found in studies of rituals and beliefs, constructions of disease and curing, kinship and social organization, and subsistence practices.

The Tzotzil and Tzeltal communities of highland Chiapas, then, became an opening to question the possibility and form of deep-historical cultural continuities. Research on Tzotzil and Tzeltal communities undertaken in the 1940s under the supervision of University of Chicago anthropologist Sol Tax offered a "baseline for the investigation of recent changes" (Vogt 1994, 83). The reader of Vogt's proposal was supposed to understand this "baseline" as a reflection of the intrinsic cultural form of Indigenous communities, effectively unchanged since the precolonial era. Against this background of cultural continuity, Vogt introduced the INI's development campaign as an independent variable. Recounting that the INI had worked in the area—introducing clinics, schools, roads, and agricultural resources—for five years, he cast the state program, in the now-risible hyperbole of midcentury grant rhetoric, as "a major force for change in the Indian culture of Chiapas—indeed, probably the most important event that has affected these cultures since the Spanish Conquest of the 1520s" (83).

The INI campaign staged a "cultural laboratory situation to describe cultural changes that are currently occurring and can be observed firsthand" (Vogt 1994,

83). Through longitudinal research across five years, Vogt planned to document the "sequences and directions of cultural change" as well as the "determinants and processes of cultural change" (83). This would entail examining both the "value systems" and "social structures" of highland Indigenous communities (84). With respect to social structure, Vogt extends the Mesoamericanist construction of Indigenous folk society as comprised of "closed corporate communities" developed substantively in Robert Redfield's ethnography and Eric Wolf's ethnology (Redfield and Villa Rojas 1934; Redfield 1941; Wolf 1955). Wolf (Wolf 1957) published his well-known comparative essay "Closed Corporate Peasant Communities in Mesoamerica and Central Java" in spring 1957; Vogt submitted his grant proposal to the NIH in March of the same year. His project, then, proposed to survey the effects of the most powerful force inducing structural and value changes in the communities of highland Chiapas since the Spanish colonists arrived.[34]

Building on research into Indigenous cultural change in the United States, Vogt's proposal parses two types of acculturation: "forced" change and "permissive" change. His elaboration of the point clarifies the distinction's analytic value: "the thesis being that changes backed by force or power are less likely to be accepted than are new patterns presented to an American Indian group under permissive conditions that allow for freedom to make choices and for a selective process of adaptation" (Vogt 1994, 84, referencing Dozier 1955). These conceptual distinctions—open versus closed communities and forced versus passive change—set up the first of three hypotheses with which Vogt closes his proposal's Research Plan: "that more acceptance of the modernization program of the National Indian Institute [INI] (and hence more cultural change) is likely to be found: (a) in 'open' communities than in 'closed' corporate communities; and (b) under conditions where the new patterns are presented in 'permissive' rather than 'forced' programs" (Vogt 1994, 85). The second and third hypotheses attempt to nuance and elaborate this first point, with the second parsing the kinds of change expected in open and closed communities, and the third specifying the prospect that religious values, in particular, will "differentially affect" "the rates and direction of changes" (85).

Vogt's construction of change here betrays a deeply liberal ideology that differentiates "force or power" from "permissive conditions that allow for freedom to make choices" (Vogt 1994, 84). He demonstrates little awareness that power may operate through "softer" forms than military or state domination. For Vogt, "power" is distinct from, rather than a condition of, "freedom." The contact zone effectuated by the development campaign, then, reads to Vogt as a field beyond power, a politically neutral "cultural" project. What follows is the tautological claim that "open" communities will be more accepting of change, and the banal (settler-colonial) claim that they will accept it all the more when change is induced by "permissive," rather than "forced," means. These concepts of power—and these concepts of freedom, choice, values, and force—lack rigor and dialectical tact. There is good reason to suspect that the applied anthropologists working in the ranks of the postrevolutionary Mexican state knew that too.

THE INI ENCOUNTERS HARVARD

On July 15, 1957, Vogt submitted the same grant to the National Science Foundation that he had sent to the NIH in March (Vogt 1994, 82). He proceeded, on that day, to mail a copy to Caso at the INI headquarters in Mexico City.[35] Given the construction of the INI's development campaign as the prevailing variable effecting Tzotzil and Tzeltal cultural change, he must have felt that his in-person conversation—in late December or early January—had resolved any concerns about the research frame.[36] The only clarification that he includes in the cover letter reads: "Footnote 1 on page 1 was necessary because the National Science Foundation emphasizes 'basic' rather than 'applied' research. It does not mean that the results of my research will not be useful to the INI—I certainly hope and expect that they will be helpful."[37] He sent basically the same letter to Mexican anthropologist Alfonso Villa Rojas, who, in 1957, had taken over as director of the Tzeltal-Tzotzil Coordinating Center in San Cristóbal.[38]

The INI was charged with bringing "integrated development" to Mexico's Indigenous populations. Historian Stephen Lewis (2018) casts INI administrators as optimists—even "utopians"—who sincerely believed that the "Indian problem," including profoundly racialized economic inequality, was resolvable through concerted development interventions. That the INI built its pilot Coordinating Center in highland Chiapas, where speakers of Tzeltal and Tzotzil had long forcefully maintained political and economic autonomy, now reads as an effort to test the power of such "indigenist mysticism" (or *mística*).

Despite its status as the premier campaign of the federal agency charged with putting the Mexican mythos-ethos of mestizaje into action, through a deeply bureaucratic internal settler colonialism, the Chiapas Coordinating Center was diminishing in political promise and importance by 1957. The center "may have reached its apogee in 1955" (Lewis 2018, 266). In an article published that year, Villa Rojas asserted, in a rather promotional voice, that the Coordinating Center "constitutes Mexico's most important center of managed social transformation . . . The region represents a true anthropological laboratory where the student has the opportunity to observe in vivo the most varied cultural forms as well as their diverse reactions to the penetration of Western civilization" (Villa Rojas [1955] 1964, 217, as translated and quoted in Lewis 2018, 266). Nonetheless, as Lewis (2018, 128), building on later HCP alumnus (and critic) Jan Rus (Rus 2004), recognizes, the work of Caso, Aguirre Beltrán, and Villa Rojas to place Vogt and his students in Zinacantán owed directly to the institute's struggle to make inroads there.

The INI center had an uneven footing in the complex political landscape of highland Chiapas. It was founded at about the same time that an alcohol monopoly, controlled by brothers Hernán and Moctezuma Pedrero Argüello, emerged (Lewis 2018, 91–112). The monopoly enabled the Pedrero brothers to raise the price and reduce the quality of liquor, which had important social and ritual functions in Tzotzil and Tzeltal communities. A proliferation of bootleg liquor production operations in the mountainous highlands resulted. The Pedreros then instigated violent, indeed "occasionally fatal," raids of Indigenous communities, where they confiscated alcohol and destroyed clandestine stills (91). The INI, as it began work in these same communities, opposed the raids, and hence gained a reputation that it sheltered bootleggers. The institute then created the Commission to Study the Problem of Alcoholism in Chiapas, which produced a critical report on the monopoly that denounced the Pedreros and revealed the complicity of the Chiapan State.[39] The state government blocked its publication. It was not released until 2009 (Lewis and Sosa Suárez 2009; Lewis 2018, 91–92).

Villa Rojas was singing the praises of the Coordinating Center as the institute began to confront the center's slow and painful demise. While the development of a traveling educational theater group, Teatro Petul, facilitated some educational and health projects, the INI could not adequately fund its bilingual schooling campaign. This included building schools, supplying them with bilingual (Tzotzil-Spanish and Tzeltal-Spanish) teaching materials, and training a cast of "cultural promoters"—young, bilingual Indigenous teachers, who often had little formal education themselves. Many promoters were former town scribes who viewed the position as a means to extend their control in a field where state power—sovereign power as well as the INI's governmentality—had not successfully displaced *caciquismo*, or strongmen-controlled bossism (Lewis 2018, 61).[40] Aguirre Beltrán, who called promoters *indígenas ladinizados*, reluctantly concluded that they served as integral intercultural agents; a critical reading could trace how the scribe turned teacher became an ambivalent "figure of mimicry" that "problematizes the signs of racial and cultural priority, so that the 'national' is no longer naturalizable" (Bhabha 1994, 125).[41]

While the schools enjoyed moderate success in some Tzeltal communities, such as Oxchuc, they struggled in the Tzotzil communities that would become core sites of US anthropological research: Zinacantán and Chamula. An INI administrative report documented that in July 1956, the municipal president of Zinacantán traveled to the Zinacanteco villages of La Granadilla and Chainatik to discourage parents from constantly pulling their children from a school and to convey the impression that the school had strong municipal support.[42] A report the next month castigated Chamulan and Zinacanteco promoters as uninterested in improving their work, despite constant guidance.[43] Lewis describes a trip that month by INI administrator Julio de la Fuente to evaluate the educational programs: "He toured some of the most difficult schools, those of the southern Tsotsil [Tzotzil] zone, mainly in Chamula and Zinacantán. 'Our achievements are extremely precarious and do not reflect this Center's many years of work and experience in the region,' he wrote" (Lewis 2018, 60).[44] They struggled, further, to educate women. They worked to provide instruction in Singer machine–based sewing as well as reading and writing, and they recruited girls and young women to the INI's Boarding School.[45]

In characterizing these challenges, one report documents Beltrán's belief that "the transformation of the Indigenous people should be their own project."[46] The indigenistas nonetheless, focused on facilitating and enabling such Indigenous transformation as they abandoned grander, utopian plans (including a broader regional industrialization project and extension of the INI's work into Ladino communities). In lieu of such shifts, INI administrators focused their attention on beleaguered campaigns in Indigenous communities (Lewis 2018, 266). Villa Rojas facilitated Vogt's entry into Maya communities by introducing him to a cultural promoter and to local caciques. Lewis (128–29) further suggests that "cultural anthropologists trained in the community study tradition were likely to pay little heed to 'outside' conditions and the overarching political and economic structures that the INI had shown itself incapable of altering." The indigenistas were happy to host Harvard anthropologists at La Cabaña and to facilitate their research connections. Harvard student Henry ("Nick") Nicholson, in an early example, visited an INI school only to find a basketball court, where he "demonstrated a few jump shots to let them know the gringos had something to do with the game," as Villa Rojas presented Chiapas to him as "one of the finest anthropological laboratories in the world."[47]

Jan Rus (2004, 205) and Stephen Lewis (2018, 129) convey an ultimate irony of the Harvard project: it constructed Zinacantán as the quintessential "Maya" community, despite its having been selected for research precisely because of its atypicality. It is evident that the HCP elevated the reputation of a faltering development campaign put on by a young postrevolutionary Mexican state institute directed by anthropologists, some of whom aspired to hold elected political offices. But what falls out of the picture in these accounts is that Vogt explicitly constructed the project as a study of the INI campaign's effects. It is not the case that Vogt, in the tradition of Redfield's community studies, simply *ignored* "external" political and economic conditions. The influence of Redfield on Vogt's earliest Chiapas research—I believe—pales compared to the influence of Kluckhohn, who was not a Mesoamericanist and had distinct ideas—value-centered ideas—about what constituted community and culture. Like Kluckhohn and—to an extent—Sol Tax, Vogt, in the 1950s, conceived the anthropologist as a knowledge broker who might aid a benevolent state.

But, in 1960, Villa Rojas concluded his Coordinating Center directorship, the HCP initiated its undergraduate field school, and Kluckhohn died. Vogt, then, restructured his ethnographic and scientific alliances, detaching the project from the INI in favor of "identifying ourselves more with the conservative segments of the Indian communities" (1994, 209). This "identification" entailed HCP students taking up residence in Indigenous households, a move that Vogt cast as *pioneering* in the context of Mesoamerican ethnography.[48] As he distanced the Chiapas project from post–Villa Rojas INI campaigns, Vogt (209) effectively abandoned the question of "culture change," reconstructing the project as research into a case of extraordinary cultural continuity: "It had become perfectly plain that we had underestimated the amount and complexity of ancient Maya social organization and culture that are still viable in these communities." The Mexican anthropologists' development interventions came to seem less a "variable" than a threat to communities that Vogt (1969, 1976) reconceived in the Rousseauian image—popularized by Sylvanus Morley (1946)—of ancient Maya cities as ritual centers ruled by peaceful "astronomer priests" (refashioned in Vogt's ethnographies as shamans).

Yes, Vogt arrived at this space of colonial fantasy and ignorance of the state after only a few years. But, to get there, to get the project off the ground, he constructed it clearly and explicitly as a study of acculturative effects: social-structural and value changes induced by the INI. The Harvard Chiapas Project did not start as a story of ignorance of the state. It started as a story of *naturalizing* the state. The cultural promoters' ambivalent status as "mimic men" destabilized and denaturalized the mestizo *nation*. But the INI shored it up by bringing in a Harvard man who would read the governmentalist power of the settler-colonial state as an incontestable natural force, something that couldn't be resisted. Naturalization produced ignorance (see also Proctor and Schiebinger 2008).

Over the next twenty years, Vogt and fellow project administrators initiated students into anthropology in this space of colonial fantasy, establishing the HCP as a—and probably *the*—premier ethnographic methods training program. Many Harvard Chiapas Project students became prominent ethnographers within and beyond Mesoamerican studies. No matter where they ultimately built their reputations and institutional influence, they were aided by methods and connections facilitated by the project. Did they—particularly early students—share Vogt's naturalization of state power?

CONCLUSION

That postwar modernist anthropologists naturalized Indigenous communities in the service of (social) scientizing the largely humanistic field of anthropology is hardly surprising today. An abundant critical literature tracking the symbolic violence of Cold War–era anthropology's reduction of colonized cultures to mechanistic, ahistorical alterities proliferated between the mid-1970s and the mid-1990s (e.g., Wagner 1975; Fabian 1983; Marcus and Fischer 1986; Behar and Gordon 1995). But such "reflexive" cultural critiques proved far less invested in modernist anthropological constructions of power and the state (let alone the state's constructions of anthropologists). Cold War–era scholars' attachments to "small-scale" societies (whether "hunter-gatherers," "folk societies," or "tribal societies") meant that understandings of power and the state remained decidedly marginal—to the modernist anthropologists and to their critics.

In Vogt's publications on Zinacantán, he brackets or excludes the state and, to a large extent, the mestizo world in its complex historical relations with Tzotzil lives. Only by turning to archives, supplemented by published reflections such as Vogt's (interestingly unreliable) memoir, can we understand how such anthropologists saw the state. In this case, Vogt naturalized Indigenous communities as, or even after, he naturalized the state. The state became a force inducing cultural change—like a natural disaster. But there are important differences between, *say*, a (once-in-a-half-millennium) earthquake and a modernizing nationalist project of postrevolutionary Mexican state development. An earthquake is a discrete, critical tectonic event that may affect social crises that—as anthropological disaster studies show—induce complex forms of cultural change and continuity (Oliver-Smith and Hoffman [1999] 2020). While that might *seem* similar in its effects, the anthropologist who studies community responses to earthquakes does not also need to understand the geological nature of tectonics; it can be bracketed. In the case of the Harvard Chiapas Project, the critical event inducing historical change—*or not*—among highland Maya communities was a state institution that directly enabled Vogt's turn to Chiapas and, ultimately, to the ideal "closed corporate community" of Zinacantán.

Earthquakes do not invite their anthropologists. State power does. Postrevolutionary Mexican nationalists *played* the postwar modernist Harvard professor, constructing political resistance as cultural conservatism for a crimson flagbearer. During the first half of the 1950s, the INI failed at least one mission of mestizaje: forging the nation out of Tzotzil lives (see Gamio [1916] 2010). Whether this cultural forge was "forced" or "permissive" had little effect in, let alone meaning for, some communities of highland Chiapas. When INI administrators found themselves struggling to assimilate Zinacantecos, they did the next best thing. They assimilated Evon Zartman Vogt Jr.—and the power of Harvard University's image with him. When Vogt realized what the INI administrators knew all along, that the development campaign was failing to induce cultural change, he deduced what seemed to him an evident conclusion: the cosmological kernel of Maya culture was so robust that the community of Zinacantán comprised the quintessential closed community, deeply conservative and resistant to change. So, if the community would not change, the Harvard project's organizing question would have to. The problem of "induced culture change" gave way to research into (the miracle of) cultural continuity. And, due to its unchanging nature, Zinacantán became the most important community in anthropology—and, hence, for anthropologists at least, the most important community in the world. Vogt shifted from naturalizing to sacralizing the closed corporate community; the habit would stick for some barely postromantic Mayanists (Watson 2020; see also Evans 2004).

The drift away from "culture change" research attended the gradual dissolution of an alliance between the Instituto Nacional Indigenista and the Harvard Chiapas Project. But, for the INI administrators, this drift would have mattered little. What mattered was the Harvard researchers' presence. Harvard faculty and students were there in droves. Development campaigns of the INI had Harvard's prestigious seal of approval. While Harvard students did not partake of Mexican mestizaje's "value orientation," they were there nonetheless, shooting hoops in the anthropological laboratory. The Harvard professor and students became an assimilating force—invited by an earthquake—by virtue, merely, of being there.

NOTES

1. Evon Z. Vogt to Leland DeVinney, April 11, 1955, Papers of Evon Zartman Vogt, 1939–2003, Harvard University Archive (hereafter Vogt Papers), HUGFP 140.6, box 1, folder 1955.

2. The project's advisory committee was comprised of Kluckhohn, Talcott Parsons, and J. O. Brew. The field directors were Vogt and John M. Roberts (Vogt and Albert 1967, viii–ix). "Rimrock," in later publications, served as a pseudonym for "Ramah."

3. For a bibliography of the Values Study publications, see Vogt and Albert (Vogt and Albert 1967, 299–305).

4. In large part due to its long-term summer field school, the Harvard Chiapas Project deeply affected the formation of twentieth-century anthropology. But it was only one of several major collaborative projects undertaken between the 1940s and the 1970s by Harvard anthropologists, and by their colleagues in anthropology programs at universities including Columbia, Cornell, and the University of Chicago. The Comparative Study of Values in Five Cultures and the Harvard Chiapas Project were followed by (and likely influenced) the

Harvard-Central Brazil Project (1962–67), run by David Maybury-Lewis, and the Harvard Kalahari Project (1963–76), run by Richard Lee and Irven DeVore. In highland Chiapas, the HCP initially ran alongside the University of Chicago's Man-in-Nature Project (1956–59), directed by Sol Tax and Norman McQuown. With respect to the broader scene of anthropological field training, Vogt collaborated with colleagues across institutions to facilitate the Columbia-Cornell-Harvard-Illinois Summer Field Research Program, which turned undergraduate research into an interinstitutional, transcontinental ethnological construction of Latin America. Other major Cold War–era collaborative ethnographies included Cornell University's Vicos Project, in the Peruvian Andes, and Julian Steward's Puerto Rico Project. On the Man-in-Nature Project, see Barrera-Aguilera (2019) and Mentanko (2020). On the Vicos Project, see also Babb (2018).

5. On Mexican indigenismo, see, e.g., Brading (1989), Lomnitz (2001, 2005), López Caballero (2020). Mauricio Tenorio Trillo (1999) traces the transnational formation of social science and nationalist indigenismo, with attention to the Boas-Gamio connection, between the 1880s and the 1930s. In turn, Giraudo (2012) attends astutely to the political and intellectual forces shaping the rise of Pan-American indigenismo, beginning with the 1940 Pátzcuaro conference.

6. It would be valuable to further examine the influence of the indigenista "action program" on Sol Tax's urgent, action anthropology (and vice versa) (see Stocking 2001; Link 2016b; see also Caso 1958, de la Fuente 1958). See also the journal *Acción Indigenista* (1953–76).

7. On the racial ideology of mestizaje in Mexico, see, e.g., Doremus (2001), Alonso (2004), and Hartigan (2013).

8. The INI's campaigns fared a bit better in some Tzeltal-speaking communities, such as Oxchuc, where Alfonso Villa Rojas—collaborator of Robert Redfield and director of the Chiapas Coordinating Center from 1957 to 1960—had completed intensive ethnographic work in the 1940s (Villa Rojas 1946; see also Corbeil 2013, Lewis 2018).

9. On what would come of "urgent anthropology," see Stocking (2001) and Link (2016a, 2016b).

10. Vogt to Leland DeVinney, April 11, 1955, Leland DeVinney to Vogt, April 12, 1955, Vogt to Leland DeVinney, April 18, 1955, Vogt Papers, HUGFP 140.6, box 1, folder 1955.

11. Leland DeVinney to Vogt, May 18, 1955, Vogt Papers, HUGFP 140.6, box 1, folder 1955.

12. Vogt to Leland DeVinney, May 31, 1955, Vogt Papers, HUGFP 140.6, box 1, folder 1955.

13. Vogt to Leland DeVinney, October 20, 1955, Vogt Papers, HUGFP 140.6, box 1, folder 1955.

14. Vogt to Leland DeVinney, November 1, 1955, Leland DeVinney to Vogt, November 4, 1955, November 15, 1955, Vogt Papers, HUGFP 140.6, box 1, folder 1955. Vogt to Leland DeVinney, November 8, 1955, Vogt Papers, HUGFP 140.6, box 1, folder 1955.

15. Leland DeVinney to Vogt, December 13, 1955, Vogt Papers, HUGFP 140.6, box 1, folder 1955.

16. E.g., Joseph Casagrande to Vogt, November 30, 1955, Vogt Papers, HUGFP 140.6, box 1, folder C-1956, enclosed in Richard Sheldon to Vogt, February 16, 1956, Vogt Papers, HUGFP 140.6, box 1, folder C-1956. George P. Murdock to Vogt, January 3, 1956, Vogt Papers, HUGFP 140.6, box 1, folder M-1956.

17. Vogt to J. Alden Mason, January 7, 1956, Vogt Papers, HUGFP 140.6, box 1, folder M-1956. Vogt to Richard C. Sheldon, December 28, 1955, Vogt Papers, HUGFP 140.6, box 1, folder S-1956.

18. Vogt to Fred Eggan, January 26, 1956, Vogt Papers, HUGFP 140.6, box 1, folder E-1956.

19. Vogt to Joe Grimes, February 8, 1956, Vogt Papers, HUGFP 140.6, box 1, folder G-1956.

20. Vogt to Isabel Kelly, February 8, 1956, Vogt Papers, HUGFP 140.6, box 1, folder J,K-1956.

21. Vogt to Howard F. Cline, February 8, 1956, Vogt Papers, HUGFP 140.6, box 1, folder C-1956; Vogt to Joe Grimes, February 8, 1956, Vogt Papers, HUGFP 140.6, box 1, folder G-1956; Vogt to John B. McIntosh, February 8, 1956, Vogt Papers, HUGFP 140.6, box 1, folder M-1956; Vogt to Gonzalo Aguirre Beltrán, February 8, 1956, Vogt Papers, HUGFP 140.6, box 1, folder A-1956; Vogt to Manuel Gamio, February 8, 1956, Vogt Papers, HUGFP 140.6, box 1, folder G-1956; Vogt to Alfonso Caso, February 8, 1956, Vogt Papers, HUGFP 140.6, box 1, folder C-1956.

22. On the science studies concept of "trading zones," which is closely linked to Tsing's construction here, see Galison (1997).

23. On contact zones, see Pratt (1992) and Haraway (2008).

24. Manuel Gamio to Vogt, February 13, 1956, Vogt Papers, HUGFP 140.6, box 1, folder G-1956. Translation by the author.

25. That Kluckhohn worked with the CIA does not, of course, mean that he was particularly savvy. But he did seem to grasp more clearly than Vogt how anthropological research was often *part* of a field of state power, rather than an objective science external to it.

26. Alfonso Caso to Vogt, February 15, 1956, Vogt Papers, HUGFP 140.6, box 1, folder C-1956. Translation by the author.

27. Gonzalo Aguirre Beltrán to Vogt, February 29, 1956, Vogt Papers, HUGFP 140.6, box 1, folder A-1956.

28. Vogt to Richard C. Sheldon, April 13, 1956, Vogt Papers, HUGFP 140.6, box 1, folder S-1956.

29. Vogt to H. A. Murray, April 20, 1956, Vogt Papers, HUGFP 140.6, box 1, folder M-1956; Vogt to W. W. Howells, April 20, 1956, Vogt Papers, HUGFP 140.6, box 1, folder H-1956; Vogt to Jerome Bruner, April 20, 1956, Vogt Papers, HUGFP 140.6, box 1, folder B-1956; Vogt to J. O. Brew, April 20, 1956, Vogt Papers, HUGFP 140.6, box 1, folder B-1956;

Vogt to David McClelland, April 20, 1956, Vogt Papers, HUGFP 140.6, box 1, folder M-1956; Vogt to Cora DuBois, April 20, 1956, Vogt Papers, HUGFP 140.6, box 1, folder D-1956; Vogt to Samuel Stouffer, April 20, 1956, Vogt Papers, HUGFP 140.6, box 1, folder S-1956; Vogt to Richard Solomon, April 20, 1956, Vogt Papers, HUGFP 140.6, box 1, folder S-1956.

30. Vogt to Howard F. Cline, April 23, 1956, Vogt Papers, HUGFP 140.6, box 1, folder C-1956; Vogt to Isabel Kelly, April 23, 1956, Vogt Papers, HUGFP 140.6, box 1, folder J,K-1956.

31. Vogt to Harry Alpert, April 26, 1956, Vogt Papers, HUGFP 140.6, box 1, folder A-1956; Vogt to Philip Sapir, April 26, 1956, Vogt Papers, HUGFP 140.6, box 1, folder S-1956; Vogt to Richard C. Sheldon, April 26, 1956, Vogt Papers, HUGFP 140.6, box 1, folder S-1956; Vogt to Leland DeVinney, April 27, 1956, Vogt Papers, HUGFP 140.6, box 1, folder D-1956.

32. Philip Sapir to Vogt, May 15, 1956, Vogt Papers, HUGFP 140.6, box 1, folder S-1956; see also Vogt (1994, 82).

33. Vogt to David Schneider, January 8, 1958, Vogt Papers, HUGFP 140.6, box 2, folder R-S-T 1956–57; Vogt to Edward ("Ned") Spicer, Vogt Papers, HUGFP 140.6, box 2, folder R-S-T 1956–57; see also Vogt (1994, 114).

34. The construction of cultural change here is relentlessly diffusionist. Vogt makes zero concessions to the role of "invention"—to invoke the language of the interwar US anthropological struggle over invention versus diffusion—in his constructions of cultural statics and dynamics.

35. Vogt to Alfonso Caso, July 15, 1957, Vogt Papers, HUGFP 140.6, box 1, folder A, B, C 1956–57.

36. Vogt to Alfonso Caso, January 25, 1957, Vogt Papers, HUGFP 140.6, box 1, folder A, B, C 1956–57.

37. Vogt to Alfonso Caso, July 15, 1957, Vogt Papers, HUGFP 140.6, box 1, folder A, B, C 1956–57.

38. Vogt to Alfonso Villa Rojas, July 15, 1957, Vogt Papers, HUGFP 140.6, box 2, folder U-V-W 1956–57. Villa Rojas was a fellow alumnus of the University of Chicago, where he worked with Robert Redfield. Redfield and Villa Rojas (Redfield and Villa Rojas 1934) had previously collaborated in a foundational study of Maya "folk" culture.

39. Julio de la Fuente, "Comisión del estudio del problema del alcoholismo en Chiapas," vols. 1–5, 1954, FD 07/012, Fondo Documental del Instituto Nacional de los Pueblos Indígenas, Biblioteca Juan Rulfo, Mexico City (hereafter, INPI, BJR). I am grateful to Octavio Murillo Álvarez de la Cadena and Alfredo Ortiz Martínez for facilitating my research in the INPI.

40. On governmentality, see Foucault (1991). A relevant discussion of *caciquismo* in the region, by a later Harvard Chiapas Project alumnus, is Rus (2005)

41. Also see the work of Wong (2019) on "marginal men" who assisted, informed, and collaborated with Robert Redfield, Sol Tax, and Manuel Andrade during their fieldwork in

Mexico and Guatemala between the 1930s and the 1950s, and the work of Mentanko (2020) on cultural intermediaries in the gendered fields of ethnographic research and INI health promotion in midcentury highland Chiapas.

42. "Informe de las visitas que practicó el Profr. Andrés Santiago Montes a las escuelas de Belisario Domínguez, Talowits, Tres Puentes, Bajobeltik y Tibó en los días comprendidos del 4 al 11 de julio," August 31, 1956, FD 07/016, p. 20, Libro Sexto (compiled by Alfonso Villa Rojas), Informes del Centro Coordinador Indigenista Tzeltal-Tzotzil (hereafter ICCITT), INPI, BJR.

43. "Informe de las labores educativos a cargo del Profr. Andrés Santiago M. correspondientes al mes de agosto," August 31, 1956, FD 07/016, p. 120, Libro Sexto (compiled by Alfonso Villa Rojas), ICCITT, INPI, BJR.

44. Here Lewis translates and quotes Alfonso Villa Rojas, "Informe de labores correspondiente al mes de agosto," 1956, FD 07/016, ICCITT, INPI, BJR.

45. "Informe presentado por la Dirección de Educación a cargo del Profr. Fidencio Montes en relación a las labores desarrolladas durante el mes de septiembre," FD 07/016, p. 179, Libro Sexto (compiled by Alfonso Villa Rojas), ICCITT, INPI, BJR.

46. "Informe presentado por la Dirección de Educación a cargo del Profr. Fidencio Montes en relación a las labores desarrolladas durante el mes de septiembre," FD 07/016, p. 179, Libro Sexto (compiled by Alfonso Villa Rojas), ICCITT, INPI, BJR. Translation by the author.

47. Henry ("Nick") Nicholson to Vogt, May 16, 1956, Vogt Papers, HUGFP 140.6, box 1, folder N-1956.

48. When he published *Zinacantan* in 1969, Vogt (1969, x) asserted that the project "has provided field experience for twenty-four graduate students, most of whom spent at least fifteen months in the field."

REFERENCES CITED

Alonso, Ana María. 2004. "Conforming Disconformity: 'Mestizaje,' Hybridity, and the Aesthetics of Mexican Nationalism." *Cultural Anthropology* 19 (4): 459–90.

Armstrong-Fumero, Fernando. 2010. "Manuel Gamio and *Forjando Patria*: Anthropology in Times of Revolution." In *Forjando Patria: Pro-Nacionalismo (Forging a Nation)*, edited by Fernando Armstrong-Fumero, 1–19. Boulder: University Press of Colorado.

Babb, Florence E. 2018. *Women's Place in the Andes: Engaging Decolonial Feminist Anthropology*. Oakland: University of California Press.

Barrera-Aguilera, Óscar Javier. 2019. "El hombre en la naturaleza: Los resultados de proyecto Chicago en Chiapas, 1956–1959." *LiminaR: Estudios Sociales y Humanísticos* 17 (1): 98–113.

Behar, Ruth, and Deborah A. Gordon, eds. 1995. *Women Writing Culture*. Berkeley: University of California Press.

Bhabha, Homi. 1994. *The Location of Culture*. New York: Routledge.

Brading, David A. 1989. "Manuel Gamio y el indigenismo oficial en México." *Revista Mexicana de Sociología* 51 (2): 267–84.

Caso, Alfonso. 1958. "Ideals of an Action Program." *Human Organization* 17 (1): 27–29.

Corbeil, Laurent. 2013. "El Instituto Nacional Indigenista en el municipio de Oxchuc, 1951–1971." *LiminaR: Estudios Sociales y Humanísticos* 11 (1): 57–72.

de la Fuente, Julio. 1958. "Results of an Action Program." *Human Organization* 17 (1): 30–33.

Doremus, Anne. 2001. "Indigenism, Mestizaje, and National Identity in Mexico during the 1940s and the 1950s." *Mexican Studies/Estudios Mexicanos* 17 (2): 375–402.

Dozier, Edward P. 1955. "Forced and Permissive Acculturation." *American Indian* 7:38–44.

Escalona Victoria, José Luis. 2009. *Política en el Chiapas rural contemporáneo: Una aproximación etnográfica al poder*. Mexico City: Universidad Nacional Autónoma de México.

Escalona Victoria, José Luis. 2018. "Encapsulated History: Evon Vogt and the Anthropological Making of the Maya." In *Beyond Alterity: Destabilizing the Indigenous Other in Mexico*, edited by Paula López Caballero and Ariadna Acevedo-Rodrigo, 244–62. Tucson: University of Arizona Press.

Evans, R. Tripp. 2004. *Romancing the Maya: Mexican Antiquity in the American Imagination, 1820–1915*. Austin: University of Texas Press.

Fabian, Johannes. 1983. *Time and the Other: How Anthropology Makes Its Object*. New York: Columbia University Press.

Fondo Documental del Instituto Nacional de los Pueblos Indígenas, Biblioteca Juan Rulfo, Mexico City.

Foucault, Michel. 1991. "Governmentality." In *The Foucault Effect: Studies in Governmentality*, edited by Graham Burchell, Colin Gordon, and Peter Miller, 87–104. Chicago: University of Chicago Press.

Galison, Peter. 1997. *Image and Logic: A Material Culture of Microphysics*. Chicago: University of Chicago Press.

Gamio, Manuel. (1916) 2010. *Forjando Patria: Pro-Nacionalismo (Forging a Nation)*. Translated by Fernando Armstrong-Fumero. Boulder: University Press of Colorado.

Giraudo, Laura. 2012. "Neither 'Scientific' nor 'Colonialist': The Ambiguous Course of Inter-American *Indigenismo* in the 1940s." *Latin American Perspectives* 39 (5): 12–32.

Graeber, David. 2001. *Toward an Anthropological Theory of Value: The False Coin of Our Own Dreams*. New York: Palgrave.

Haraway, Donna J. 2008. *When Species Meet*. Minneapolis: University of Minnesota Press.

Hartigan, John. 2013. "Mexican Genomics and the Roots of Racial Thinking." *Cultural Anthropology* 28 (3): 372–95.

Hayden, Cori. 2003. *When Nature Goes Public: The Making and Unmaking of Bioprospecting in Mexico.* Princeton, NJ: Princeton University Press.

Lamphere, Louise. 2002. "The Long-Term Study Among the Navajo." In *Chronicling Cultures: Long-Term Field Research in Anthropology*, edited by Robert V. Kemper and Anya Peterson Royce, 108–34. Walnut Creek, CA: AltaMira Press.

Lewis, Stephen E. 2018. *Rethinking Mexican Indigenismo: The INI's Coordinating Center in Highland Chiapas and the Fate of a Utopian Project.* Albuquerque: University of New Mexico Press.

Lewis, Stephen E., and Margarita Sosa Suárez, eds. 2009. *Monopolio de aguardiente y alcoholismo en los Altos de Chiapas: Un estudio "incómodo" de Julio de la Fuente.* Mexico City: Comisión Nacional para el Desarrollo de los Pueblos Indígenas.

Link, Adrianna. 2016a. "Documenting Human Nature: E. Richard Sorenson and the National Anthropological Film Center, 1965–1980." *Journal of the History of the Behavioral Sciences* 52 (4): 371–91.

Link, Adrianna. 2016b. "Salvaging a Record for Humankind: Urgent Anthropology at the Smithsonian Institution, 1964–1984." PhD diss., Johns Hopkins University.

Lomnitz, Claudio. 2001. *Deep Mexico, Silent Mexico: An Anthropology of Nationalism.* Minneapolis: University of Minnesota Press.

Lomnitz, Claudio. 2005. "Bordering on Anthropology: Dialectics of a National Tradition in Mexico." In *Empires, Nations, and Natives: Anthropology and State-Making*, edited by Benoît de L'Estoile, Federico Neiburg, and Lygia Sigaud, 167–96. Durham, NC: Duke University Press.

López Caballero, Paula. 2020. "Desarticular el indigenismo oficial: Miradas al Instituto Nacional Indigenista (1940–1960)." *Cahiers des Amériques latines.* https://doi.org/10.4000/cal.12410.

Marcus, George E., and Michael M. J. Fischer. 1986. *Anthropology as Cultural Critique: An Experimental Moment in the Human Sciences.* Chicago: University of Chicago Press.

Mentanko, Joshua. 2020. "The Gendered Politics of Fieldwork and State Medicine in the Altos of Chiapas, 1940–1960." *History and Anthropology.* https://doi.org/10.1080/02757206.2020.1830388.

Oliver-Smith, Anthony, and Susanna M. Hoffman, eds. (1999) 2020. *The Angry Earth: Disaster in Anthropological Perspective.* New York: Routledge.

Pratt, Mary Louise. 1992. *Imperial Eyes: Travel Writing and Transculturation.* New York: Routledge.

Price, David H. 2016. *Cold War Anthropology: The CIA, the Pentagon, and the Growth of Dual Use Anthropology.* Durham, NC: Duke University Press.

Proctor, James D., and Londa Schiebinger, eds. 2008. *Agnotology: The Making and Unmaking of Ignorance*. Stanford, CA: Stanford University Press.

Redfield, Robert. 1941. *The Folk Culture of Yucatán*. Chicago: University of Chicago Press.

Redfield, Robert, and Alfonso Villa Rojas. 1934. *Chan Kom: A Maya Village*. Washington, DC: Carnegie Institution of Washington.

Rus, Jan. 2004. "Rereading Tzotzil Ethnography: Recent Scholarship from Chiapas, Mexico." In *Pluralizing Ethnography: Comparison and Representation in Maya Cultures, Histories, and Identities*, edited by John M. Watanabe and Edward Fischer, 199–230. Santa Fe, NM: School of American Research Press.

Rus, Jan. 2005. "The Struggle against Indigenous Caciques in Highland Chiapas: Dissent, Religion and Exile in Chamula, 1965–1977." In *Caciquismo in Twentieth-Century Mexico*, edited by Alan Knight and Wil Pansters, 169–200. London: Institute for the Study of the Americas.

Scott, James C. 1998. *Seeing Like a State: How Certain Schemes to Improve the Human Condition Have Failed*. New Haven, CT: Yale University Press.

Stocking, George. 2001 *Delimiting Anthropology*. Madison: University of Wisconsin Press.

Strathern, Marilyn. 1996. "Cutting the Network." *Journal of the Royal Anthropological Institute* 2 (3): 517–35.

Tenorio Trillo, Mauricio. 1999. "Stereophonic Scientific Modernisms: Social Science between Mexico and the United States, 1880s–1930s." *Journal of American History* 86 (3): 1156–87.

Tsing, Anna Lowenhaupt. 2005. *Friction: An Ethnography of Global Connection*. Princeton, NJ: Princeton University Press.

Villa Rojas, Alfonso. 1946. "Notas sobre la etnografía de los indios tzeltales de Oxchuc, Chiapas, México." In *Microfilm Collection of Manuscripts on Middle American Cultural Anthropology*. Chicago: University of Chicago Library.

Villa Rojas, Alfonso. (1955) 1964. "Adiestramiento de personal." In *La antropología social aplicada en México: Trayectoria y antología*, edited by Juan Comas, 211–27. Mexico City: Instituto Indigenista Interamericano.

Vogt, Evon. 1969. *Zinacantan: A Maya Community in the Highlands of Chiapas*. Cambridge, MA: Harvard University Press.

Vogt, Evon. 1976. *Tortillas for the Gods: A Symbolic Analysis of Zinacanteco Rituals*. Norman: University of Oklahoma Press.

Vogt, Evon Z. 1994. *Fieldwork among the Maya: Reflections on the Harvard Chiapas Project*. Albuquerque: University of New Mexico Press.

Vogt, Evon Z., and Ethel M. Albert, eds. 1967. *People of Rimrock: A Study of Values in Five Cultures*. Cambridge, MA: Harvard University Press.

Vogt, Evon Z., and Richard M. Leventhal, eds. 1983. *Prehistoric Settlement Patterns: Essays in Honour of Gordon R. Willey.* Albuquerque: University of New Mexico Press.

Wagner, Roy. 1975. *The Invention of Culture.* Chicago: University of Chicago Press.

Watson, Matthew C. 2020. *Afterlives of Affect: Science, Religion, and an Edgewalker's Spirit.* Durham, NC: Duke University Press.

Wolf, Eric. 1955. "Types of Latin American Peasantry: A Preliminary Discussion." *American Anthropologist* 57 (3): 452–71.

Wolf, Eric. 1957. "Closed Corporate Peasant Communities in Mesoamerica and Central Java." *Southwestern Journal of Anthropology* 31 (1):1–18.

Wong, Perry. 2019. "Biographies of a Sociological Type: 'Marginal Men' in the Establishment of 'Middle American' Anthropology." *Journal of Latin American and Caribbean Anthropology* 24 (4): 823–42.

6

Distilling the Past through the Present

*Discussions with Contemporary US Rum Makers for Understanding
Nineteenth-Century Rum Making in the Yucatán Peninsula*

JENNIFER P. MATHEWS AND JOHN R. GUST

For more than a decade, we have been studying historic sugarcane and rum distillery sites from the late nineteenth and early twentieth centuries in Quintana Roo, Mexico.[1] These distilleries were small haciendas located in remote jungle and mangrove environments. Foreigners (sometimes from the US) often managed the small operations that relied on a primarily Maya labor force to produce a high-quality rum that was only consumed in the Yucatán peninsula. Despite the recent occupation of these archaeological sites, they often lack many artifacts, as local peoples have either reused them for other purposes, recycled them, or sold them for scrap. Because we are dealing with such a partial material record and the archival records for this region are few, we have had to turn to other sources for understanding and interpreting this history. One resource that we have found useful are interviews with contemporary rum distillers in the United States. Through our discussions with boutique rum distillers, we are gaining insight into the *chaîne opératoire* (operational chain) related to the use of equipment and distillation process that nineteenth-century Indigenous laborers and distillers were using in the Yucatán peninsula. In particular, we are interested in the art and skill of distillation that would have been needed for producing high-quality rum in isolated locations. This chapter will discuss the results of our findings from these interviews and our attempt to infer some clarity from an often murky archaeological past.

https://doi.org/10.5876/9781646424276.c006

BACKGROUND ON THE HISTORIC PERIOD
IN NORTHERN QUINTANA ROO

In 1821, Mexico celebrated its independence from Spain, marking the recoup of Indigenous land rights. However, in the Yucatán peninsula, although the Mayan residents had abolished noble titles and abolished slavery (Orosa Diaz 1994, 139), Indigenous Maya labor rights and their land ownership were degraded in the government's attempt to encourage foreign investment in industry in an attempt to "modernize" the economy (Cline 1947, 32–34). Haciendas expanded their production of beans, beef, corn, cotton, and, later, henequen (Rugeley 1996, 16; Andrews, Burgos Villanueva, and Millet Cámara 2006, 179–80) for the urban centers of Mérida and Campeche City. By 1840, Maya villages were surrounded by hacienda lands, cutting off their access to schools, and limiting their ability to develop infrastructure, or sustain themselves with traditional agricultural methods (Rugeley 1996, xiv, xvi–xvii). Maya peoples were then forced to attach themselves as hacienda laborers, where they had to engage in brutal work for little pay and purchase high-cost goods from company stores. They placed them into a cycle of continuous service as indentured servants. It was in this context in which Maya initiated the Caste War in 1847 (Turner 1910; Meyers and Carlson 2002; Alston, Mattiace, and Nonnenmacher 2009). Years of rebellion and upheaval resulted in casualties of roughly 40 percent on both sides. However, by 1850, Mexican and Yucatecan armies had secured the western part of the peninsula, forcing Maya peoples to retreat to the remote "uncontrollable wilds" of the east of what is now Quintana Roo (Reed 2001, 177; Rugeley 2001, 162–63).

Maya residents in the community of Kantunilkin, of northern Quintana Roo, signed a treaty in 1855 that asked for the cessation of hostilities and affirmed their autonomy (Sullivan 2004, 36). The Mexican government responded by giving two major land grants in this region (Reed 2001, 288) as an attempt to lure whites from Europe and North America to establish themselves as colonists (Sullivan 2004, 19). The climate and moist soils with high levels of lime and salt of the east coast were ideal for growing sugar (De Portas 1872, 13–14). Multiple sugarcane haciendas were established, where they were also producing aguardiente, which is a kind of high-quality rum that was widely popular in the area (Rugeley 1996, 17).

One such hacienda, known as San Antonio Xuxub (figure 6.1), was located in the remote mangrove swamps of the "Costa Escondida" on the north coast of Quintana Roo. The small hacienda of Xuxub was founded by Mauricio Palmero around 1870 and then sold to a wealthy Mexican from Mérida named Ramón Aznar in 1872. He provided the financing for the land and equipment, partnering with an engineer from New Jersey known as Robert L. Stephens, who would serve as manager (Sullivan 2004).

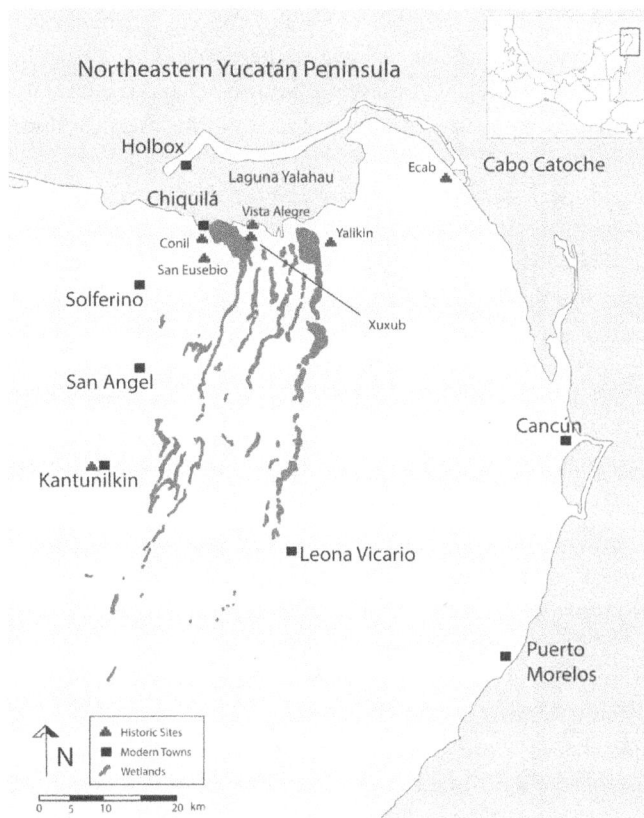

Figure 6.1. Map showing the locations discussed in the text, including Xuxub, San Eusebio, and Kantunilkin. (Map drawn by Jeffrey Glover.)

Stephens was originally from New Jersey, where he had trained as an engineer. However, he had an adventurous spirit and moved to Yucatán for work. He was hired by Andrés Urcelay to install machinery at a sugar mill in Solferino. The equipment had to be transferred from Progreso to Puntachen, so Urcelay contracted the boat *Fulita* to do so. None of the laborers showed up to load the equipment on the appointed day. The following day, Stephens ordered that the *Fulita* be brought to the dock for loading. However, it would take half a day to load the equipment and a storm was coming in, so the captain refused. Stephens insisted and had the boat loaded anyway, but the captain left in protest and got drunk. Although the boat owner was able to find a new captain, he ordered that the boat be unloaded before the storm. Stephens argued instead that they should leave soon to miss the rest of the storm, but the replacement captain refused to do so. That night, the fully loaded *Fulita* was smashed to pieces against the pier. The sugar-milling equipment was dumped into the shallow waters of the port, where it was damaged. Stephens maintained that had the boat departed when he ordered it, there would have been no problem. However, it took over a week to retrieve the equipment and the Urcelays blamed Stephens for the damage to the machinery and the resulting delay (Sullivan 2004, 34–35)

Despite this setback and a lack of capital, Stephens saw the promise of sugar production and wanted to purchase an operation of his own. He had operated sugar mills on plantations in Cuba (Sullivan 2004, 16) and thus was able to convince Ramón Aznar, a member of a wealthy Mexican family seeking further moneymaking opportunities, to purchase the property of Xuxub. The plan was that Stephens would oversee rum production and manage the Maya laborers for ten years and then sell the property and split the profits (132). During the first few years, they worked to develop infrastructure for small-scale sugarcane and rum production, including a cane-crushing mill and a cookhouse for boiling down the cane juice into syrup. Sullivan (247) believes that approximately thirty Maya families lived on site and were essential to developing the rum distillery business. John Gust found labor records for a slightly later and nearby hacienda known as San Eusebio, giving us a point of comparison for the roles that these Indigenous laborers would have played (Gust 2016, 133–57; Gust and Mathews 2020, 35).

Salaried laborers included the *mecánico*, who oversaw the sugar works; *plataformeros*, who operated the mule-drawn Decauville narrow-gauge railways; *carpinteros* (carpenters), who tended the sugar cauldrons; and the distiller. Piece-rate workers most often were responsible for a task tied to an area, or for cutting a prescribed number of pieces of wood or cane (Gust and Mathews 2020, 34–36). Wages for the workers were extremely low, and they were sometimes paid in the form of rum (Wells 1985; Rugeley 1996; Alston, Mattiace, and Nonnenmacher 2009). Workers' wives were also expected to perform the domestic duties not only of their household but of the managers' households as well. This labor may have taken the entire workday to complete and was unpaid (Peniche Rivero 1994, 78–79). Additionally, the work schedule on sugar plantations was uneven. There were times of the year when little labor was required, and at other times work continued around the clock. As sugarcane is perishable and, once cut, degrades quickly, workers had to process it quickly during harvest time (Erik Vonk, personal communication, 2014; see also Solomon 2009, 110). In part because of the low wages paid, sugar haciendas were highly profitable for owners and managers. The return on investment was up to 700 percent, and initial startup costs could be recouped by the second year (Reed 2001, 10).

San Antonio Xuxub, which today sits on Solferino-San Angel ejido land (agricultural land held communally by an Indigenous community), is located approximately 7.1 kilometers east-southeast of the contemporary town of Chiquilá. Due to its remote location, and probably because he was a white foreigner, Stephens feared attack by contentious neighbors (including the Urcelays), Caste War holdouts, and bandits (Sullivan 2004, 27). To make an approach to the Xuxub property more difficult, he demanded that no one should cut a road,[2] which would allow access by land to the operation. In spite of this, Balthazar Montilla, a commander of the local National Guard garrison who had been harassing Stephens, ordered a road cut to Xuxub on June 18, 1875 (Sullivan 2004, 27–29, 126; see also Sullivan 1998, 57).

In April 1875, a former Cruzo'ob rebel leader named Bernardino Cen, and dozens of his loyal rebels left the stronghold of Chan Santa Cruz (Sullivan 1998, 56; Reed 2001, 272; 2004, 117). In October, they used Montilla's road to approach and attack Xuxub. Cen and his men pillaged the operation, killing dozens of the Maya workers and Stephens (Sullivan 1998, 60; 2004, 79; Reed 2001, 272). Xuxub was eventually reoccupied and production was restarted, but the sugarhouse and cane fields were ultimately destroyed by a fire in May 1880 (Sullivan 2004, 177).

When we initiated an archaeological project at the site of Xuxub in 2010, we were unaware of the challenges we would face in trying to interpret the site. First, upon locating and clearing these structures for mapping, we realized that while much of the stone features were still standing (figure 6.2), there was almost no metal left from the machinery that had been originally in use. When we later studied the site of San Eusebio (see figure 6.1), a larger-scale rum production hacienda located south of Xuxub (first owned by La Compañía Agrícola del Cuyo y Anexas, and then sold at a fire sale price to Compañía Colonizadora de la Costa Oriental de Yucatán around 1908 during an economic downturn), we found the same pattern of standing stone structures but no metal machinery. Notably, according to informant Sean Devlin, curator of archaeological collections at George Washington's Mount Vernon, this is a common phenomenon at distilleries for a couple of reasons. (1) As we have previously inferred, once abandoned, the equipment is still inherently valuable and can be reused in other ways or sold; and (2), distilleries are often subject to fires and structures and artifacts would be severely damaged or destroyed entirely (Sean Devlin, personal communication, January 5, 2021). This lack of the artifacts related to sugarcane processing and rum distillation was a severe impediment to our understanding of the productive capacity and operation of these sites (Gust and Mathews 2020); however, archaeologists studying the historical period can generally supplement their knowledge with available archival records.

Unfortunately for us, a second challenge we faced was that our study area also lacks the archival documentation that is found in other areas of the Yucatán peninsula. For example, archaeologists studying the Yucatecan henequen haciendas of the nineteenth century have been fortunate to have a rich source of documents related to labor records, commodity production, and operations (see, e.g., Millet Cámara

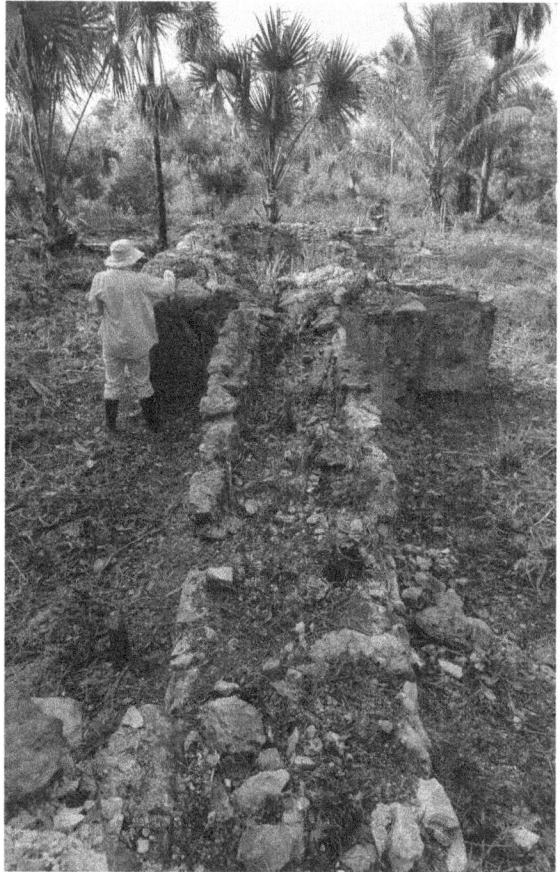

Figure 6.2. The standing stone walls of the sugarhouse building at Xuxub. Within the structure at the far end would have been three cauldrons for cooking down the sugarcane juice. (Photo courtesy of Scott L. Fedick, 2014.)

1984; Benavides Castillo 1985; Alexander 1997, 2003; Meyers and Carlson 2002; Alston, Mattiace, and Nonnenmacher 2009; Meyers 2012; Newman 2014). While we have found a few documents pertaining to the forestry concessions in the area and Paul Sullivan graciously gave us access to his data from his book *Xuxub Must Die*, these documents were mostly about Stephens's political problems with his neighbors. Further, the Roman Catholic Church had a reduced presence in the area compared to the rest of the peninsula, as this area had low population density and was considered "dangerous." This has meant that the usual documents such as bills of lading or birth, death, and marriage records for the area have been unavailable to us.

Third, while we did eventually find a small number of important labor records from San Eusebio (Gust 2016; Gust and Mathews 2020, 34–35), we have learned that sugar haciendas had very different work schedules and living arrangements from those at the henequen haciendas of western Yucatán. The growing cycle for sugarcane has "crunch" times, when a lot of labor must be deployed, but many fewer workers are needed most of the year. While some henequen haciendas in western Yucatán such as Tabí also grew sugar and distilled rum (Barceló Quintal 1981), it is difficult to parse out the daily labor assignments of sugar work from the more predominant henequen work. The two years' worth of sugar work labor records that Gust found for San Eusebio (Gust 2016, 133–57) reinforced the seasonal nature of work in this industry. He also found labor roles for other El Cuyo operations in our study area such as cattle lots (at unidentified sites of Solferino and a related site referred to as Moctezuma), and salt production (in the town of El Cuyo). None of the workers listed at San Eusebio appear on the labor rolls for these other worksites, further reinforcing the seasonal nature of their work for the company, differentiating them from the work done at henequen haciendas. Lee J. Alston, Shannan Mattiace, and Tomas Nonnenmacher (2008) also note that seasonal laborers at most sugar haciendas would most likely have continued to live in their own villages and "commute" to the hacienda. However, the operations at Xuxub were impossible to access without a boat, which surely meant that the site had a seasonal work camp instead of a year-round village. As Bernadette Cap (2015) has explored in her work on ancient Maya marketplaces through the comparative study of modern, temporary open-air Belizean markets, structures such as vendor stalls leave few permanent marks on the archaeological record, and the larger trash left behind is generally swept up and tossed. Thus, temporary living quarters for workers at Xuxub would help explain why we had difficulty locating evidence of house foundations and found a fewer number than expected of quotidian artifacts typical of Maya workers. In fact, we only found a single fragment of a comal (a flat griddle used in cooking) and were much more likely to come across glass cologne bottles of Florida Water, medicine bottles, or fragments of fancy earthenware sherds—all imported from the United States (Mathews and Gust 2017, 151–55). The seasonal residency at Xuxub also presumably eliminated the need for an on-site cemetery, as we also never found evidence of any kind of burial markers, and families would have wanted their loved ones buried at home.

Due to these three major challenges outlined above, by necessity, we turned to interviews in Mexico and the United States to fill the gaps in our understanding. The remainder of this chapter will focus on a subset of these interviews that emphasize the specialized knowledge of contemporary rum distillers and archaeologists associated with distilleries in the US.[3] This information provided us with the knowledge to understand the operational chain, including how this equipment worked, the distillation process, and thinking about the role of Indigenous labor that went into the creation of rum at Xuxub.

TWENTY-FIRST-CENTURY CRAFT DISTILLATION AS A
WINDOW INTO NINETEENTH-CENTURY DISTILLATION

Craft distilling is a fast-growing and competitive industry in the United States, with over 2,000 known craft distillers as of 2020 (Micallef 2020). Many in this young craft distiller movement compare it to the wine industry in Napa in the 1970s, with the intention of producing a high-quality product that can rival established distillers in places such as Scotland, Ireland, and Kentucky. In addition to relying on the use of high-quality ingredients, some craft distillers are engaging in-depth research into the science of distilling (Richter 2018, 12) or are being informed by traditional distilling methods and equipment of the eighteenth and nineteenth centuries. It was these latter distillers that we were particularly interested in interviewing; several experts have provided insight into the nineteenth-century distillation techniques that we are attempting to reconstruct in the Costa Escondida of Yucatán.

EXPERT INSIGHTS INTO INGREDIENTS AND YIELDS

In March 2015, we visited the Richland Rum Distillery in Richland, Georgia, owned and operated by Karin and Erik Vonk. While this craft distilling company uses modern sterilization methods and new equipment, they are updated versions of the same simple machinery that was used to make rum in the 1800s. We interviewed Karin and Erik as well as Master Distiller Roger Zimmerman to discuss their distillation process and to get their insights into some of our research questions on the sites we are studying in Mexico.

For example, we asked Erik about information from the literature that stated that once cut, sugarcane must be processed within twenty-four hours (i.e., Rogoziński 1999, 118; Meyers and Carlson 2002, 230). He confirmed that once cut, sugarcane will lose its moisture, become hard to extract, and start to ferment on its own, giving the final product off flavors if not used almost immediately (Erik Vonk, personal communication, March 18, 2015). We were also able to get insight into the raw ingredients that they may have been using in the 1800s. At Richland Rum their process starts with cane syrup. Although molasses is the base for approximately 97 percent of modern rum, this requires a lot of processing and bleaching to produce drinkable rum. Thus, distillers at Richland model their process on the recipe for "rhum agricole," which starts with cane syrup or juice. The Vonks informed us that for a time, many producers viewed molasses as a virtually worthless byproduct that would result in an inferior product (Erik and Karin Vonk, personal communication, March 18, 2015). French distillers in the nineteenth-century colonies, in particular, preferred to use cane syrup (Williams 2005, 265), while Jamaican rums that relied on molasses were known for their harsh flavor and high alcohol content

(Barty-King and Massel 1983, 89). Based on the fact that the rum produced at Xuxub had a reputation for being good tasting (Sullivan 2004, 39) and rudimentary equipment would have made additional processing challenging, we infer that these distillers were using cane syrup as the base for their product. There would have been a trade-off, however, as using cane syrup as their base limited their production to only rum and not sugar. However, at the larger and later production site of San Eusebio, we believe their rum would have been molasses based. They are known to have had centrifuges capable of spin-separating molasses from sugar and ran advertisements in the United States for sugar cubes ("El hacendado mexicano y fabricante de azúcar" 1906, 273, 369; "El hacendado mexicano y fabricante de azúcar" 1907, 399; *El hacendado mexicano y fabricante de azúcar* 1908, 9, 129, 249, 440).

Another aspect that has been elusive in the literature is the yield produced from cane juice. Erik Vonk told us that one acre produces 2,500 gallons of cane juice, which produces 250 gallons of cane syrup, which produces three barrels, or 750–900 bottles, of the final product (Erik Vonk, personal communication, March 2015). While we understand that yields will vary based on different sugarcane varieties, these statistics for high-quality, simply produced rum give us a general starting point.

WHAT IS *THIS* USED FOR?

One of the key pieces of equipment in the processing of sugar is the mill or cane grinder. Xuxub's cane fields were likely located just south of the equipment area and would have been transported to the processing area to produce cane syrup. Although larger sugar mills on islands such as Antigua would have used windmills to grind large stores of cane stocks (Gasper 1985, 98; Carstensen 1993, 9; Davis 2016, 26–27), at Xuxub the mill was quite small and animal driven. The standing feature is a circular ring-of-rocks (figure 6.3) that would have held an *arrastre*, or primitive grinder for crushing cane. Fortunately, in March 2015, we visited Historic Westville in Columbia, Georgia. While there, we were able to meet with Gillian Wong, collections manager and archaeologist, where she showed us around the museum grounds made up of regional nineteenth-century buildings, including trade buildings and equipment saved from destruction and relocated. Gillian was able to direct us to a sugar-milling machine (figure 6.4) that is still used to extract juice from small amounts of cane produced on site.

It was helpful to see the actual process of feeding sugarcane stocks into the mill and photograph the various parts that made up the machine to help us identify anything that we do come across archaeologically. It also made it clear how dangerous this machinery could have been for Maya workers working long shifts in hot, humid

Figure 6.3. Rock outline showing the original mill at Xuxub. (Photo and illustration by John R. Gust, 2016.)

Figure 6.4. The sugarcane mill at Historic Westville in Columbus, Georgia. (Photo by Jennifer P. Mathews 2015.)

conditions. Additionally, we learned that following the cane-crushing process at Richland Rum, the distiller pours the cane syrup into a large and open stainless-steel fermenting vat to which water and yeast are added (figure 6.5). Fermentation takes four to seven hours, depending on the temperature in the distillery, as their facility is not temperature controlled and can get quite warm during Georgia summers (Roger Zimmerman, personal communication, March 18, 2015). This finding implies that even with a rudimentary setup in the middle of the jungles of Yucatán, an experienced distiller would have known how to adjust the process accordingly. Seeing the fermenting vat with no lid on it also led us to ask them about the use of large open stone tanks at sites such as Xuxub (figure 6.6), San Eusebio, and a third site we documented known as Rancho Aznar.

We had initially thought that these were water cisterns, as they have been identified as such elsewhere in Yucatán; however, they are located immediately adjacent to a water well. When we showed owner Erik Vonk photos and drawings of the feature from Xuxub, he noted that the structure has thick stone walls and that the interior appears to have been plastered, making it quite possibly a fermentation tank. He also said that if they had a large quantity of cane syrup available, it was possible for the tanks to be used continuously instead of on a batch-by-batch basis (Erik Vonk, personal communication, March 18, 2015).

In December 2020 and January 2021, we held two interviews with Steve Bashore, director of historic trades at George Washington's Mount Vernon. Part of his many duties includes his management of the distillery, where he oversees runs of craft whiskey and of brandy in a reconstruction of Washington's Distillery that opened in the 1780s. The current distillery (which opened in 2006) is a reconstruction based on the archaeology of the original building foundations and equipment that operated during the eighteenth and nineteenth centuries. We showed him photographs of the Xuxub's Structure 2 and asked his opinion about what it might be. He acknowledged that it could have been a water cistern, as the location close to a well would have made it easier for them to pump or bucket water. This would allow the distillers to keep a large amount of water on hand, since distillers do not always know how much of a given ingredient will be needed for the fermentation process. He also noted that in a photo from an earlier visit by our project colleagues Dominique Rissolo and Jeffrey Glover showing two large metal rings (figure 6.7) that they could have been large barrels used for fermentation.[4] These could have allowed Maya laborers to move the cane juice from the cooking cauldrons in the sugarhouse (cane juice would be ladled from kettle to kettle, as more water evaporated and the juice became a thicker and thicker syrup) to keep them free for the next batch and keeping the production line moving (Steve Bashore, personal communication, December 30, 2020).

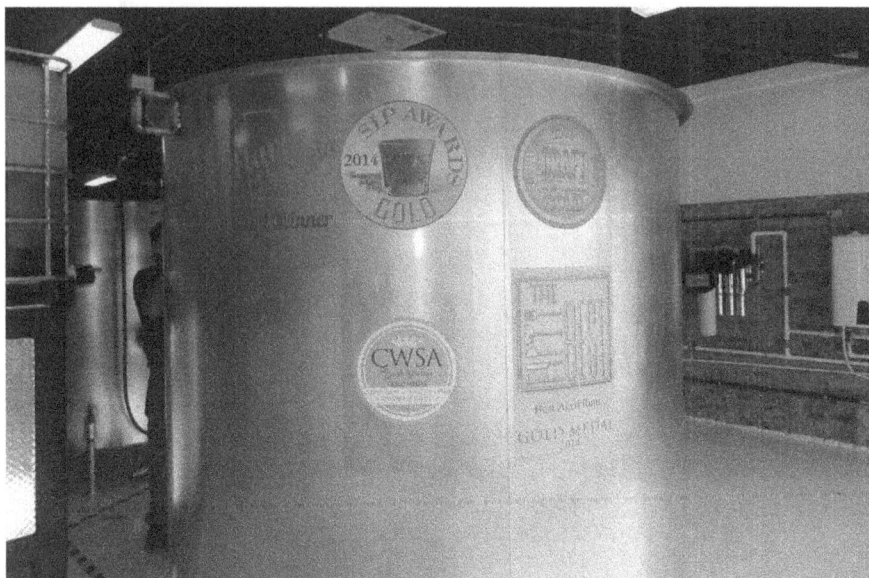

Figure 6.5. Open distilling vat at Richland Rum in Georgia. (Photo by Jennifer P. Mathews, 2015.)

Figure 6.6. Interior of a Structure 2 at the site of Xuxub with cement on the interior of the walls and floor, used as a possible cistern or fermentation tank for rum distillation. (Photo courtesy of Scott L. Fedick, 2014.)

Figure 6.7. Informants showing two large metal rings (estimated to be approximately 1.5 meters in diameter) from the site of Xuxub. (Photo courtesy of Dominique Rissolo and Jeffrey Glover, Proyecto Costa Escondida, 2009.)

However, Bashore also emphasized that the stone structure could have been used as a fermenter, as it looked extremely similar to a feature that he had learned about at Buffalo Trace Distillery in Kentucky, now nicknamed "Bourbon Pompeii" (Steve Bashore, personal communication, December 30, 2020). In 2016, Buffalo Trace Distillery was going to renovate a storage building and discovered the foundation of the original O.F.C. Distillery from 1873. Further work revealed what they thought initially was a cistern but what turned out to be a virtually intact fermentation tank that could have held a total of 11,000-gallons of mash (Patton 2016). Col. E. H. Taylor, who constructed the tanks, indicated that they were made of brick and laid in Portland cement, and then lined in sheet copper. The dimensions of each of the three in-ground whiskey fermentation tanks are approximately 5 meters by 3.35 meters by 1.21 meters deep, allowing each tank to hold 3,200 gallons of mash where it would ferment for five to seven days ("Buffalo Trace" 2019). In comparison, Structure 2 at Xuxub is constructed aboveground (bedrock would prevent it from being built in-ground) of locally sourced limestone and mortar and lined on the floor and all four walls with limestone-based cement, making it watertight. It is nearly the exact same dimensions, standing 4.0 by 5.0 meters and 1.5 meters tall (Gust 2016, 150). The contemporaneity of the structures, similar construction, and size seems to make a compelling argument that Structure 2 at Xuxub was in fact a fermentation tank that could have accommodated over 3,000 gallons of cane juice.

After fermentation, Roger Zimmerman, the master distiller at Richland Rum went on to explain that the cane syrup liquid is then pumped into one of their copper stills (Zimmerman, personal communication, March 3, 2015). As we have no remnants of the stills or equipment at our sites that would indicate how the cane syrup liquid that Maya workers would transport across the grounds, we have to infer from comparisons at other distilleries. For example, Steve Bashore said that at the Mount Vernon distillery, though they could pump water, any thicker substances had to be moved using long-handled wooden ladles with buckets attached on the end, or they would engage in a bucket brigade, passing the materials between a chain of workers (Steve Bashore, personal communication, December 30, 2020).

DISTILLERY SKILLS, EXPERIENCE, AND INVISIBLE LABOR

Distiller Roger Zimmerman went on to explain that once the cane syrup contents are in the still, it heats up slowly, and eventually, the high-proof liquid evaporates and condenses. The first of this liquid is known as the "heads" and is a potentially poisonous mix of ethyl alcohol, various nonethyl alcohols, and other chemicals produced during fermentation. Zimmerman said that with experience, the distiller knows by smell and taste when the best of the distilling rum is being produced and diverts the flow into the specially prepared wooden barrels of American white oak. The heads are saved and added to the next batch, as much of it is ethyl alcohol. Once most of the alcohol has been evaporated from the tank, the distiller diverts the flow of the evaporating liquid again and continues to condense what he calls the "tails." This liquid is a mix of a little ethyl alcohol but is more noxious, with unflavorful chemicals. Richland retains this mixture for use in their other nonconsumable products such as fuel. This part of the distillation run at sites in our study area could have similarly been used for cleaning products, fuel, and so on (Roger Zimmerman, personal communication, March 18, 2015).

Although Zimmerman had modern gauges and equipment at his disposal at Richland Rum, he seemed not to trust them and said that he really made the rum by experience and taste (Roger Zimmerman, personal communication, March 18, 2015). Further, Steve Bashore said that the equipment at Mount Vernon had no gauges to monitor temperatures and rather that the fires used in the distillation process were the key to success. Through trial and error, he and his team have learned how to build and feed fires, using different sizes and amounts of wood depending on the stage of the distillation process they were in. He brought in an expert from England who had worked in the kitchens of Henry VIII at Hampton Court and informed them that they were creating temperature spikes in the still by the way they were laying the wood. After showing them best practices, Bashore reported that his team became better still operators. Moreover, he said that with experience, although he had charts that tracked the fermentation protocols and handheld thermometers for double-checking temperature checks, he had developed an "internal clock." He now has a sense about when it is time to add ingredients and can tell by smell how to not let it ferment too long and ruin the batch. He also knows that once it is in the still, he has developed an instinct about when it is going past the hearts (the usable portion of the distillation run) and by smell and taste can tell when it is headed into the tails (the poisonous portion of the distillation run). He summed it up by saying, "It's like cooks that don't have to reach for the recipe after a while" (Steve Bashore, personal communication, December 30, 2020).

These expert details convince us of how important the human element was in the distillation process in the nineteenth century. The difference between profitability and ruin for an operation, even if everything else is done right, is and was in the hands of the distiller. The literature on rum production often (rightly) focuses on the harshness of the work and the large number of people needed to perform monotonous tasks such as harvesting sugarcane, but it is easy to forget that in order to produce a good product an operation needs a number of highly skilled artisans in key positions. We asked Sean Devlin and Steve Bashore at Mount Vernon about the role that enslaved and indentured workers might have played in the distillation process of George Washington's whiskey and whether they would have been an "invisible" contributor to the skilled labor.

Sean Devlin mentioned that despite the lack of records of where enslaved peoples working in the distillery lived, he believed that they were sleeping up on the second floor between shifts and would have been integral to the process (Sean Devlin, personal communication, January 5, 2021). Steve Bashore reflected that although enslaved peoples might have had varying levels of motivation for participating in producing a good product, there were several aspects that might have encouraged them to do so. First, they would have gotten in trouble for not doing the process correctly. Second, they would have had a large investment of time in learning the trade, and the process would have become easier to manage over time. Third, there would have been individuals who demonstrated a real skill for particular tasks and the managers of the distillery would have likely prioritized those laborers with the best skills to work at key tasks. This would have allowed managers to run a productive operation, produce the highest-quality products, and take some of the workload off of their plates (Steve Bashore, personal communication, December 30, 2020). We cannot know what working conditions would have been for Maya laborers at a small hacienda like Xuxub, but this logic allows us to presume that younger, less-experienced workers may have been weeding, harvesting cane and transporting it to the mill, crushing the cane, and helping with transporting water and other supplies across the grounds, while those Indigenous laborers with the most experience would have been running the sugar cookhouse and still and served as essential skilled workers in the operation. The only non-Indigenous person at the Xuxub operation would have been Mr. Stephens, and he simply would not have been able to do all of the skilled tasks himself. Like the enslaved workers at Mount Vernon, Maya laborers would have been key in managing the skilled distilling tasks.

CONCLUSIONS

Since the 1990s, historical archaeologists have been using oral sources or testimonies to help with the interpretation of archaeological data. Generally, these interviews occur with individuals who have some kind of direct connection to the site or that can provide memories, interpretations, and discussion points through the presentation of artifacts from the site. One of the benefits of this approach is that it invites the broader community to participate in scholarly research (Toulson 2014, 4, 9). Our research has absolutely enhanced from our having conducted interviews with local and regional residents in the Yucatán peninsula about aspects of the site of the Xuxub, including their knowledge of artifacts and features, site abandonment and state of preservation, and the use of small-scale railroads in the region (Mathews, Gust, and Fedick 2023). However, these informants lacked specific and more specialized knowledge of distillation or the rum production industry. Thus, for this chapter, we have turned to experts with no connection to our archaeological sites of study per se but rather with deep knowledge of eighteenth- and nineteenth-century distilling processes. Through interviews with contemporary distillers and archaeologists who are studying historic distilleries, we have gained insight into interpretations of buildings with questionable identifications, the ingredients that would have been used, and the operation chain that includes the process of traditional harvesting and distillation, as well as the art and skill of the distillation process in which Indigenous workers would have engaged. While we recognize that there are limitations to how much we can infer from these sources, we are severely hampered by the limited number of associated archival sources and artifacts with our sites. Further, we have found this interview process incredibly helpful for our own understanding, as we have not participated in the distillation process ourselves. Last, we have greatly enjoyed the enthusiasm that these experts have for the subject matter and have benefited from their willingness to put us in touch with other experts. We anticipate that we will continue to expand our insights into this elusive but rich history with their help.

NOTES

1. The authors would like to thank Fernando and Ben for including them in this volume; their informants in Yucatán and the US for their time, insight, and enthusiasm; Jeffrey Glover, Dominique Rissolo, and Scott Fedick for their assistance in this research; and Marco Martinez and Lauren Swartz for their continuing love and support. Research funding came from Trinity University and the University of California, Riverside.

2. In context this is more of an access path or walking trail than a true road.

3. All interviews in the US were conducted with permission of the Institutional Review Board (IRB) at Trinity University. In all cases, interviewees confirmed their consent to be interviewed; and asked to be identified by their real names and titles, and to identify the distilleries. All interviews in Mexico were conducted with permission of the IRB at Trinity University. In all cases, interviewees confirmed their consent to be interviewed, and we kept all names anonymous, as is practice in anthropology with vulnerable informants.

4. Although we don't know how deep this barrel may have been originally, knowing that it was 1.5 meters in diameter and estimating that it was at least 1 meter deep, we can calculate that it could have a capacity of at least 1,750 gallons or 6,675 liters (total capacity estimated using inchcalculator.com).

REFERENCES CITED

Alexander, Rani T. 1997. "Haciendas and Economic Change in Yucatan: Entrepreneurial Strategies in the Parroquia de Yaxcaba, 1775–1850." *Journal of Archaeological Method and Theory* 4 (3/4): 331–51.

Alexander, Rani T. 2003. "Architecture, Haciendas, and Economic Change in Yaxcabá, Yucatán, Mexico." *Ethnohistory* 50 (1/2): 191–220.

Alston, Lee J., Shannan Mattiace, and Tomas Nonnenmacher. 2009. "Coercion, Culture, and Contracts: Labor and Debt on Henequen Haciendas in Yucatán, Mexico, 1870–1915." *Journal of Economic History* 69 (1): 104–37.

Andrews, Anthony, Rafael Burgos Villanueva, and Luis Millet Cámara. 2006. "The Historic Port of El Real de Salinas in Campeche, and the Role of Coastal Resources in the Emergence of Capitalism in Yucatán, México." *International Journal of Historical Archaeology* 10 (2): 179–205.

Barceló Quintal, Raquel. 1981. "La tierra y sus dueños: San Juan Bautista Tabi." In *Yucatán: Peonaje y liberación*, edited by Blanca González, José Luis Sierra Villarreal, Luis Aboites Aguilarm, and José Luis Domínguez. Mérida: Fonapas-Yucatán, Comisión Editorial del Estado, INAH.

Benavides Castillo, Antonio. 1985. "Notas sobre la arqueología histórica de la Hacienda Tabi, Yucatán." *Revista Mexicana de Estudios Antropológicos* 21:45–58.

"Buffalo Trace Restarts Col. E. H. Taylor Jr's 1883 Fermentation Tank for the First Time in a Century." 2019. *Distillery Trail: Tales from the Trail Blog*, January 23. https://www.distillerytrail.com/blog/buffalo-trace-restarts-col-e-h-taylor-jrs-1883-fermentation-tank-for-the-1st-time-in-a-century/.

Cap, Bernadette. 2015. "Classic Maya Economies: Identification of a Marketplace at Buenavista del Cayo, Belize." PhD diss., University of Wisconsin, Madison.

Carstensen, Birgit. 1993. *Betty's Hope: An Antiguan Sugar Plantation*. St. Johns: Antiguan Printing and Publishing Ltd.

Cline, Howard F. 1947. "The 'Aurora Yucateca' and the Spirit of Enterprise in Yucatan, 1821–1847." *Hispanic American Historical Review* 27 (1): 30–60.

Davis, Catherine. 2016. "The Panoptic Plantation Model: Geographical Analysis and Landscape at Betty's Hope, Plantation, Antigua, West Indies." MA thesis, California State University, Chico, Department of Anthropology. https://scholarworks.calstate.edu/downloads/6t053g69w.

De Portas, Rafael. 1872. *Tratado sobre el cultivo de la caña y elaboración de azúcar*. Mérida: Imprenta del Gobierno.

"El hacendado mexicano y fabricante de azúcar." 1906. Advertisement. *El hacendado mexicano y fabricante de azúcar* (vol. 12). Document incomplete. HathiTrust Digital Library. https://babel.hathitrust.org/cgi/pt?id=nyp.33433008869194&view=1up&seq=1.

"El hacendado mexicano y fabricante de azúcar." 1907. Advertisement. *El hacendado mexicano y fabricante de azúcar* (vol. 13). Document incomplete. HathiTrust Digital Library. https://babel.hathitrust.org/cgi/pt?id=nyp.33433008869228&view=1up&seq=1.

"El hacendado mexicano y fabricante de azúcar." 1908. Advertisement. *El hacendado mexicano y fabricante de azúcar* (vol. 14). Document incomplete. HathiTrust Digital Library. https://babel.hathitrust.org/cgi/pt?id=nyp.33433008869194&view=1up&seq=1.

Gasper, David Barry. 1985. *Bondmen and Rebels: A Study of Master-Slave Relations in Antigua*. Durham, NC: Duke University Press.

Gust, John R. 2016. "Bittersweet: Porfirian Sugar and Rum Production in Northeastern Yucatán." PhD diss., University of California, Riverside.

Gust, John R., and Jennifer P. Mathews. 2020. *Bittersweet History: Sugarcane, Rum, Labor and Life on the Yucatán Peninsula*. Tucson: University of Arizona Press.

Mathews, Jennifer P., and John Gust. 2017. "Cosmopolitan Living? Examining the Sugar and Rum Industry of the Costa Escondida, Quintana Roo Mexico." In *The Value of Things: Prehistoric to Contemporary Maya Commodities*, edited by Jennifer P. Mathews and Thomas Guderjan, 144–62. Tucson: University of Arizona Press.

Mathews, Jennifer P., John Gust, and Scott L. Fedick. 2023. "Preserving the Nineteenth Century in the Throes of Twenty-First-Century Development: Twenty Years of Historical Archaeology in the Yalahau and Costa Escondida Regions of Quintana Roo, Mexico." In *Beyond Conquest: New Perspectives on the Historical Archaeology of the Maya World*, edited by Kasey Diserens Morgan and Tiffany C. Fryer. Boulder: University Press of Colorado.

Micallef, Joseph V. 2020. "The American Distilling Institute Announces The 2020 Craft Spirits Awards" *Forbes*, April 8. https://www.forbes.com/sites/joemicallef/2020/04 /08/the-american-distilling-institute-announces-the-2020-craft-spirits-awards/?sh= 6f5e50c766a4.

Meyers, Allan, D. 2012. *Outside the Hacienda Walls: The Archaeology of Plantation Peonage in Nineteenth-Century Yucatan*. Tucson: University of Arizona Press.

Meyers, Allan D., and David L. Carlson. 2002. "Peonage, Power Relations, and the Built Environment at Hacienda Tabi, Yucatan, Mexico." *International Journal of Historical Archaeology* 6 (2002): 225–52.

Millet Cámara, Luis. 1984. "De las estancias y haciendas en el Yucatán Colonial." In *Hacienda y cambio social en Yucatán: Colección raíces*. Mérida: Instituto Nacional de Antropología e Historia.

Newman, Elizabeth Terese. 2014. *Biography of a Hacienda: Work and Revolution in Rural Mexico*. Tucson: University of Arizona Press.

Orosa Díaz, Jaime. 1994. *Historia de Yucatán*. Mérida: Ediciones de la Universidad Autónoma de Yucatán.

Patton, Janet. 2016. "Buffalo Trace Unearths 'Bourbon Pompeii' of 1873 Distillery on Kentucky River." *Lexington Herald Leader*, October 14. Accessed January 6, 2021. https://www.kentucky.com/news/state/article108222782.html.

Peniche Rivero, Piedad. 1994. "Women, Bridewealth and Marriage: Peonage and Social Reproduction in the Henequen Hacienda of Yucatan." In *Women of the Mexican Countryside, 1860–1990*, edited by Heather Fowler-Salimini and Mary Kay Vaughan, 74–98. Tucson: University of Arizona Press.

Reed, Nelson. 2001. *The Caste War of Yucatan*. Palo Alto, CA: Stanford University Press.

Richter, Marice. 2018. "The New Brew: Craft Distillers Want to Pour it on in Texas." *Fort Worth Business Press* 30, no. 29 (August 20): 12–25.

Rogoziński, Jan. 1999. *A Brief History of the Caribbean: From the Arawak and the Carib to the Present*. New York, NY: Facts on File, Inc.

Rugeley, Terry. 1996. *Yucatán's Maya Peasantry and the Origins of the Caste War*. Austin: University of Texas Press.

Rugeley, Terry. 2001. *Maya Wars: Ethnographic Accounts from Nineteenth-Century Yucatán*. Norman: University of Oklahoma Press.

Solomon, S. "Post-harvest Deterioration of Sugarcane." *Sugar Tech* 11 (2): 109–23.

Sullivan, Paul R. 1998. *Para que lucharon los mayas rebeldes, y vida y muerte de Bernardino Cen*. Chetumal: Universidad de Quintana Roo.

Sullivan, Paul R. 2004. *Xuxub Must Die: The Lost Histories of a Murder on the Yucatan*. Pittsburgh: University of Pittsburgh Press.

Toulson, Louise. 2014. "Toward a Methodology for the Use of Oral Sources in Historical Archaeology." Historical Archaeology 48 (1): 3–10.

Turner, John Kenneth. 1910. *Barbarous Mexico*. Chicago: Charles H. Kerr and Company Co-Operative.

Wells, Allen. 1985. *Yucatán's Gilded Age: Haciendas, Henequen, and International Harvester, 1860–1915*. Albuquerque: University of New Mexico Press.

Williams, Ian. 2005. *Rum: A Social and Sociable History of the Real Spirit of 1776*. New York: Nation Books.

7

Indígenas and International Influences of Modern Medicine in Twentieth-Century Guatemala

DAVID CAREY JR. AND LYDIA CRAFTS

The transnational movement of ideas, people, medicines, and machines has been crucial to the development of scientific medicine (Tilley 2004; Cueto 2007b; Packard 2007; Carter 2012).[1] With its medical and public health engagement with Colombia, Venezuela, Mexico, El Salvador, and the United States, Guatemalan health care during the first half of the twentieth century bears this out. At the turn of the twentieth century, Guatemalan officials looked abroad for effective vaccines and models of health and hygiene. By midcentury—when the Pan American Sanitary Bureau (PASB) infected marginalized Guatemalans (including many Indigenous people) with syphilis, gonorrhea, and chancroid—US and Guatemalan authorities and medical professionals had well-established networks that enabled medical experimentation in Guatemala (A. Adams and Giraudo 2020, 176–78, 191).

From 1946 to 1948, PASB targeted the most vulnerable Guatemalans—prisoners, mental hospital inmates, military recruits, *indígenas* (Indigenous people), sex workers, and orphans—as research subjects in sexually transmitted infection (STI) experiments. Intent on experimenting on "pure Indians" so he could practice "pure" science, the lead doctor, John C. Cutler, elevated the role of race in the trials. Like Cutler, many of the doctors who were on contract with PASB were from United States Public Health Service (USPHS), which had considerable influence on PASB. Trained on a USPHS fellowship, Guatemalan Dr. Juan Funes collaborated with Cutler. Instead of obtaining informed consent, they offered research subjects "cigarettes or some soap" (A. Adams and Giraudo 2020, 190; Funes 1950). Those blatant

https://doi.org/10.5876/9781646424276.c007

violations of human rights were all the more shocking since they were perpetrated during the Guatemala Revolution (1944–1954), a democratizing moment that spurred widespread labor organizing, agrarian reform, and the extension of social services to the poor (Gibbings and Vrana 2020; Gleijeses 1991; Handy 1994; Harms 2011; Forster 2001).

Such experimentation challenges the notion of Guatemala as a backward space of disease that could serve as a natural laboratory for the United States. Instead, US institutions such as the Rockefeller Foundation (RF), USPHS, and US military established colonialist medical networks in the Americas that propagated disease in Central America. Even as medical doctors and scientists celebrated their "tropical triumphalism," the US presence in the Panama Canal Zone contributed to the spread of malaria (Stern 2005; Sutter 2007). Shortly after the RF director in Guatemala, Alvin Struse, declared the nation free of yellow fever in 1918, influenza struck, likely originating from US military camps in Guatemala that RF sought to shield from yellow fever (Palmer 2010, 189–92). More than twenty years later, *indigenista* writer and doctor Epaminondas Quintana traced the spread of venereal diseases in Guatemala (prior to the PASB STI experiments) to the US military (A. Adams and Giraudo 2020, 187). While authorities represented themselves as clean and modern saviors of supposedly dirty and depraved *indios* (Indians), foreign and national medical professionals often were the vectors of disease in Guatemala.

Disparaging discourse about Indigenous health notwithstanding, most Latin American rural poor (especially Indigenous) people lacked adequate health and sanitary services. Guatemala was no exception with its national oligarchy that exploited Indigenous labor and exacerbated significant economic and health disparities between *indígenas* and other Guatemalans.

In a manifestation of visceral racism, Guatemalan medical professionals tended to portray *indígenas* as culprits in their ill health. Informed by Guatemalan elites' prejudices and their own biases, foreign health-care interlopers similarly disparaged indígenas. Referencing geophagy whereby (particularly rural poor) people eat dirt in response to iron deficiency, one of the first RF representatives in Guatemala dubbed indígenas "dirt eaters" at a time when RF officers often associated filth with disease (Stern 1999, 64, 67). Those shared beliefs facilitated the conditions whereby most US and Guatemalan medical professionals approached marginalized Guatemalans as test subjects first and patients second (if at all).

Transnational humanitarian approaches to public health often discounted Indigenous health-care epistemologies, practices, and knowledge. Reflecting Latin America's long Cold War, US philanthropic institutions such as RF, USPHS, and PASB viewed scientific medicine as "soft power" that could strengthen US cultural influence and capitalist expansion (Birn 2006, 3; Cueto and Palmer 2015, 109–10;

Birn and Necochea López 2020). Guatemalan authorities likewise saw scientific medicine as a means for civilizing indígenas and nation-building. When authorities redefined *curanderismo* from healing to charlatanism and *brujería* from social healing to witchcraft and then criminalized their practitioners for putting patients at risk by not adhering to scientific medicine, they persecuted Indigenous and other traditional healers. By marginalizing the broad range of services provided by empirical health-care providers, authorities effectively reduced health-care options for large swaths of the population, particularly rural indígenas. Such marginalization informed RF, USPHS, and other US officials' and public health experts' perceptions that Guatemala was comprised largely of "ignorant indios." Those perceptions beg the question of whether US researchers conducted medical experiments in Guatemala because of the population or the place (or some combination thereof). In addition to indígenas, foreign and national researchers experimented on other marginalized groups: women, Afro-Guatemalans, and poor Ladinos (non-Indigenous Guatemalans). Still, US researchers often referred to Guatemalans as *indígenas* in their medical notes. Both Guatemala's location in "America's backyard" and population served as draws for US researchers intent on finding human subjects.

Revealing the ambiguity that marked many transnational influences, as much as elites and officials deployed and distorted medical science to support national goals, Indigenous approaches to health care shaped learned medicine. In a publication that attracted European attention, Guatemalan Dr. José Flores (1751–1824) studied Indigenous remedies for cancer (Few 2010, 519–37; Cueto and Palmer 2015, 48–49). Impressed by the experience and knowledge of Indigenous midwives, some Ladino doctors praised and consulted them on natal care procedures and practices (Carey 2018, 137–56). By educating doctors and nurses, Indigenous healers mitigated the power of scientific medicine and elevated the legitimacy of traditional healing. If *La Gaceta*: *Revista de Policía y Variedades* (*Police Gazette*) was any indication, most medical professionals and Ladinos had some knowledge of Indigenous and other traditional medicines. Targeting the literate upper to lower middle class, *La Gaceta* regularly reported on arrests of *curanderos* (popular healers), *brujos* (social healers, spiritual guides, witches), and other traditional practitioners who operated beyond the bounds of scientific medicine (Gibbings 2020a, 288–89).[2]

After World War I, scientific medicine and Indigenous healing practitioners collaborated and clashed as international entities such as the League of Nations Health Organization (LNHO), RF, and the Pan American Sanitary Bureau (founded as the International Sanitary Bureau in 1902 before becoming the PASB in 1923 and the Pan American Health Organization in 1949) advanced medical science internationally and adapted it to local conditions. Based out of Washington, DC, the

PASB ensured that Latin American nations were aware of international interventions throughout the region including RF's collaboration with the Costa Rican government to eradicate *anquilostomiasis* (hookworm) since 1915.[3] Formed to promote peace in the aftermath of World War I, the League of Nations created its Health Organization to track and investigate the Spanish Influenza pandemic (1918–20), a typhus outbreak in Eastern Europe, and other international epidemics. In the early 1920s, the LNHO sought to improve public health systems in members states that requested such assistance—a charge that often put the LNHO, its member states, and its collaborators such as the PASB on a collision course with traditional medicine.

Partly because some Latin Americans associated RF (LNHO's primary funder) with US imperialism, Brazil and other countries that generally supported LNHO's coordination and dissemination of epidemiological information were suspicious of LNHO's imperialist underpinnings (Tworek 2019, 816, 820, 829, 830–32). Latin Americans also distrusted US calls for Pan-American health, even as they regularly attended PASB conferences. Operating on a shoestring budget, PASB passed the 1924 American Sanitary Code to facilitate member states' ability to organize public health agencies and programs aimed at stemming infectious disease (Palmer 1998; Cueto 1994; Cueto 2007a; Cueto and Palmer 2015; Palmer 2010). The unwritten assumption in that document privileged scientific over Indigenous approaches to diseases. Such coordinated international promotion of scientific medicine in the first part of the twentieth century had profound effects in nations with large Indigenous populations. Training a lens on Guatemala magnifies medical professionals and officials' diverse responses to promoting scientific medicine in the face of innovative Indigenous healing practices.

To understand the historical processes at the intersections of indígenas, medicine, and international interlopers in Guatemala, we conducted research at Guatemalan and US archives. Replete with silences, archives are particularly muted around the intersections of Indigeneity, modernization, and medicine in nations committed to advancing scientific medicine in ways that disparaged Indigenous healing. Evidence of complex and contradictory approaches to scientific medicine abound in Guatemalan, RF, and USPHS archives that were organized, in part, to capture the unitary power of modern medicine. Archival materials generated by the very authorities intent on contrasting clean, modern, scientific medicine against filthy, retrograde, superstitious Indigenous practices ironically argue against those categories by revealing the complexity, dynamism, and heterogeneity of health care and healing in twentieth-century Guatemala. This chapter explores how such archives and conducting research in nations such as Guatemala, where history is hotly contested, inform what scholars can learn about the past.

INTERNATIONAL IMAGINARIES

Three days after her cows escaped their pasture in Ciudad Vieja in 1850, Bernarda Ramírez found them tied to a public post in the town square, where they "were considerably worse off." Irate that the mayor who confiscated them had not informed her of their whereabouts and "fearful of the consequences" of vigilantism, Ramírez petitioned the president of Guatemala.[4] In what the illiterate cattle owner considered an extreme abuse of the law "that even in Turkey could not be carried out against citizens much less a hard working family," the governor refused to release the animals to her.[5] In another indication that Guatemalans did not necessarily hold glowing opinions of foreign countries or their citizens, Ramírez's contemporary, the mayor of the village of Dueñas, responded to an absentee landowner's negligence by questioning whether "the town should accept seditious foreigners."[6] A few decades earlier, Dr. Narciso Esparragosa had referenced Egypt to conjure images of Blackness (and women with large clitorises) (Few 2007, 170). To underscore their and their nation's problems, these Guatemalans invoked ideas of distant foreign countries (and people) with which Guatemala had little contact.

Those anecdotes shed light on nineteenth-century popular perceptions of foreign nations. Although many Guatemalan residents were aware of happenings that directly affected their nation, such as border negotiations with Honduras in 1933, by the twentieth century few paid much heed to countries that rarely engaged with Guatemala.[7] Such seemingly random references contrast sharply with the more systematic international relations scientists, doctors, agronomists, and other professionals in Guatemala developed with colleagues, companies, patients, authorities, and institutions in the Americas and Western Europe.[8] Professionals throughout Latin America sought to engage broader intellectual, scientific, and medical communities. In some cases, governments funded scholarships for study abroad. Latin American physicians and public health professionals attended international conferences not just to learn but also to disseminate their own countries' research and innovative procedures, techniques, and treatments (Palmer 2003, 81, 84, 90).

According to many journalists and authorities, ignoring international expertise and knowledge was detrimental. The official daily of the government, the *Diario de Centro América*, criticized farmers for overlooking brochures and other publications from foreign countries that the Ministry of Agriculture distributed. Such willful ignorance helped explain why, according to one writer, "our harvests [are] poor in comparison to those obtained in North America."[9]

The influence of European and US progenitors notwithstanding, transnational humanitarianism often reflected the national race, gender, and class relations where it was implemented. US imperialism and neocolonialism were seldom unitary hegemonic forces but rather shaped by national dynamics and thus played out distinctly in different Latin American countries (Carey 2023). Through transnational human-itarianism, US and Guatemalan doctors exchanged and created racialized knowl-edge about indígenas. In the 1946–48 STI experiments, US and Guatemalan doctors strengthened their relations through medical voyeurism and efforts to manipulate people they aimed to render medical subjects. Interpreted through the lens of their ideas about science and distinct approaches to public health, Guatemalan medical professionals' approaches to health care offer a window into the ways Latin Americans applied transnational expertise. Suggesting transnational humanitarian efforts often did little to address the underlying structural conditions such as pov-erty, racism, and sexism that undermined many Guatemalans' well-being, improved public health in some areas contrasted starkly with anemic responses in others that exacerbated the vulnerability of disenfranchised populations.

Although there is some truth to historical portrayals of Guatemala as a nation that sought to emulate and engage Europe and the United States, international influences were complicated, multidirectional, and fraught with pitfalls such as reliance on US resources and expertise. Guatemalan medical professionals followed their Latin American counterparts in resisting US eugenicists who derided immigrants from the region as racially inferior (Stepan 1991, 173, 177). Yet a shared perception of white-ness also strengthened solidarities between US and Guatemalan doctors. One RF worker lauded Guatemalan elites "as the cream of Central America. The unfortunate mixture of negro blood so common in Spanish countries is almost nil," he wrote to his RF superiors.[10] Those perceptions facilitated the bonding of US and Guatemalan doctors across borders. To cultivate collaboration, Guatemalan dictator Manuel José Estrada Cabrera (1898–1920) appointed Struse president of the Guatemalan Consejo de Salubridad (Public Health Council) in 1918. That the dictator selected a foreigner to serve as Guatemala's highest public health official demonstrates how closely connected RF representatives were with Guatemalan political elites. When Struse died of influenza later that year, the next RF director in Guatemala delicately avoided the same offer as RF prohibited that practice and encouraged national gov-ernments to assume responsibility for RF-sponsored projects (and their own proto ministries of health) (McCreery 1994, 233; Stepan 2011a, 500–501).[11]

Generally dismissive of and often derogatory toward indígenas and Afro-Guatemalans (Garifunas), Guatemalan elites and intellectuals frequently looked to Europe for ideas and inspiration. An August 19, 1933, *Diario de Centro América* editorial lamented that Africans and "*nuestros indios Americanos*" did little with "all the opulence of their continents . . . In contrast, we see the Italian nation lift itself up on pulverized rock and scientific abundance, [and produce] the most porten-tous harvests of every kind of agricultural product. There is the courage of man succeeding against natural obstacles."[12] Juxtaposing intelligent, scientific Europeans

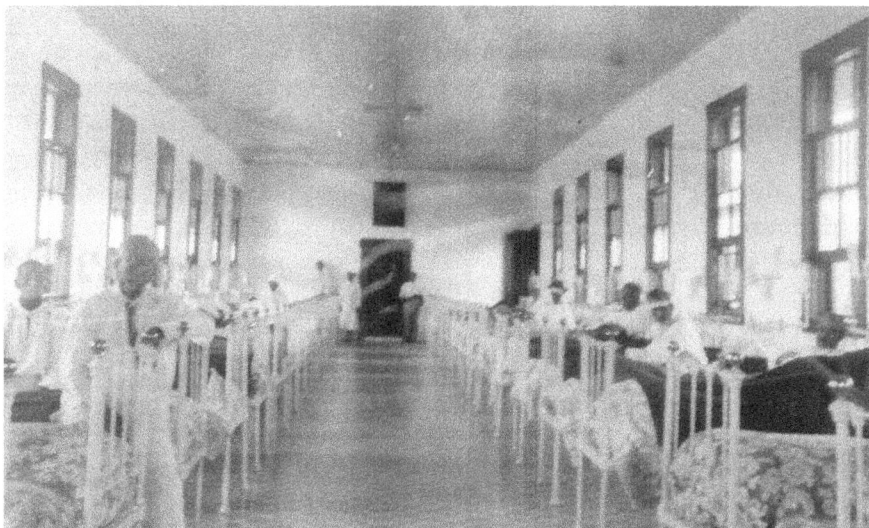

Figure 7.1. "Rockefeller photo of colored bedspreads and brass knobs 'reflecting Indian in-fluence' in a new public ward, 1922" (Source: RAC, RG 1.1 Projects, series 319, box 1, folder 1.)

with decadent, "ignorant indios" and Africans was a common trope in nineteenth- and twentieth-century Guatemala. Guatemalan elites insisted those *razas* hindered modernization.

Yet on occasion, medical professionals and RF agents made accommodations intended to attract indígenas to scientific medicine. Similar to how the Mexican National Indigenist Institute built hospital rooms with niches to burn copal to reassure Maya patients and their families, Guatemalan and RF officials recognized the potential of ethnic overtures (Lewis 2018). Revealing a Guatemalan hospital's attempt to incorporate Indigenous culture, the caption of a 1922 photograph (figure 7.1) reads, "Interior of one of new public wards. Note colored bedspreads and brass knobs on beds—reflecting Indian influence."[13] The black-and-white photograph muted such influence, but the sentiment to incorporate Indigeneity into hospital furnishings if not medical care was clear. Some hospital authorities and RF representatives tried to make medical institutions more welcoming to indígenas. The effect of such concessions is difficult to discern, but over time Guatemalan indígenas increasingly availed themselves of hospital care.

The attention to material culture and its ability to convey meaning suggests some RF and Guatemalan officials understood how clothing and other public markers denoted Indigenous identities and cultures. Yet the assertion that colorful blankets and brass knobs reflected "Indian influence" betrays a superficial understanding of

Indigenous cultures where symbols and colors represented larger narratives about the past, not just efforts to enliven outfits or spaces. In San Juan Comalapa, the red stripes along the shoulders of Kaqchikel Maya women's huipiles represented the violence (either blood or fire depending on the weaver and wearer) of the Spanish invasion. As such, red on a blanket in a Hispanic institution may have been less than inviting for some Indigenous women. Although designers may have been thinking of the staffs Indigenous leaders carried to denote their authority, the brass knobs are even more difficult to relate to Indigenous culture. Viewed from these perspectives, the black-and-white photograph's attempt to capture colorful blankets is an apt analogy for RF's inability to see the complexity and completeness of Indigenous culture in Guatemala (Carey 2023).

TRANSNATIONAL SCIENTIFIC MEDICINE

By the turn of the twentieth century, most Latin American nations had developed robust and complex medical sciences. As Ecuador's Eugenio Espejo (1747–95) had done before them, Latin American doctors and researchers like Carlos Finlay (1838–1915) in Cuba, Oswaldo Cruz (1872–1917) in Brazil, and Rodolfo Robles (1878–1915) in Guatemala offered proof that Latin Americans' contributions were crucial to the global development of medical sciences and public health practices (Espinosa 2009; Cueto and Palmer 2015; A. Adams and Giraudo 2020). During the colonial period and early twentieth century, the University of San Carlos in Guatemala City prepared many Central American (especially Honduran and Costa Rican) doctors, some of whom enjoyed illustrious careers (Carey ca. 2019). Trained in Guatemala, Dr. Ernesto Argueta produced the Honduran Health Code in 1910 (Martínez García 2017, 15). Resisting US and European claims to scientific authority, Latin American doctors combatted disparaging views of the region. Dr. Luis Galich of Guatemala believed that doctors held intimate knowledge of their country's population, which granted them authority to maintain the "complete organism" of society (Galich 1949, 28). Yet, when doctors tested new technologies to understand their applicability to Guatemala, they thought more about economic concerns than the needs of indígenas, Garifunas, and other marginalized Guatemalans. Galich's perception of what constituted a healthy entity reflected the patriarchy and racism prevalent in Guatemalan society. In their quest to build modern nation-states, doctors also drew upon international medicine that reinforced entrenched hierarchies in their countries (Stepan 1991, 17; Eraso 2007, 793–822; Stern 2011, 431–43; Otovo 2016, 170; Córdova 2017; Lambe 2017, 11; Roth 2020, 51–52).

Many medical professionals remained intent on maintaining Guatemala's strong medical tradition (Few 2015, 8). Yet the dictatorships of Estrada Cabrera and Jorge

Ubico Castañeda (1931–44) stripped autonomy from the University of San Carlos. The university was severely underfunded; doctors taught at the school on a voluntary basis.[14] An earthquake followed by a series of tremors between December 1917 and January 1918 destroyed the medical school building. In 1921, arsonists burned the school archives (Abad 1996). Facing these setbacks, the medical school still aimed to prepare students according to standard practices in the United States, Europe, and Latin America. Students conducted "daily dissection of cadavers" in anatomy classes (Abad 1996). They also developed an active medical discourse on topics including hygiene, legal medicine, and medical ethics. Still, the repressive climate of the Ubico dictatorship led more Guatemalan doctors and intellectuals to study and move abroad.

As the century wore on, Central American medical students increasingly studied in the United States (Martínez García 2017). Some students developed south-south solidarities by pursuing educational opportunities in Cuba and Mexico (Martínez García 2017; Birn 2020, 5). The presence of RF and the United Fruit Company (UFCO) hospital facilitated students' development of local ties with those organizations. Guatemalan students participated in medical research on indígenas and Afro-Guatemalans who labored on coffee and banana plantations. Those organizations also facilitated Guatemalans' study at prestigious US universities. The rapport that Dr. Luis Gaitán had built with RF and UFCO during a 1918 campaign to contain yellow fever placed him in good stead to receive a RF fellowship to study at Johns Hopkins University's School of Public Health and Hygiene.[15] He later became the minister of health in Guatemala. Gaitán's ties with US researchers and institutions heightened his professional prestige.

Through study at US institutions, Guatemalan students were exposed to a medical culture that increasingly focused on animal and human-subject research. Established in 1916 with a grant from the Rockefeller Foundation, Johns Hopkins School of Public Health and Hygiene had the first and one of the most preeminent public health academic programs in the United States. In his survey on medical education, Abraham Flexner, known for his reform of medical education in the United States to focus on laboratory instruction and clinical experience, held Johns Hopkins medical school to be the ideal (Lederer 1995, 55). Folklorist Gladys-Marie Fry traced the African American oral tradition about "night doctors," who allegedly kidnapped African Americans for experimentation and dissection, to the period between the 1880s and World War I, when more Black people were migrating north to cities such as Baltimore (7).

Between the 1920s and 1940s, Johns Hopkins University grew into an epicenter of research on venereal disease. Guatemalan medical professionals received fellowships to study syphilis at Johns Hopkins University.[16] The Rockefeller Institute also devoted considerable resources to the study of syphilis and funded programs at Johns Hopkins University (Lederer 1995, 82). Because venereal diseases posed a serious problem to the US Army, which lost almost 7 million days of active duty to these diseases, the US government began focusing on venereal disease control during World War I (Brandt 1987, 115). Even though the US government significantly curtailed funding for venereal disease in the 1920s, groups such as USPHS, RF, and Johns Hopkins University continued to view these infectious diseases as a priority.

As postcolonial scholars have demonstrated, power relations between people in developed (Western Europe and the United States) and developing (Latin America) nations often yielded shifting fields of knowledge, practice, and interactions where contestation and collaboration were as likely as hegemony and subordination. Such complex exchanges were particularly evident in the local-global health nexus (Stoler 2002; Birn and Necochea López 2011). Just as traditional and Indigenous healers at times inverted scientific medical power by educating doctors and nurses, so too did Latin American doctors and public health officials upend neocolonial relations by contributing to international scientific medical knowledge production and the practices of US and European physicians (Cueto 1989; Carey 2006, 31–60). Suspicious of its support for Estrada Cabrera, some Guatemala City doctors refused to work with RF (Palmer 2010, 86). Yet RF and other multilateral agencies were crucial to developing public health programs and national health ministries. As was true elsewhere in Latin America, reciprocity often marked relationships between foreign and national actors who forged public health institutions and programs (Cueto and Palmer 2015, 106–8). Collaborations among medical professionals across the Americas indicate that national borders did not bound medical knowledge production despite the very different resources and challenges in each nation (Gómez de Cruz 2008; Soto-Laveaga 2009; Birn and Necochea López 2011, 523).

The relative (authoritarian) stability enjoyed in late nineteenth-century Guatemala facilitated an effort to beautify the capital. In addition to Parque la Reforma (modeled after New York City's Central Park) and a sewer system that drained the capital, Guatemala City boasted streetcars, electric lights, photoshops, bicycles, and cinemas by the turn of the century. Workers repaired aqueducts and relocated the cemetery with an eye toward improving public health. A modernized police force and newly outfitted national army similarly contributed to that goal (Kirkpatrick 2017, 231–52; Kirkpatrick 2020).

To complement those modernizing efforts, Guatemalan officials looked abroad for models of good health and hygiene. In a report to the Guatemala City mayor in 1899, a group of doctors referenced the work of the "prominent Finnish medical hygienist Dr. Alberto Palmberg" to underscore "that the health of the *pueblos* is the supreme law" and to demonstrate that people "should not fear filtering" because "the modern process of purifying water is proven" by "scientific data."[17] As the government planned to construct potable water infrastructure in the capital nine years earlier, they turned to the international market for "iron pipes [*hierro tubos*] and other materials" (*Despacho de Gobernación y Justicia* 1890, 6). When engaging the international community of medical professionals and companies throughout the first half of the twentieth century, Guatemalan authorities and medical personnel often approached their situations from positions of strength. Some stressed their contributions, talents, intelligence, and research as they sought to collaborate in medical communities beyond their borders.

Invitations to Guatemalan medical professionals came from the United States, Colombia, El Salvador, and Cuba. In 1922, Guatemalan medical and public health practitioners were invited to an international exposition on hygiene in Cuba.[18] In February 1924, the director of the American College of Surgeons visited Guatemala to invite physicians to become fellows in the college. He hoped, "to promote a closer affiliation between the professions of the Americas."[19] In addition to asking for a list of their top surgeons, he solicited their ideas about bringing fellows throughout the region closer together. In contrast to broader trends in Latin American relations with the US government and the American Public Health Association (Carrillo and Birn 2008, 225–54; Ross 2009, 573–602), such overtures were aimed at promoting cultural diplomacy through medical expertise as well as spreading US (scientific) medicine in Latin America (Vieira de Campos 2006; Reggiani 2007; Hochman 2008, 161–91).[20] While medical professionals in the Americas regularly sought to work together, collaborating with US doctors and scientists could be perilous (Espinosa 2009). The director enjoyed more resources and power than most Latin American surgeons. Nonetheless, his use of the term Americas to denote the region suggested his attempt to mitigate US centrism. Akin to José Marti's notion of "Nuestra América," regional professional organizations in Latin America provide evidence that transnational exchanges of ideas, people, and materials were not contingent on the United States. Fruitful interactions regularly evolved absent its participation (Löwy 2001; Birn 2006b, 675–708).

Throughout the 1920s and the Ubico dictatorship, the scientific medical establishment continued to flourish in ways that built upon Estrada Cabrera's cozy relationship with RF (Palmer 2010; Carey 2021). Informed by public health experts, the Ubico administration coordinated antimalaria campaigns (*Memoria de los trabajos realizados* 1939, 122; Administración del Señor General Don Jorge Ubico 1942, 125). In San Jerónimo (Baja Verapaz Department), constructing canals to drain lowland water had reduced the malaria infection rate from 87.5 percent to 34.7 percent in one year. By 1941, the rate had dropped to 12.5 percent. In Santa Rosa, the reduction in malaria incidence was even more dramatic, from 100 percent of the population in

1929 to 28 percent 1938 thanks to "canalization" (Administración del Señor General Jorge Ubico 1942, 125). Convinced the key to those achievements was maintaining canals, Ubico made "a very special effort in favor of the health of the Indigenous race [*raza indígena*]," though it entailed coercing their labor to do so (9).

Although intermittent and irregular foreign assistance facilitated Guatemalan solutions to epidemics, Guatemalan public health officials and medical professionals enjoyed success independent of foreign interventions. By the time the Pan American Sanitary Bureau offered aid and cooperation, Guatemalans had already contained an April 1944 typhus outbreak.[21]

In an effort to highlight "the splendid case that Guatemala today presents to the eyes of the world,"[22] the Ministry of Agriculture's 1932 annual report insisted the government would balance budgets, punctually pay off loans, and build useful public works.[23] For doctors and public health officials, enhancing the nation's international reputation was contingent upon advancing scientific medicine, improving health care, and preempting epidemics. During the first half of the twentieth century, Guatemalan public health officials' strategies ranged from improving hygiene (particularly among the poor and Indigenous people) and compelling Indigenous midwives to undergo formal training, to deploying eugenics and instituting measures to reduce hookworm, syphilis, tuberculosis, and malaria. With interactions that ranged from desperate pleas for foreign expertise or resources to proud contributions to medical and scientific communities, transnational humanitarian efforts in Guatemala shed light on the nation's bifurcated sense of identity.

At times, indígenas and other marginalized Guatemalans rejected international overtures. Some Guatemalan sex workers refused to participate in PASB syphilis experiments. More than twenty years earlier in 1922, to his superiors' chagrin, the mayor of the tiny Ladino town of Alotenango in the heavily Indigenous department of Sacatepéquez denied a RF International Health Commission assistant a room, a lavatory, and moral support.[24] Generally medical directors would visit communities to gain local authorities' support and secure a site for a laboratory. Such resistance was not singular, however. In neighboring Nicaragua, residents regularly refused RF assistants admittance to their homes when they arrived to conduct hygiene inspections. That resistance was as much about the politics of municipalities refusing to succumb to an inept central state as a critique of "Yankee interference" (Peña Torres and Palmer 2008, 62).

FOREIGN ALLURE AND DRUGS

With its skeletal health care and public health infrastructure, Guatemala was dependent on foreign assistance to conduct public health campaigns. While the primary objective of most Guatemalan medical professionals was to staunch the spread of disease, USPHS and PASB officers had different priorities. Pan American Sanitary Bureau officer M. F. Haralson explained that typhus campaigns "may be considered more as investigative or research in nature than as definite public health programs" (Haralson 1948, 923). To his and his colleagues' minds, delousing and vaccinating highland indígenas offered critical data. The PASB shared their research findings and techniques with typhus committees in Colombia and Mexico (Crafts 2019; Padilla B 1948). Indiscriminately spraying highland indígenas with DDT without asking their consent suggests officials approached them as subjects rather than citizens. By the 1940s, when US agents were spraying indígenas in highland Guatemala and Mexican migrant workers in the US Southwest, scientists had begun to express concern about DDT's harmful effects (Cohen 2011, 98–100).

Eager to tap into medical expertise and public health products from abroad, Guatemalan officials regularly engaged with international intellectual and business communities. Both deployed science. With its German factories and cross— allegedly the largest electric sign in the world at the time—Bayer offers one such example (see figure 7.2).

> The great substance of that electric sign is small compared to the moral magnanimity of the **Bayer Cross** in the modern scientific skyline where its lights shine like a celestial body of the first magnitude. **She symbolizes the constant effort, scientific preparation and . . . integrity of an organization that has contributed to the relief and wellbeing of humanity everywhere, with products** [that are] **always pure, always effective, and always deserving of confidence**. For that reason, noble and loyal **Bayer Cross** is an infallible point of orientation for the scientist in his laboratory, doctor in his clinic, and family in their home.[25]

Grounding its claim of expertise and efficacy in science, Bayer promoted its brand as a worldwide elixir. Like other German pharmaceutical companies, Bayer enjoyed a strong presence in twentieth-century Latin America (Cueto and Palmer 2015, 89). Even though scientific medicine was intimately intertwined with disparaging Indigenous healing in Guatemala and other parts of Latin America, Indigenous healers incorporated and Indigenous patients consumed such medications when deemed effective. In turn, some Guatemalans were curious about alternative medicine in international locations.[26]

The Guatemalan government regularly engaged foreign companies and experts. Dating to late nineteenth-century South American sanitation cooperation efforts, the Americas developed robust programs to encourage sanitation policies and practices. A precursor to the Organization of American States, the International Conference of American States hosted international sanitation conferences

El anuncio eléctrico más grande del mundo

En esta fotografía, tomada de noche, puede apreciarse el anuncio eléctrico más grande del mundo, construido recientemente por la famosa Casa Bayer en una de sus fábricas de Alemania. Este anuncio tiene 2,200 bombillos eléctricos, mide 72 metros de diámetro y 220 metros de circunferencia. Puede verse hasta de una distancia de 10 kilómetros.

● La grandeza material de este signo eléctrico es pequeña comparada a la grandeza moral de la **Cruz Bayer** en el horizonte científico moderno, donde brilla con luz propia como astro de primera magnitud.

● Ella simboliza el constante esfuerzo, la preparación científica y la invariable honradez de una organización que ha contribuído al alivio y bienestar de la humanidad en todas partes del mundo, con productos siempre puros, siempre eficaces y siempre dignos de confianza.

● Es por eso que la noble y leal **Cruz Bayer** es un infalible punto de orientación para el hombre de ciencia en su laboratorio, para el médico en su clínica, para la familia en el hogar.

Si es Bayer es Bueno

Figure 7.2. Electric sign. (Source: *La Gaceta: Revista de Policía y Variedades,* November 10, 1934.)

beginning in 1902 (Birn 2002, 19, 25, 35). Guatemala embraced efforts to improve sanitation. In 1911, the government purchased Clayton system equipment to initiate large-scale disinfection campaigns with "a powerful element" (*Memoria de la Secretaria* n.d., 6). As machinery aged and broke down though, parts could be difficult to replace, rendering equipment useless (as was true of Westinghouse X-ray machines some thirty years later).[27] Even after RF opened its International Health Commission (IHC) offices in Guatemala in 1914, Guatemalan officials cast a wide net for public health advice and information. In December 1926, the government approved a contract with the J. G. White Engineering Corporation of New York to study of the capital's sanitation situation, including analysis of potable water; drainage and pavement; and underground telegraph, telephone, and electrical wires

(*Memoria de la Secretaria* ca. 1927, 6). By engaging in a marketplace of ideas rather than simply adopting RF approaches, Guatemalan officials enjoyed some autonomy and agency in developing public health programs and practices. Perceptions that foreign resources bolstered sanitation and hygiene campaigns continued into the 1930s, when the government imported hospital-grade paint from the United States to achieve "maximum hygienic conditions."[28]

Informed by perceptions of progress and modernization, officials requested foreign medicine that often failed to live up to its billing. When Dr. Xoza asked the municipal council of Guatemala City to order the French typhoid vaccine "that had such brilliant results in World War I," he added that it "naturally would give a note of culture" to the city; the drug's life-saving potential was apparently of secondary concern.[29] Such insistence on elevating culture could come at a high cost. If past experience was any indication, French vaccines' ability to protect Guatemalans from disease was dubious at best. On August 31, 1886, the Guatemala City municipal council imported "abundant vaccination fluid" from France.[30] Two years later, the vaccination inspector reported it had been ineffective.[31] Nonetheless, in 1889, the council asked for more vaccine from France.[32] Apparently news of the existence of the vaccine was spreading more quickly than reports of its ineffectiveness. One week later, February 22, the mayor of San Salvador asked the Guatemala City council to send him the vaccine.[33]

Increasingly convinced the French vaccine was ineffective, the Guatemala City municipal council concurrently earmarked money to import vaccines from San Francisco and London.[34] Within a month of the San Francisco vaccination arriving in Guatemala, however, the official vaccine caretaker reported it "did not work."[35] Undeterred, the council ordered more from San Francisco on August 2, 1889, because the vaccine "imported from France did not produce results" either.[36] Perhaps because the California vaccine was equally ineffective, the council earmarked 41.35 pesos for another shipment of French fluid on October 5, 1894.[37] Such faith in the superiority of foreign drugs, despite so much evidence to the contrary, flew in the face of their Colombian contemporaries, who were quick to point to the irrelevance of foreign medicines and expertise for national diseases (Obregón 2002, 105, 106). Without studying local conditions, distributing foreign medicine and imposing foreign strategies often were ineffective measures, and at times disastrous (Obregón 2002, 104). Beyond a simplistic explanation that Guatemalans lacked confidence in their ability to produce vaccines, the archives offer few clues as to why late nineteenth-century officials were wedded to foreign solutions whereas their late eighteenth- and nineteenth-century predecessors developed their own smallpox vaccine (Few 2010). As political turmoil undermined Guatemala's once flourishing medical school and community, the nation may have become more dependent on foreign medicine (Palmer 2003, 52).

As the twentieth century progressed, authorities were increasingly vigilant of domestic and foreign medications. "To guarantee health and defend the public against the deceitful traffickers," the Guatemalan secretary of state curtailed "the importation and sale of specific patents whose application is not necessarily medical" in 1926 (*Memoria de la secretaria* ca. 1927). When Guatemalan doctors received foreign drugs to prevent the spread of syphilis in the 1940s, they carried out their own studies to ensure that they would be useful for local populations.[38] Guatemalan public health officials also pointed to the limits of medical science. Dr. Epaminondas Quintana insisted that chemical analysis of breast milk was useless to infants without increasing nourishment.[39] Establishing medical potency or even applicability was challenging when faced with a health crisis that demanded immediate solutions.

Notwithstanding continued questions about the efficacy about foreign medicine, some Guatemalan public health experts were convinced they could "import heroic drugs."[40] Many medicines enjoyed favorable customs status. On October 5, 1922, the treasury minister allowed drugs from New York to enter the country free of taxes; a few weeks earlier a box of syrups and fluid extracts and "three bundles of Catgut" similarly avoided customs duties.[41] The following year, serums from the National Hygiene Department in Buenos Aires were admitted free of charge.[42] In sharp contrast in February 1922, requests to import Cyrasal, a new treatment for syphilis, duty free were denied.[43] By the end of the month, he had given up: "Being exorbitant the customs duties, we could not sell Cyrasal, because it is unknown in this republic."[44] Without a reputation of efficacy or political connections, Cyrasal faced such high taxes that its sale was prohibitive. Further evidence in the archives of such differential customs treatment suggests a drug's political potency was as important as its medical efficacy.

In addition to high prices, concerns about dangerous side effects inhibited the sale of certain drugs. When the American Medical Association (AMA) warned in 1937 that sulfanilamide (Para-aminobenzol-sulfonamide) should only be used "under prescription and medical vigilance," the general director of Guatemalan public health followed suit "in light of the accidents that occurred using" it.[45] Such adherence to AMA warnings hints at some Guatemalan officials' trust in the US public health systems that facilitated the USPHS's syphilis experiments in Guatemala less than a decade later. Although some Guatemalan medical professionals critiqued foreign medicine, many lacked the infrastructure for research and accessibility to foreign drugs that would have facilitated more independent decision-making. The regimes of Estrada Cabrera, Ubico, and Juan José Arévalo (1945–51) all depended to some degree on US and RF resources for public health projects (Adams and Giraudo 2020, 176, 186; Carey 2023). Guatemalan doctors eschewed local healing practices and presumed the superiority of foreign medical knowledge. Unfortunately, that trust trumped the other sentiment in the director's sulfanilamide warning: concern for citizens' well-being.

GERMAN AID AND INDIGENOUS INFLUENCES

Although the motives for their altruism were not always clear, foreigners and foreign nationals regularly contributed to health care in Guatemala. When the General Hospital in Guatemala City was in the process of reconstruction in the early 1930s, the German minister Wilhelm Von Ruhlmann donated thirty (US) dollars to the cause.[46] After the onset of World War II, Guillermo "Willi" Dieseldorff (son and heir of German-born coffee planter and merchant Erwin Paul Dieseldorff) pledged to invest his plantations' profits in local hospitals and other public works. Both small and grand, his philanthropy was partly a response to the geopolitical context and local political pressure. As a German national, Dieseldorff had to defend himself and prove his politics. In a February 5, 1942, letter to *jefe político* Brigadier General Fidel Torres, Dieseldorff insisted on his "true pro-democratic position . . . and his unchanging proposition of cooperation with . . . the great Interamerican movement of continental defense."[47]

To improve health care (and his standing) in Guatemala, Dieseldorff solicited (and enthusiastically fulfilled) requests for donations from hospitals, doctors, the Guatemalan Red Cross, and other beneficent societies.[48] He also envisioned expanding and modernizing the Hospital del Norte in Cobán, Alta Verapaz. Since government funding failed to cover the costs of health care institutions, Dieseldorff's generosity was especially impactful. In his June 8, 1942, request for Q$196 to pay for such medical implements as forceps, knives, and Davis mouth gags, the director of the Sociedad Protectora del Niño explained, "This society lives and maintains itself thanks to the altruism of generous persons."[49] A hospital administrator similarly underscored that Dieseldorff's donation would allow the maternity ward to "operate indefinitely under superb conditions."[50]

Living and operating their plantations and other enterprises in the heavily Indigenous department of Alta Verapaz, the Dieseldorffs and other Germans who settled in the area had regular interactions with Q'eqchi's. When Dieseldorff argued that progress would improve the lives of those who embraced it, he included indígenas in that assertion (Gibbings 2019). While most German coffee planters exploited (and often abused) Indigenous laborers, a few, such as the Dieseldorffs, espoused Q'eqchi' ethics of reciprocity and instructed foremen to facilitate the fluorescence of Indigenous religions (Gibbings 2020b). Intent on making Guatemala their new home even as their loyalties remained to their families overseas, many Germans started families with Q'eqchi' women. Early twentieth-century Guatemalan intellectuals such as Miguel Angel Asturias promoted such miscegenation between European immigrants and indígenas to improve the stock of the latter. He celebrated "robust and well-endowed" Q'eqchi'-German children (Gibbings 2016, 214–36; see also Asturias [1921] 1977, 101–3).

While he supported institutions of scientific medicine, Dieseldorff also conducted ethnographic studies of Indigenous medicine and treated plantation workers with cures from such *curanderos* as Félix Cucul. Some German planters exoticized Indigenous healing by associating it with "wizards . . . and fortune-tellers," which dovetailed nicely with police conflations of Indigenous curanderismo and brujería (Gibbings 2020a, 291). Whereas RF and Guatemalan officials generally disparaged Indigenous medicine, some Germans lauded and researched it. Some Ladinos too studied and documented Indigenous medicine (Gibbings 2020a, 288–89; see also Selis Lope 1931). That interest lent legitimacy to curanderos. It also piqued the government's attention. In 1939, the Ubico administration requested medicinal plant and seed samples from all municipalities to investigate the potential of cultivating them for export. Although the value some Germans placed on Indigenous medicinal plants must have buoyed Q'eqchi' healers, not all Q'eqchi' embraced the attention. Domingo Caal accused Dieseldorff of appropriating and commodifying Indigenous knowledge and customs (Gibbings 2020a, 292).

Although the government publicized and distributed public health guidelines "with the greatest profusion" since at least the early twentieth century,[51] not until the 1940s did authorities develop public health educational materials in Indigenous languages. In 1943, Dr. Quintana proposed creating antityphus education materials—namely, posters and records—in the four most widely spoken Indigenous languages: K'iche' Kaqchikel, Mam, and Q'eqchi'. Insisting those media were the "most appropriate means to achieve Indigenous comprehension . . . of contagion," he explained, "the efficacy of flyers is nonexistent because the majority are illiterate."[52] For some of Dr. Quintana's contemporaries, delivering public health information in Indigenous languages did not suffice. According to Quetzaltenango public health representative Rigoberto de León, "Much of the work is lost because of the indifference of the inhabitants where the Indigenous element prevails" (*Memoria de los trabajos realizados* 1945, 350). The absence of any evidence of outreach in Indigenous languages in the archival record prior to the 1940s suggests monolingual and illiterate indígenas had little access to public health initiatives. That ignorance made them more susceptible to epidemics and police persecution.

IMPERIALISM, EXPERIMENTATION, AND INDIGENEITY

At first glance, the experiments carried out by PASB when its doctors infected Guatemalan prisoners and mental hospital inmates with syphilis and gonorrhea from 1946 to 1948 suggest a starkly different story about international humanitarian health care than this chapter portrays. When initial experiments involving sex workers failed to yield statistically significant infection rates, Cutler employed the more direct, invasive, and painful methodology of abrading subjects' penises with a hypodermic needle and dripping drops of syphilitic emulsion onto the abraded area for one to two hours. Guatemalan doctors in the military and public health departments, including Dr. Funes, who ran the venereal disease hospital, assisted US doctors with their research, conducted their own experiments on sex workers, and selected their "patients" for study.[53] Instead of seeking the consent of each subject or their family members, researchers established cooperation with institutions. Overcrowded and underresourced, institutions such as Guatemala City's Central Penitentiary and National Mental Health Hospital were ill prepared to refuse PASB inducements, which included donated drugs, even after Cutler and Funes explained the experiments.

Cutler described the majority of people he experimented upon as "Mayans from the backwoods," even though medical records suggest that some were Ladinos, Ladinas, or Afro-Guatemalans.[54] Tracing the names of people subjected to experimentation through institutions that participated in the research has revealed that some hospital patients only spoke Indigenous languages such as Kaqchikel and would not have understood US and Guatemalan doctors, even if they had tried to explain their research.[55] Associations between criminality and Indigenous culture meant that *indígenas* were more vulnerable to imprisonment and confinement in the national mental health hospital where the experiments occurred (Carey 2013, 102). Conscripted into the army, *indígenas* comprised the majority of soldiers as well. Language barriers, illiteracy, and low rank of soldiers was a boon to researchers who sought to find the most defenseless and vulnerable people in the country upon whom to experiment. Conducting research on *indígenas* who did not speak English or Spanish also helped doctors hide their research from people in the United States and Latin America who would have denounced the experiments as reprehensible (R. Adams 1968; Carey 2010).

Capitalizing upon *indígenas'* marginality, Cutler and other PASB researchers believed *indígenas* were ideal test subjects. No evidence indicates that PASB doctors initially went to Guatemala because they were specifically interested in researching the disease in Indigenous people, as opposed to the 40-year study in Tuskegee, Alabama (1932–72) (Jones 1993; Reverby 2009). The belief that "syphilis was almost a different disease" in African Americans compared to people of European descent motivated the central question in that study (Brandt 1973, 23). In contrast to research on onchocerciasis which Guatemalan researchers deemed an "Indigenous disease," syphilis was not thought to be endemic in Indigenous communities (Adams and Giraudo 2020). When Cutler arrived in Guatemala, US researchers studying onchocerciasis relayed the benefits of conducting research on *indígenas*. Assistant chief of the USPHS Venereal Disease Division and PASB Caribbean sector chief Dr. Joseph Spoto secured Indigenous subjects including prisoners and orphans. Ignoring (or oblivious to) Dr. Quintana's refutation of racist ideas that "Indians" were "uncooperative" and "superstitious," Cutler complained, "The Indians had . . . very widespread prejudices against frequent withdrawals of blood. . . . [they were] uneducated and superstitious" (Adams and Giraudo 2020, 190). Convinced *indígenas* were acquiescent by nature rather than in response to longstanding structural inequalities in the country, Spoto advised Cutler not to explain the experiments to *indígenas* or pay them much for the research.[56] PASB interests in Guatemala were more akin to RF researchers who chose Central America as a site to launch pilot programs on hookworm because it offered a location in which "experiments could be tried out on a small scale and in a comparatively quiet way."[57] US doctors also sought to take advantage of legalized sex work in Guatemala to gain access to sex workers as experimental "subjects." Abiding by laws in Guatemala, PASB doctors exported their ethical and legal justifications for their research, reflecting a practice in medical research that continues in the current day.

When they encountered problems with the accuracy of diagnostic tests for syphilis, Cutler and his team became more focused on questions of race. They sought to study whether factors in the population, tropical environment, or presence of malaria confounded study results. Cutler scoured the countryside looking for a "pure Indian" upon whom he could research this problem.[58] Among Guatemalan researchers, debates had circulated in the 1930s and 1940s over whether Indigenous Guatemalans had acquired immunity to syphilis (Jacobsthal 1942, 1955). The long-standing myth that Indigenous people of the Americas had given syphilis to Spanish conquistadores influenced these disputes. For his part, Funes rejected these notions and advocated that the government extend venereal disease control measures to highland communities. Reflecting the assimilationist and interventionist bent of political leaders during the Guatemalan Revolution (1944–54), Funes argued that these public health campaigns would "civilize" indígenas and uplift the nation (1949, 3–4).

Cutler concluded indígenas had no "racial immunity" to syphilis.[59] As noted previously, some Guatemalan doctors inverted neocolonial relations by influencing PASB doctors' understandings of race and disease. In making this claim in his final report, Cutler upheld the notion that Guatemala was an ideal laboratory for studying sexually transmitted diseases. Cutler refuted the idea that biological characteristics in indígenas affected the manifestation of disease, but he upheld racist notions that they made ideal experimental subjects. Cutler did not, however, challenge his superiors who had made race a central question in Tuskegee, Alabama (Reverby 2009; Jones 1993). As opposed to the Alabama study that focused just on African American groups, PASB researchers aimed to make the results of their experiments on Guatemalan indígenas universal (namely, applicable to people of European descent). These conclusions bolstered the idea that Guatemala could serve as a "Third World" model for research during the Cold War. As a result, Guatemala became a center for research on malnutrition and reproduction. Rumors still persist in Guatemala about the widespread sterilization of indígenas during the Cold War, which also occurred in marginalized groups in the United States and other parts of Latin America (Briggs 2003, 146–47; Stern 2005, 99–100; Eraso 2007; Córdova 2017, 146).

Despite rumors about indígenas' docility, they were not yielding. Doctors' research methods clashed with popular perceptions of health. Since typically only midwives physically examined Indigenous women and poor Ladinas, they resisted doctor's medical inspections (Carey 2006, 36). Doctors also faced protests in prisons and Indigenous towns during diagnostic blood tests. In one Kaqchikel town about an hour from Guatemala City, parents wielded machetes and drove PASB researchers out of town after they drew blood from children at the local school without obtaining their families' consent.[60] Parents and prisoners, subscribing to popular understandings of medicine, believed that blood draws would weaken children's bodies.

Despite Guatemalans' claims to bodily sovereignty, doctors managed to conduct their experiments with few constraints. US and Guatemalan researchers' convictions that they were on the precipice of eradicating a disease that had plagued armies since at least the fifteenth century curtailed possibilities to mitigate the experiments (Stepan 2011b). In World War II, USPHS researchers had discovered that penicillin cured syphilis, but questions remained about the efficacy of the drug and methods to curb the spread of disease. Doctors hoped to resolve these questions in Guatemala. Cutler told his superiors that Guatemala offered the "opportunity to study syphilis just as Chesney studies it in the rabbit."[61] Dr. Alan Chensey was a researcher at Johns Hopkins University and a staunch proponent of "unrestricted research" on both humans and animals for the advancement of science.[62] Researchers built upon Guatemala's inequitable racial structures to locate people for study and conduct experiments without the "red tape" that apparently hampered their work in the United States.

Both place and population attracted US researchers to Guatemala. As a nation firmly ensconced within the US sphere of influence, Guatemala maintained racial and class structures that marginalized a large swath of the population. Those people in that place made for an ideal setting for conducting unfettered (and unethical) research.

When the syphilis study came to light in 2010, US and Guatemalan media and officials portrayed it as a horrific anomaly, particularly since the experiments occurred during the Guatemalan Spring. In truth, the experiments were not so much an aberration as a manifestation of longer histories of Guatemalan health care professionals' and politicians' approaches to transnational humanitarian campaigns and medical advancement. As politicians, doctors, and intellectuals strove to regenerate Guatemalans' bodies and minds to become productive workers, the Guatemalan Revolution brought new energy for scientific research. Guatemalans did not simply adopt drugs touted by the United States; they performed their own experiments to examine their utility and applicability to local populations.[63] Guatemalan doctors who did not obtain informed consent from research subjects revealed a shared ethics that crossed national borders. Despite an intensification of research during the Guatemalan Revolution, the experiments suggest a continuation of Guatemalan medical professionals' earlier attempts to build a nation by inviting professional expertise from abroad.

US doctors took advantage of this moment of reform to further their research. As historian Greg Grandin (2006) argues, the United States had long approached Central America as a workshop where it could experiment with programs before pursuing them at home or on the world stage. In this case, however, the USPHS was expanding upon a domestic program. Thanks to the rich historiography of the Tuskegee study on untreated syphilis in African American men, much is known about the US political and public health climate and the USPHS's objectives (Reverby 2009; Jones 1993). Yet little is known about the history of public health, disease, and medicine in Guatemala that set the stage for the syphilis experiments. Without this context, our understanding of these human rights violations remains obtuse.

CONCLUSION

The seeds of those human rights abuses can be found in histories of public health in Guatemala. The Guatemala City municipal council's insistence on importing vaccines from France and San Francisco even after they regularly had proven ineffective reveals a faith in foreign health-care knowledge and medicine. In the syphilis experiments, the possibility to gain access to penicillin and work with doctors who had recently gained international renown for their findings made Guatemalan institutions and doctors eager to seek US researchers' help. As the United States grew to become a leading producer of pharmaceuticals during World War II, small Central American and Caribbean countries such as Guatemala struggled to resist opportunities to gain access to medicines, even if that meant surrendering human lives (Lambe 2016, 489–516).

The collaboration between Funes and Cutler too can be read as part of a longer historical trajectory of Guatemalan and foreign doctors and researchers collaborating to address vexing health care and public health problems. Even if Funes's USPHS fellowship and hopes to gain medical resources from the United States compromised his ability to critique the experiments, the foundation of trust in foreign medical expertise (if not ethics) had been laid far earlier. Two years before the experiments, the US ambassador facilitated blood plasma donations from US soldiers to Guatemalan hospitals.[64] He too was building on a long-standing relationship of transnational humanitarianism that had developed between the United States and Guatemala. At the same time, we should not assume that Funes and other Guatemala medical professionals approached the experiments with an inferiority complex. Their predecessors had been invited abroad to study, research, and practice; were praised by health care professionals in other countries; and regularly engaged in international communities of doctors and scientists. Even though hospitals and health care in general were woefully underfunded in Guatemala, there were many reasons to be proud of what its doctors and medical researchers had accomplished.

Even as Guatemalan professionals stood proud of their collective accomplishments and knowledge, the nation's health care system was strikingly unequal, particularly between urban and rural areas (where indígenas dominated demographically), and it often depended on the largesse of foreign companies and nationals. Dieseldorff almost singlehandedly constructed, furnished, and modernized the hospital in Cobán that served so many indígenas. His generosity made business and political sense for him, but it also underscored the dependence of Guatemala's health care and public health systems on outside support. For many Guatemalan health care and public health professionals, there were no illusions of national autonomy. They needed foreign funding and knowledge. Even the few lone voices of concern for how certain aspects of public health campaigns and health-care practices adversely affected the poor may have been muted in the face of donations to flailing institutions. As rich as many of the transnational exchanges of information, medicine, techniques, and technology were, the Guatemalan government's inability (or unwillingness) to adequately fund national health care and public health initiatives made it vulnerable to foreign control and exploitation. Ranging from resistance to acquiescence, indígenas' responses to foreign medical influences echoed those of non-Indigenous medical professionals.

NOTES

1. Since the term Maya only became common during Guatemala's multicultural turn in the 1990s, we use the terms most often found in the archival documents that inform this essay: *indígena* (Indigenous person) and *indio* (Indian). The latter remains a pejorative term used by non-Indigenous Guatemalans to disparage, denigrate, and discount Indigenous people. Although it distinguishes people by ethnicity in a nation with rampant racism, *indígena* is a neutral term that simply denotes (but does not denigrate) an individual's ethnic identity. When historical actors use the term Maya, we do too. For the development and evolution of the term Maya, see Hale (2005, 10–28).

2. See, e.g., *La Gaceta: Revista de Policía y Variedades*, March 19, 1933, May 5, 1935, July 19, 1942, and February 14 and June 18, 1943.

3. Museo de Medicina, Quito, Ecuador, FEM0121, Oficina sanitaria Panamericana, publication number 102, Washington, DC, September 1935.

4. Loyola Notre Dame Library, Special Collections (henceforth LNDLSC), Baltimore, MD, Guatemala Collection, box 26, Varios, leg. 28551, exp. 21, 1850, Supremo Gobierno de Juan Izquierdo por Bernarda Ramírez.

5. LNDLSC, Guatemala Collection, box 26, Varios, leg. 28551, exp. 21, 1850, Supremo Gobierno de Juan Izquierdo por Bernarda Ramírez.

6. LNDLSC, Guatemala Collection, box 21, Agricultura, Sr. Corregidores del departamento de Sacatepéquez de Celesino Tamayo, 1850.

7. "Desbordante entusiasmo en la Antigua Guatemala por el fallo," *Diario de Centro América*, January 25, 1933.

8. "La agricultura vuelve a ser ocupación costeable," *Diario de Centro América* August 4, 1933; "Sección agrícola," *Diario de Centro América*, July 7, 1933.

9. Héctor Barahona, "Método para fertilización del suelo y aumento de las cosechas," *Diario de Centro América*, September 3, 1936.

10. Rockefeller Archive Center (RAC), Record Group (RG) 5, series 2, 319 Projects, box 31, folder 183, Memorandum to Dr. William Rose Regarding Guatemala, January 26, 1918?

11. On the important role of foreigners during Estrada Cabrera's dictatorship, see McCreery (1994, 233).

12. Italics added. "Página editorial: Prelación de los cultivos agrícolas," *Diario de Centro América*, August 19, 1933.

13. RAC, RG 1.1 Projects, series 319, box 1, folder 1; RF Photographs, series 317, box 85, folder 1706.

14. RAC, RF, RG 5, series 2, box 31, folder 183, Dr. Padilla, "Organization of the Administration of Public Health in Guatemala," ca. 1920.

15. RAC, RF Records, RG 10, subgroup 2, Fellowship Card, Dr. Luis Gaitán, October 1, 1921.

16. RAC, RF, RG 1.1, series 319E, box 171, folder 2639, Fellowship Card, Dr. Enrique Padilla.

17. Archivo General de Centroamérica (henceforth AGCA), Guatemala City, B81.3. legajo (leg.) 1092, expediente (exp.) 23945, Municipalid de la capital, 1899, "Informe por doctores sobre la inconveniencia de la existencia de la presa del río de 'Las Vacas,'" July 4, 1899.

18. AGCA, Inventario 1884–1924, índice leg. 23097, Dirección del hospital general, November 26, 1922.

19. AGCA, Inventario 1884–1924, índice leg. 23107, Dirección del hospital general, 1924, letter from American College of Surgeons, February 10, 1924.

20. AGCA, indice de salud, leg. 23225, 1942 correspondencia, letter to Director General de Hospital, Guatemala, July 25, 1942, from Sanidad Pública.

21. AGCA, leg. 23240, 1944–46 correspondencia, Asilo de Alienados a Sr. Presidente, "Informe relación con la epidemia de Tifus Exantematico que sufre el Asilo de Alienados," 1944.

22. "Resumen de las labores del Ministerio de Agricultura durante el año de 1932," *Diario de Centro América*, February 14, 1933.

23. "Resumen de las labores del Ministerio de Agricultura durante el año de 1932," *Diario de Centro América*, February 14, 1933.

24. AGCA, Jefatura Política Sacatepéquez, 15 de noviembre, 1922 Carta al Jefatura Política del Director del Fundación Rockefeller Commissión Internacional de Sanidad.

25. *La Gaceta*, November 10, 1934; bold in the original.

26. *Diario de Centro América*, March 19, 1910.

27. AGCA, índice de salud, leg. 23240, 1944–46 Correspondencia, carta de Servicio de Radiología a Director de Hospital Dr. Mariano Zecena, Guatemala City, October 11, 1944.

28. AGCA, índice, 140 ministerio de salud, Memoria del 1935 de Beneficencia Pública, January 17, 1935, p. 4.

29. AGCA, B81.3, leg. 1092, exp. 23981, municipalidad de la capital, higiene: mociónes de Drs. Goza y Ortega relativas a hygiene pública, 1923.

30. AGCA, B82.3, leg. 1100, exp. 24332, August 31, 1886, "el conservador de la vacuna, sugiere a la municipalidad de la capital, se proceda importar de Francia abundantes fluido vacuno."

31. AGCA, B82.3, leg. 1100, exp. 24339, September 25, 1888, "el regidor inspector de la vacuna, informa a la municipalidad de la capital que no ha dado buen resultado el fluido que últimamente se pidió a Francia."

32. AGCA, B82.3, leg. 1100, exp. 24339, February 14, 1889, "jefe político participa a la municipalidad de la capital."

33. AGCA, B82.3, leg. 1100, exp. 24339, February 22, 1889, "El alcalde San Salvador, El Salvador, solicita del Guatemala."

34. AGCA, B82.3, leg. 1100, exp. 24345, June 11, 1889, "jefe político transcribe a la munici-pal de la capital . . . relativo a que el cónsul de Guatemala en San Francisco, CA, anunciaba el

próximo envío del fluido vacuno que se le solicitó"; B82.3, leg. 1100, exp. 24346, July 1, 1889, "D. Federico Arévalo, obsequió a la municipal de la capital tubos conteniendo fluido vacuno, que hizo venir de Londres."

35. AGCA, B82.3, leg. 1100, exp. 24341, July 3, 1889, "el conservador de la vacuna, informa a la municipal de la capital, que el fluido recientemente importado de San Francisco, CA, no dio resultados."

36. AGCA, B82.3, leg. 1100, exp. 24345, fol. 1, August 2, 1889, "el conservador de la vacuna, indica a la municipal de la capital que debería pedirse a San Francisco, CA, cierta cantidad de fluido, porque el importado de Francia no dio resultado."

37. AGCA, B82.3, leg. 1100, exp. 24366, October 5, 1894, "la municipal de la capital eroga la cantidad de 41 pesos con 35 centavos, valor del fluido importado de Francia."

38. The National Archives, Atlanta, Georgia (henceforth NA), Dr. Juan Funes M. Funes and Srta. Casta Luz Aguilar, "La solución de mafarside-orvus en la profilaxis de la blenorragia en la mujer," *Boletín de la Oficina Sanitaria Panamericana* (August 1952), 121–26; AGCA, Ref. Number 4816, Boletín Número 1 from the Ministerio de Salud Pública y Asistencia Social; Galich (1947).

39. AGCA, Epanimondas Quintana, "En alimentación infantil el análisis químico de la leche de madre o nodriza, tal como se hace aquí, es inútil," *Boletín Sanitario de Guatemala* 12, no. 49 (January–December 1941): 148.

40. AGCA, B101.1, leg. 3638, exp. 23141, Salubridad Pública 1930, Dirección General de Guatemala, January 18 and 21, 1930, Salubridad Pública, Dirección General de Guatemala, July 19, 1930.

41. AGCA, Inventario de salud pública 1884–1924, exp. 23097, Presidente y sus ministros 1922, Ministerio de Hacienda y Crédito, September 20, 1922, Ministerio de Hacienda y Crédito, October 5, 1922, Ministerio de Hacienda y Crédito, September 22, 1922.

42. AGCA, Inventario de salud pública 1884–1924, exp. 23100, Presidentes y sus ministerios folder, sueros de departamento nacional de higiene de Buenos Aires, July 5, 1923.

43. AGCA, Inventario de salud pública 1884–1924, exp. 23097, Presidente y sus ministros 1922, Ministerio de Hacienda y Crédito, February 2, 1922.

44. AGCA, Inventario de salud pública 1884–1924, exp. 23097, carta de Max Paetau, February 20, 1922.

45. AGCA, índice 140, ministerio de salud, leg. 23178, Sanidad Pública Guatemala, December 6, 1937.

46. AGCA, B101.1, leg. 3638, exp. 23145, Deutsche Gesandschaft Guatemala, November 25, 1931.

47. Tulane University Latin American Library (TULAL), Dieseldorff Collection (DC) box 9, carta a Sr. Fidel Torres, jefe político departamental, February 8, 1942.

48. TULAL, DC, box 9, "Dieseldorff acude a otra obra de caridad," *El Liberal Progresista*, April 20, 1943; Gibbings (2020a).

49. TULAL, DC, Personal Correspondence box 9, Sociedad Protectora del Niño, June 8, 1942.

50. TULAL, DC, box 9, Hospital Nacional Central de Zona, Cobán, Alta Verapaz, October 20, 1942.

51. AGCA, B81.3, leg. 1092, exp. 23971, fol. 7, carta de Carlos F. Novella a Concejal de la municipalidad de la capital, July 22, 1914.

52. Quintana (1943, 69). In another instance of racism and diminishing an ethnic or racial group's way of speaking, Epaminondas was the name of the African American boy who was featured in the stories of *Little Black Sambo*, which was based on a book about Epaminondas published in 1907.

53. NA, Records of John C. Cutler, "Experimental Studies in Gonorrhea," October 29, 1952, p. 7.

54. NA, Records of John C. Cutler, John C. Cutler to RC Arnold, "Correspondence," September 16, 1947.

55. AGCA, Fondo de la Salud Pública, Los expedientes de los pacientes del asilo, leg. 24120.

56. NA, Records of John C. Cutler, John C. Cutler to Richard Arnold, "Correspondence," August 21, 1946.

57. Lewerth (1949, 2, 411), cited in Palmer (2010, 1). In colonial Africa too, research accompanied health-care services and Africans were frequently subjects of research; see Tilley (2016 746–47).

58. NA, Records of Dr. John C. Cutler, John C. Cutler, "Final Syphilis Report," February 24, 1955.

59. NA, Records of Dr. John C. Cutler, John C. Cutler, "Final Syphilis Report," February 24, 1955.

60. Raymond L. Scheele, "Dual Report on Field Work in Santo Domingo Xenocoj, Sacatepéquez, Guatemala," July 4, 1951, 10–11, Richard Adams personal library, Panajachel, Guatemala.

61. NA, John C. Cutler to John Mahoney, John C. Cutler Records, "Correspondence," September 18, 1947.

62. NA, John C. Cutler to John Mahoney, September 18, 1947, Correspondence, John C. Cutler Records. See also "Dr. Alan Chesney of Johns Hopkins; Ex-Dean of Medical School Dies in Baltimore at 76," *New York Times*, September 23, 1964.

63. NA, Funes and Aguilar, "La solución de mafarside-orvus en la profilaxis de la blenorragia en la mujer," *Boletín de la Oficina Sanitaria Panamericana* (August 1952), 121–26; Galich (1947).

64. AGCA, B101.1, leg. 3638, exp. 23240, 1944–46 correspondencia, letter from US embassy, July 11, 1944.

REFERENCES CITED
ARCHIVOS

AGCA: Archivo General de Centroamérica, Guatemala City, Guatemala

LNDLSC: Loyola Notre Dame Library, Special Collections, Guatemala Collection, Baltimore, MD, Guatemala Collection

Museo de Medicina, Quito, Ecuador

NA: The National Archives, Atlanta, GA

RAC: Rockefeller Archive Center, Sleepy Hollow, NY

TULAL: Tulane University Latin American Library, New Orleans, LA

GENERAL

Abad, Amaya. 1996. *Facultad de Ciencias Médicas, 1895–1995: Historia y recopilación.* Editorial Oscar de León Palacios, La Facultad de Ciencias Médicas, 1895–1995, Universidad de San Carlos, Guatemala City.

Adams, Abigail E., and Laura Giraudo. 2020. "'A Pack of Cigarettes or Some Soap': Race, Security, International Public Health and Human Medical Experimentation during Guatemala's October Revolution." In *Out of the Shadow: Revisiting the Revolution from Post-peace Guatemala*, edited by Julie Gibbings and Heather Vrana, 175–98. Austin: University of Texas Press.

Adams, Richard N. May 1968. "The Development of the Guatemalan Military." *Studies in Comparative International Development* 4 (5): 359–90.

Administración del Señor General Don Jorge Ubico. 1942. *Dos lustros de obra sanitaria en la república de Guatemala.* Guatemala City: Publicaciones del Partido Liberal Progresista.

Asturias, Miguel Ángel. (1921) 1977. *Guatemalan Sociology: The Social Problem of the Indian / Sociología Guatemalteca: El problema social del indio.* Tempe: Arizona State University.

Birn, Anne-Emanuelle. 2002. "'No More Surprising than a Broken Pitcher'? Maternal and Child Health in the Early Years of the Pan American Sanitary Bureau." *Canadian Bulletin of Medical History* 19 (1): 17–46.

Birn, Anne-Emanuelle. 2006. *Marriage of Convenience: Rockefeller International Health and Revolutionary Mexico.* Rochester: University of Rochester Press.

Birn, Anne-Emmanuelle. 2020. "Alternative Destinies and Solidarities for Health and Medicine in Latin America before and during the Cold War." In *Peripheral Nerve: Health and Medicine in Cold War Latin America*, edited by Anne-Emmanuelle Birn and Raúl Necochea López, 1–28. Durham, NC: Duke University Press.

Birn, Anne-Emanuelle, and Raúl Necochea López. 2011. "Footprints on the Future: Looking Forward to the History of Health and Medicine in Latin America in the Twenty-First Century." *Hispanic American Historical Review* 91 (3): 521–22.

Birn, Anne-Emanuelle, and Raúl Necochea López, eds., 2020. *Peripheral Nerve: Health and Violence in Cold War Latin America*. Durham, NC: Duke University Press.

Brandt, Allan M. 1987. *No Magic Bullet: A Social History of Venereal Disease in the United States Since 1880*. New York: Oxford University Press.

Brandt, Allan. 1973. "Racism and Research: The Case of the Tuskegee Syphilis Study." *Hastings Center Report* 8 (6): 21–29.

Briggs, Laura. 2003. *Reproducing Empire: Race, Sex, Science, and U.S. Imperialism in Puerto Rico*. Berkeley: University of California Press.

Carey, David, Jr. 2006. *Engendering Mayan History: Kaqchikel Women as Agents and Conduits of the Past, 1875–1970*. New York: Routledge.

Carey, David, Jr. 2010. "Mayan Soldier-Citizens: Ethnic Pride in the Guatemalan Military 1925–1945." In *Military Struggle and Identity Formation in Latin America: Race, Nation and Community 1850–1950*, edited by Nicola Foote and René D. Harder Horst, 136–56. Gainesville: University Press of Florida.

Carey, David, Jr. 2013. *I Ask for Justice: Maya Women, Dictators, and Crime in Guatemala, 1898–1944*. Austin: University of Texas Press.

Carey, David, Jr. 2018. "Heroines of Healthcare: Germana Catu and Maya Midwives." In *Faces of Resistance: Maya Heroes, Power, and Identity*, edited by Ashley Kistler, 137–56. Tuscaloosa: University of Alabama Press.

Carey, David, Jr. Ca. 2019. "The Politics and Culture of Medicine and Disease in Central America." In *Oxford Research Encyclopedia of Latin American History*. New York: Oxford University Press. https://doi.org/10.1093/acrefore/9780199366439.013.52.

Carey, David, Jr. 2021. "A Cautionary Tale of Environmental Management: Water Management, Land Reclamation, and Malaria in Twentieth-Century Guatemala." *Environmental History* 26 (3): 449–79.

Carey, David, Jr. *Health in the Highlands: Indigenous Healing and Scientific Medicine in Guatemala and Ecuador*. Berkeley: University of California Press, 2023.

Carrillo, Ana María, and Anne-Emanuelle Birn. 2008. "Neighbors on Notice: National and Imperialistic Interests in the American Public Health Association, 1872–1921." *Canadian Bulletin of Medical History* 25 (1): 225–54.

Carter, Eric. 2012. *Enemy in the Blood: Malaria, Environment, and Development in Argentina*. Tuscaloosa: University of Alabama Press.

Cohen, Deborah. 2011. *Braceros: Migrant Citizens and Transnational Subjects in Postwar United States and Mexico*. Chapel Hill: University of North Carolina Press.

Córdova, Isabel M. 2017. *Pushing in Silence: Modernizing Puerto Rico and the Medicalization of Childbirth*. Austin: University of Texas Press.

Crafts, Lydia. 2019. "Mining Bodies: Medical Experimentation and Ethics during the Guatemalan Spring, 1944–54," PhD diss, University of Illinois, Urbana.

Cueto. Marcos. 1989. *Excelencia científica en la periferia: Actividades científicas e investigación biomédica en el Perú, 1890–1950*. Lima: GRDE-CONCYTEC.

Cueto, Marcos, ed. 1994. *Missionaries of Science: The Rockefeller Foundation in Latin America*. Bloomington: Indiana University Press.

Cueto, Marcos. 2007a. *The Value of Health: A History of the Pan American Health Organization*. Washington, DC: Pan American Health Organization.

Cueto, Marco. 2007b. *Cold War, Deadly Fevers: Malaria Eradication in Mexico, 1955–75*. Baltimore: Johns Hopkins University Press.

Cueto, Marcos, and Steven Palmer. 2015. *Medicine and Public Health in Latin America: A History*. Cambridge: Cambridge University Press.

Despacho de Gobernación y Justicia presenta a la asamblea legislativa de la República de Guatemala en sus sesiones ordinarias de 1890. ca. 1890. Guatemala City: Establecimiento Tipográfico de La Unión.

Eraso, Yolanda. 2007. "Biotypology, Endocrinology, and Sterilization: The Practice of Eugenics in the Treatment of Argentinean Women during the 1930s." *Bulletin of the History of Medicine* 81 (4): 793–822.

Espinosa, Mariola. 2009. *Epidemic Invasions: Yellow Fever and the Limits of Cuban Independence, 1878–1930*. Chicago: University of Illinois Press.

Few, Martha. 2007. "'That Monster of Nature': Gender, Sexuality, and the Medicalization of a 'Hermaphrodite' in Late Colonial Guatemala." *Ethnohistory* 54, no. 1 (Winter): 159–76.

Few, Martha. 2010. "Circulating Smallpox Knowledge: Guatemalan Doctors, Maya Indians and Designing Spain's Smallpox Vaccination Expedition, 1780–1803." *British Journal for the History of Science* 43 (4): 519–37.

Few, Martha. 2015. *For All of Humanity: Mesoamerican and Colonial Medicine in Enlightenment Guatemala*. Tucson: University of Arizona Press.

Forster, Cindy. 2001. *The Time of Freedom: Campesino Workers in Guatemala's Revolution*. Pittsburgh: University of Pittsburgh Press.

Funes, Juan. 1949. "Proyecto de nueva legislación antivenérea, Consideraciones Generales." *Salubridad y Asistencia: Organo del Ministerio de Salud Publica y Asistencia Social* 2, no. 3 (March): 3–4.

Funes, Juan M. 1950. "Plan General de acción de la lucha antivenérea." *Salubridad y Asistencia Social* 1 (October): 11.

Galich, Luis F. 1947. "Tratamiento de la sífilis primaria con oxofenarisina-bismuto en veinte días, según el método de Pillsbury." Guatemala City.

Galich, Luis F. 1949. "Coordinación de los servicios asistenciales y de sanidad pública." *Salubridad y Asistencia Social* (March): 28.

Gibbings, Julie. 2016. "*Mestizaje* in the Age of Fascism: German and Q'eqchi' Maya Interracial Unions in Alta Verapaz, Guatemala." *German History* 34 (2): 214–36.

Gibbings, Julie. 2019. "Progressive Mothers, Populist Politics: Eugenics, Race, and Progress during Jorge Ubico's Guatemala." Paper presented at Latin American Studies Association Conference, Boston, May.

Gibbings, Julie. 2020a. *Our Time Is Now: Race and Modernity in Postcolonial Guatemala.* Cambridge: Cambridge University Press.

Gibbings, Julie. 2020b. "'Their Debts Follow Them into the Afterlife': German Settlers, Ethnographic Knowledge, and the Forging of Coffee Capitalism in Nineteenth-Century Guatemala." *Comparative Studies in Society and History* 62 (2): 380–420.

Gibbings, Julie, and Heather Vrana, eds. 2020. *Out of the Shadow: Revisiting the Revolution from Post-peace Guatemala.* Austin: University of Texas Press.

Gleijeses, Piero. 1991. *Shattered Hope: The Guatemalan Revolution and the United States, 1944–1954.* Princeton, NJ: Princeton University Press.

Gómez de Cruz, Magda. 2008. "Smallpox Vaccination, the Establishment of Vaccination Boards, and State Formation in Venezuela and Cuba in the Nineteenth Century." PhD diss., Florida International University, University Park, FL.

Grandin, Greg. 2006. *Empire's Workshop: Latin America, the United States, and the Rise of the New Imperialism.* New York: Henry Holt Company.

Hale, Charles R. 2005. "Neoliberal Multiculturalism: The Remaking of Cultural Rights and Racial Dominance in Central America." *Political and Legal Anthropology Review* 28, no. 1 (May): 10–28.

Handy, Jim. 1994. *Revolution in the Countryside: Rural Conflict and Agrarian Reform in Guatemala, 1944–1954.* Chapel Hill: University of North Carolina Press.

Haralson, M. F. 1948. "The Organization and Aims of the Pan American Sanitary Bureau in the Americas and along the United States–Mexico Border." *Boletín de la Oficina Sanitaria Panamericana* 27, no. 10 (October): 917–25, 923.

Harms, Patricia. 2011. "God Doesn't Like the Revolution: The Archbishop, the Market Women, and the Economy of Gender in Guatemala, 1944–1954." *Frontiers: A Journal of Women's Studies* 32 (2): 111–39.

Hochman, Gilberto. 2008. "From Autonomy to Partial Alignment: National Malaria Programs in the Time of Global Eradication, Brazil, 1941–1961." *Canadian Bulletin of Medical History* 25 (1): 161–91.

Jacobsthal, Erwin. 1942. "Sobre el problema del tratamiento de la sífilis en Centro América." *Boletín Sanitario de Guatemala* 8, no. 59 (January–December): 125.

Jones, James H. 1993. *Bad Blood: The Tuskegee Syphilis Experiment*. New York: Free Press.

Kirkpatrick, Michael D. 2017. "Phantoms of Modernity: The 1894 Anarchist Furor in the Making of Modern Guatemala City." *Urban History* 44 (2): 231–52.

Kirkpatrick, Michael D. August 2020. "Consumer Culture in Guatemala City during the 'Season of Luis Mazzantini,' 1905: The Political Economy of Consumption." *Journal of Latin American Studies*. https://doi.org/10.1017/S0022216X2000067X.

Lambe, Jennifer. 2016. "Drug Wars: Revolution, Embargo, and the Politics of Scarcity in Cuba, 1959–1964." *Journal of Latin American Studies* 49 (3): 489–516.

Lambe, Jennifer. 2017. *Madhouse: Psychiatry and Politics in Cuban History*. Chapel Hill: University of North Carolina Press.

Lederer, Susan E. 1995. *Subjected to Science: Human Experimentation in America before the Second World War*. Baltimore: Johns Hopkins University Press.

Lewis, Stephen. 2018. *Rethinking Mexican Indigenismo: The INI's Coordinating Center in Highland Chiapas and the Fate of a Utopian Project*. Albuquerque: University of New Mexico Press.

Löwy, Ilana. 2001. *Virus, moustiques, et modernité: La fièvre jaune au Brésil entre science et politique*. Paris: Archives Contemporaines.

Martínez García, Yesenia. 2017. "Michel Foucault y su planteamiento teórico para estudiar los enfermos, las enfermedades y las políticas de salud en Honduras, 1880–1954." Paper presented at I Congreso Nacional de Historia, Tegucigalpa, October.

McCreery, David. 1994. *Rural Guatemala, 1760–1940*. Stanford, CA: Stanford University Press.

Memoria de la Secretaria de Gobernación y Justicia, 1911. n.d. Guatemala City: Tipografía Nacional.

Memoria de la Secretaria de Gobernación y Justicia presentada a la asamblea legislativa de la República de Guatemala, 1926. ca. 1927. Guatemala City: Tipografía Nacional.

Memoria de los trabajos realizados por la dirección general de Sanidad Pública durante el año de 1939, presentada a sus jefes, supremo e inmediato, señor presidente de la República y señor secretario del estado en el despacho de Gobernación y Justicia. December 1939. Guatemala City: Tipografía Nacional.

Memoria de los trabajos realizados por la dirección general de Sanidad Pública y sus dependencias, durante, el año de 1945. 1945. Guatemala City: Tipografía Nacional.

Obregón, Diane. 2002. "Building National Medicine: Leprosy and Power in Colombia, 1870–1930." *Social History of Medicine* 15, no. 1 (April): 89–108.

Otovo, Okezi T. 2016. *Progressive Mothers, Better Babies: Race, Public Health, and the State in Brazil*. Austin: University of Texas Press.

Packard, Randall. 2007. *The Making of a Tropical Disease: A Short History of Malaria.* Baltimore: Johns Hopkins University Press.

Padilla B, Enrique. 1948. "Las Rickettsiasis en Guatemala." *Boletín de la Oficina Sanitaria Panamericana* 25, no. 6 (July): 519–24.

Palmer, Steven. 1998. "Central American Encounters with Rockefeller Public Health, 1914–1921." In *Close Encounters of Empire: Writing the Cultural History of U.S.–Latin American Relations,* edited by Gilbert M. Joseph, Catherine C. LeGrand, and Ricardo D. Salvatore, 311–32. Durham, NC: Duke University Press.

Palmer, Steven. 2003. *From Popular Medicine to Medical Populism: Doctors, Healers, and Public Power in Costa Rica, 1800–1940.* London: Duke University Press.

Palmer, Steven. 2010. *Launching Global Health: The Caribbean Odyssey of Rockefeller Foundation.* Ann Arbor: University of Michigan Press.

Peña Torres, Ligia María, and Steven Palmer. 2008. "A Rockefeller Foundation Health Primer for US-Occupied Nicaragua, 1914–1928." *CBMH/BCHM* 25 (1): 43–69.

Quintana, Epaminondas. 1943. "Proyecto de educación sanitaria contra el Tifus Exantematico en Guatemala." *Gaceta Médica Centroamericana* 1 (2): 69.

Reggiani, Andres Horacio. 2007. *God's Eugenicist: Alexis Carrel and the Sociobiology of Decline.* New York: Berghahn Books.

Reverby, Susan M. 2009. *The Infamous Syphilis Study and Its Legacy: Examining Tuskegee.* Chapel Hill: University of North Carolina Press.

Ross, Paul. 2009. "Mexico's Superior Health Council and the American Public Health Association: The Transnational Archive of Porfirian Public Health, 1887–1910." *Hispanic American Historical Review* 89 (4): 573–602.

Roth, Cassia. 2020. *A Miscarriage of Justice: Women's Reproductive Lives and the Law in Early Twentieth-Century Brazil.* Stanford, CA: Stanford University Press.

Selis Lope, Mario. 1931. *Secretos de la raza: Creencias, costumbres, medicina y supersticiones de los indígenas de la Verapaz.* Cobán, A.V.: Tipografía "El Norte."

Soto-Laveaga, Gabriela. 2009. *Jungle Laboratories: Mexican Peasants, National Projects, and the Making of the Pill.* Durham, NC: Duke University Press.

Stepan, Nancy Leys. 1991. *"The Hour of Eugenics": Race, Gender, and Nation in Latin America.* Ithaca, NY: Cornell University Press.

Stepan, Nancy Leys. 2011a. "The National and the International in Public Health: Carlos Chagas and the Rockefeller Foundation in Brazil, 1917–1930s." *Hispanic American Historical Review* 91 (3): 469–502.

Stepan, Nancy. 2011b. *Eradication: Ridding the World of Diseases Forever?* Ithaca, NY: Cornell University Press.

Stern, Alexandra Minna. 1999. "Buildings, Boundaries and Blood: Medicalization and Nation Building on the U.S.-Mexico Border 1910–1930." *Hispanic American Historical Review* 79, no. 1 (February): 41–81.

Stern, Alexandra Minna. 2005. *Eugenic Nation: Faults and Frontiers of Better Breeding in Modern America*. Berkeley: University of California Press.

Stern, Alexandra Minna. 2011. "'The Hour of Eugenics' in Veracruz, Mexico: Radical Politics, Public Health and Latin America's Only Sterilization Law." *Hispanic American Historical Review* 91 (3): 431–43.

Stoler, Ann Laura. 2002. *Carnal Knowledge and Imperial Power: Race and the Intimate in Colonial Rule*. Berkeley: University of California Press.

Sutter, Paul S. 2007. "Nature's Agents or Agents of Empire? Entomological Workers and Environmental Change during the Construction of the Panama Canal." *Isis* 98 (4): 724–54.

Tilley, Helen. 2004 "Ecologies of Complexity: Tropical Environments, African Trypanosomiasis and the Science of Disease Control in British Colonial Africa, 1900–1940." *Osiris* 19: 21–38.

Tilley, Helen. July 2016. "History of Medicine: Medicine, Empires, and Ethics in Colonial Africa." *AMA Journal of Ethics* 18 (7): 746–47.

Tworek, Heidi J. 2019. "Communicable Disease: Information, Health, and Globalization in the Interwar Period," *American Historical Review* 124, no. 3 (June): 813–42.

Vieira de Campos, André Luiz. 2006. *Políticas internacionais de saúde na Era Vargas: O Serviço Especial de Saúde Pública, 1942–1960*. Rio de Janeiro: Fiocruz.

8

A Cartography of Tourist Imaginaries

M. BIANET CASTELLANOS

Tourist brochures, guidebooks, and maps tell us a story about a place. Over time, this story may shift or become fixed in time. The tourist center of Cancún exemplifies both processes. Despite its attempt to rebrand itself as an upscale ecotourism center (in order to generate more revenue) after Hurricane Wilma in 2015, it remains tied to the sun, sand, and sea tourism associated with mass tourism and spring break revelers.[1] These shifting tourist imaginaries are indicative of more than just fickle tourist tastes. They also reflect racial ideologies central to settler colonial projects rooted in Indigenous elimination and dispossession. While studies of settler colonialism primarily focus on the Anglophone world, an investigation of settler colonial projects in Latin America is also sorely needed (Castellanos 2017).[2] I suggest that settler colonialism has been central in producing and shaping transnational Mayanness. Cancún is a perfect example of a settler colonial project reliant on the tropes of vanishing Indians and vacant lands to justify the elimination and displacement of Indigenous peoples. These settler tactics of erasure reinforce a transnational tourist imaginary of Maya peoples as exotic and ahistorical. Through an examination of an assortment of travel guidebooks, brochures, and maps of Cancún that I have collected since 1991, I explore the racial ideologies and settler colonial tropes that buttress tourist imaginaries in one of the most popular tourist destinations in the Americas.

I begin by analyzing two guidebooks—*The Mexican Caribbean* (Green 1984) and *Maya Riviera: Cancun–The Islands–Tulum* (2013)—because they mark two

https://doi.org/10.5876/9781646424276.c008

distinct phases of tourism development in the region. *The Mexican Caribbean* represents a phase of development oriented to sun, sand, and sea, whereas *Maya Riviera* represents a phase oriented toward luxurious ecotourism and geared toward conserving the environment and promoting sustainable relationships with local communities. Sold in hotel gift shops and local bookshops, the guidebooks are made up of photo-essays and maps intended to capture the history, beauty, and mystery of this region. Both guidebooks were endorsed by the Mexican government and published by international presses. *The Mexican Caribbean* includes an introduction by Armando Herrerias, the former director of the Escuela Mexicana de Turismo (Mexican School of Tourism). The text was written by M. Green and endorsed and published by Grijalbo, a Spanish press.[3] *Maya Riviera* was written by Mexican archaeologist Luis Alberto Martos and published in a collaboration between Mexican press Monclem Ediciones, Italian press Casa Editrice Bonechi, and Mexican institutions Conaculta (El Consejo Nacional para la Cultura y las Artes, or National Council for Culture and Arts) and the Instituto Nacional de Antropología e Historia (INAH, or National Institute of Anthropology).[4] As transnational productions, these guidebooks construct an idea of Mayanness rooted in US setter colonialism. While these popular guidebooks may have been published three decades apart, I show that they both rely on settler colonial narratives of "discovery" and whiteness to construct a particular story about place, time, space, and Maya peoples. In *Mapping Latin America*, Karl Offen and Jordana Dym suggest that "what the map does not reveal is as important as what it does" (2011, 3). To trace settler colonial narratives, I consider what these guidebooks and their maps occlude, as well as what they show. By erasing a history of Indigenous insurrection in the Yucatán peninsula and relegating contemporary Maya peoples into cultural icons, these materials transformed the region into a consumable site for American tourism and foreign investment. *The Mexican Caribbean* and *Maya Riviera* solidify a settler colonial narrative of the Mexican state of Quintana Roo as a site that is ahistorical, devoid of Indians, and primed for discovery.

I conclude by examining the *Atlas de turismo alternativo en la peninsula de Yucatán* (2015). Written by scholars Ana García de Fuentes, Samuel Jouault, and David Romero, in coordination with the Centro de Investigación y de Estudios Avanzados del Instituto Politécnico Nacional or CINVESTAV-IPN—Unidad Mérida (Center for Research and Advanced Studies of the National Polytechnic Institute, Mérida) and the Facultad de Ciencias Antropológicas—Universidad Autónoma de Yucatán or UADY (Department of Anthropology Sciences at the Autonomous University of Yucatán), this multidisciplinary collection forms part of a movement made up of local scholars, nonprofit organizations, and higher education and research institutions to promote an alternative approach to tourism that is oriented around local community decision making and participation. This type of tourism is growing rapidly and represents a new phase in tourism development: community-based tourism (CBT) (Castellanos and Córdoba Azcárate 2021). Through small-scale tours that historicize local practices and emphasize sustainability and collective decision making, community-based tourism challenges settler ways of knowing, even if it cannot dispel settler narratives of discovery.

A SETTLER COLONIAL PROJECT

In the late 1960s, the Mexican government scoured the countryside in search of perfect locations to establish tourist centers to boost the national economy. They selected Cancún as the first tourist pole to develop because it was considered to be "paradise" with miles of "usable beach" (Martí 1991, 18). Plans for a modern city envisioned a tourist utopia buttressed by an industrious Mexican middle class. Although the construction of this city and the tourist industry relied on cheap, Indigenous labor, housing for these workers initially was not included in these plans. Due to this oversight, housing remains a site of struggle for working-class and Indigenous residents. Housing insecurity, however, did not stymie migration to this city. Within three decades, Cancún became a thriving metropolis with over half a million settlers.

As a settler colonial fantasy based on vanishing Indians and empty lands, Cancún has papered over histories and conflicts that challenge this fantasy (Castellanos 2021). This narrative erases a long history of Indigenous revolt and land struggles. In 1847, Maya farmers and small landholders successfully fought to secede from the Mexican nation. While this victory was short lived with the arrival of additional Mexican troops, this war, known as the Caste War, lasted fifty years.[5] For villages such as Xcacal Guardia in the state of Quintana Roo, the war is ongoing (Sullivan 1989). The city of Cancún is also a contested site. The thousands of workers who built the city struggled to find housing; squatting on ejido lands (communally owned lands) became a tactic to address housing shortages (McLean n.d.). In 2015, sixty-eight informal settlements were scattered throughout the city. Who owns land and who can develop it have shaped local politics and have led to the emergence of grassroots land struggles led by Maya women (Castellanos 2021). Maya struggles for autonomy and land rights have been well documented ethnographically (Sullivan 1989; Castellanos 2010a, 2021; Armstrong-Fumero 2013). Nonetheless, these stories have been excised from tourist imaginaries of Cancún. Inspired by recent studies that aim to decolonize cartography by constructing critical social histories (Craib 2004; Offen and Dym 2011), my analysis provides a critical analysis of the settler colonial narratives embedded in the maps, photographs, and texts of tourist guidebooks.

MAPPING TOURISM

When tourists land in Cancún, they are immediately handed a free copy of the *Mapa Cancun-Xcaret-Xel-Ha Pocket Guide* as they exit the airport.[6] Over 36 million copies have been disbursed. This ubiquitous bilingual (Spanish and English) guidebook includes maps and advertisements of local restaurants and tourist attractions. Its primary objective is to promote consumer spending. Yet, the *Mapa* also orients tourists to a particular worldview about the region's history, geography, and infrastructure. It narrates a tourist fantasy of mass consumption, heteronormativity, and Indigenous spectacles. This vision is reinforced in the videos tourists are exposed to as they travel from airport to hotel; the *combis* (white passenger vans) that ferry show films that narrate this sense of discovery and heteronormative whiteness, making it impossible for tourists to escape this imaginary. Raymond Craib (2004) suggests that coherence and homogeneity are central features of mapmaking; they create spatial realities that paper over conflict and disorder to produce a representational fixity of particular landscapes. *The Mexican Caribbean* and *Maya Riviera* guidebooks are larger tomes, with close to 100 pages of text, photographs, and maps. What worlds and worldviews do they invite us to imagine? What conflicts do they paper over?

I begin by paying attention to the maps located at the end of these guidebooks. At first glance, the tourist maps included in *The Mexican Caribbean* and *Maya Riviera* appear to be basic renderings of the region. But as Walter Little (2011) explains, tourist maps are more than just renderings that provide spatial orientation; they make geopolitical statements. The maps in *The Mexican Caribbean* and *Maya Riviera* feature vast, empty spaces that serve to foreground one of the central tropes of settler colonial narratives—a terra nullius waiting to be discovered and the elimination of Indigenous peoples.

The map of the Yucatán peninsula included in *The Mexican Caribbean* is colorful with cartoonish illustrations.[7] Bold brown lines demarcate the boundaries of the states of Yucatán, Campeche, and Guatemala, segmenting the landscape into vast empty spaces. In contrast, the state of Quintana Roo shows signs of occupation, crowded with a pictorial geography filled with pyramids, Chacmools, hotels, and palm trees. Only tourist destinations are noted on the map; Spanish place-names are translated into English, but Maya place-names are not, thereby generating a sense of the unknown. Published by Spanish-based Editorial Grijalbo in 1984, a decade after Cancún opened its first hotel, this guidebook circulated long before Cancún and the Riviera became the most popular tourist centers in Latin America. The guidebook forms part of government efforts to brand this newly developed tourist region as "The Mexican Caribbean." The empty space also reinforced the sense of discovery for tourists bent on traveling off the beaten track, but close enough to the amenities of sun, sand, and beach. The Maya place-names invite tourists to explore ancient ruins such as Kohunlich and places with exotic names Akumal. A lone white male surfer and two sailboats, one of which is manned by a white male, lay claim to the expanse of deep blue sea. These two figures dwarf the icons of the ruins and hotels, converting Anglo tourists as larger-than-life figures that figuratively dominate this landscape and thus displace Maya people inhabiting the region from the tourist imaginary.

The map in Monclem Ediciones' *Maya Riviera: Cancun–The Islands–Tulum* (2013) is also located at the end of the guidebook (see figure 8.1). It looks like a standard road map with Quintana Roo as its focal point. All major towns, archaeological sites, and tourist attractions are marked and sorted with simple signs: a black dot, square, and triangle. Hovering at its edges, the country of Belice [*sic*] and states of Yucatán, Campeche, and Quintana Roo are marked in bold capitalized letters. The background is filled in muted colors, mint green for biospheres and parks, light blue for the ocean, a sandy color for Quintana Roo, and a light yellow for the other states and countries. Since there are no illustrations, you can follow the road to discover well-known places *and* those off-the-beaten path, most of which are concentrated along the beach. As your eyes move down the coastline, the abundant dots coalesce into a region now called the "Maya Riviera." While this map includes more place-names and thus hints at the presence Maya people in the region, the place-names primarily serve to mark routes through "La Ruta Maya" (Maya Route) made popular by *National Geographic* in 1989.[8]

As Raymond Craib (2004) suggests, maps rely on particular signifiers to produce a homogenized space. In the map in *The Mexican Caribbean*, images of sailboats and white male surfers mark a white leisure space, while images of archaeological ruins hint at an ancient past waiting to be discovered. The map in *Maya Riviera* eschews images and instead turns to modern cartographic routines emblematic in road maps to homogenize space. The peninsula is made knowable—discoverable—because it looks like other road maps. Space is oriented around specific markers such as the beach and archaeological sites. The maps intentionally draw our eyes to the coastline. Indeed, the coastline is the only area to show signs of density and habitation. The whole point of these cartographic practices is to attract foreign tourism. The untranslated Maya place-names add mystery and a sense of the exotic, but they speak to a past, not a present. What is missing in both these maps is the presence of Maya peoples and a sense of the peninsula as more than just a place to see and tour. The only history presented to us is an ancient past and a recognition of a colonial past marked by Spanish place-names, but the history of colonial conflict and revolutionary movements and the contemporary land rights struggles remain unmarked. By erasing the bulk of the villages and towns in the peninsula, these maps funnel tourists along tourism corridors that

Figure 8.1. Map from the Martos, *Maya Riviera.*

are highly traveled and well known, and direct them away from communities that may be impoverished, urbanized, industrialized, or ecologically devastated; speak Yucatec Maya (instead of English); and/or may be ambivalent, even averse to foreigners and tourism (Baños Ramírez 1996; Re Cruz 1996; Juárez 2002; Breglia 2006; Castellanos 2010b; Córdoba Azcárate 2020). Such encounters might challenge the vision of the peninsula as a welcoming and unpopulated tropical haven.

DISCOVERING MAYA CULTURE

Guidebooks, like maps, can also transform our relationships to space, time, and history. The opening line to the text of *The Mexican Caribbean*, written by Armando

Herrerias, harkens back to the Spanish conquest. "During the second decade of the 16th century, white men from Spain discovered Mexico" (Green 1984, 2). To begin with the discovery of Mexico is an intentional reminder of tourism's objective—to mimic this sense of discovery. To focus on white men from Spain draws our attention to settlers, rather than Indigenous peoples. Maya peoples may have inhabited the peninsula for centuries before the Spanish "conquerors" arrived, but it is the conquest that is the focal point. History that matters begins in the sixteenth century. The peninsula is depicted as "untouched . . . virginal tracts" that remained "underdeveloped" because it was the Aztec empire that attracted the Spanish conquistadors. The "splendid capital of the Aztec empire, Mexico-Tenochtitlan" was considered to have economic potential because it provided a "'reservoir' of Indian manual labor" and served as "the gateway to the mining regions that were soon to become the main center for settlement and economic exploitation" (2). While Herrerias acknowledges that the Yucatán peninsula was noted for the presence of "one of the world's greatest Indian cultures," this culture remains nameless and its ghostly presence resulted in keeping the peninsula "basically underdeveloped." According to Herrerias, the peninsula did not experience an economic boom until the nineteenth century with the advent of a plantation economy based on the cultivation of sisal (sisal fibers are used to make rope). Herrerias finally identifies this culture as Maya in relation to tourism. He proclaims Maya culture as the "most fascinating cultural adventures of man" and exemplified by the "Mayan route" of archaeological wonders. We are provided with a literal road map without discussing any people and the history of debt peonage endemic to sisal cultivation.

The main text of *The Mexican Caribbean*, written by M. Green, begins with a discussion of myths popularized in Mexican and Maya folklore. The reference to the myth of Quetzalcoatl justifies colonial domination, and the reference to spiritual life found in the Maya chronicles of Chilam Balam link contemporary Maya peoples with an ancient past. Maya people are introduced as "a happy, healthy beautiful people" and as "descendants of a noble, proud Mayan people" (1984, 4). Like Herrerias, Green associates Maya people with henequen production used to "produce hats, handbags, and mats." We are told that "the Indian is a happy lover of fiestas" and song. Maya peoples are portrayed as mystical, spiritual people who can only be understood in relation to tourism economies and traditions rooted in an ancient past. There is no mention of the debt peonage that made henequen production profitable and the war it sparked. Nor is there a reference to Maya people as a key source of labor for the tourism industry and as urban dwellers (Castellanos 2010b).

Indeed, the discussion of the history of the state of Quintana Roo is framed in relation to Mexican independence and the construction of Cancún. Green writes:

> Until recent times, this region was one of the last unexplored Mexican areas. In 1975, the government decided to aid the development of the coastal area, creating the State of Quintana Roo, with a name that is much esteemed by the Mexicans. Andres Quintana Roo was not only an exceptional writer, but also a prominent leader in the struggle for Mexican independence . . . All manner of tourist services have been created since 1975 in an unprecedented campaign that has taken place with the assistance of the most modern technical means. Some cities, like Cancun [*sic*], have resulted from these recent development[s], always in accordance with a demanding overview program that respects the natural attractions of the region. (1984, 16)

Local history continues to pivot between an ancient Maya civilization and national history Mexican independence, even as the region continues to be depicted as an empty space in need of development.

The text of *Maya Riviera* opens with a bold attempt to brand a region as exotic and empty of all but tourists. Written by archaeologist Luis Martos, it begins:

> The coast of the Mexican state of Quintana Roo, known today as the Maya Riviera, is remarkable for its impressive tourist complexes alternating with dense jungle, savanna, and mangroves, extensive beaches with fine white sands, and warm, crystalline, blue-hued waters. A land of eternal spring, a region of enigmatic Maya cities whose temples stand proudly to this day, between sea and jungle (2013, 3).

Published in coordination with Mexico's Conaculta and INAH, the book immediately introduces us to Maya archaeology, but once again people are missing. Instead, these descriptions invite tourists to explore this lush geography and to uncover the "mystery" of Maya city-states. The emphasis on Maya ruins, instead of contemporary Maya people and culture, speaks to nationalist projects that exalt specific Indigenous groups over others. Sheila Contreras argues that the glorification of Aztec culture serves to construct a "national telos that moves from Teotihuacan to Tenochtitlan to present-day Mexico City" (2008, 6). Similar tactics are at work in the Yucatán peninsula, where the emphasis on an ancient Maya civilization fixates us on Chichén Itzá as historical past and present and thus erases a history of Maya insurrection and contemporary land struggles. Martos narrates the history of this transformation, making the transition from pre-Hispanic settlements to Maya Riviera appear seamless.

The two sections, "Maya Culture" and "Cancún," that follow the introduction reinforce Maya erasure. The section "Maya Culture" focuses exclusively on the political geography of precolonial Maya city-states. Martos then jumps into a description of Cancún's archaeological history, followed by its discovery by foreign explorers such as John Lloyd Stephens and Augustus Le Plongeon. Martos declares:

"In the middle of the 20th century some archeological reconnaissance expeditions were launched along the coastline, which at that time formed part of the territory of Quintana Roo and where only small fishing villages, a few ranches and coconut groves were to be found. However, in 1970 Cancún became the focus of an ambitious tourist project." On page 20, Martos introduces contemporary Maya peoples in relation to the environment. As explained in the section "The Mayas and their Environment":

> The Mayas of the Riviera took full advantage of the natural environment in which they lived; archeological work in the jungle has revealed the existence of a complex network of lots fenced in by walls which functioned as a nucleus of domestic and economic activity.

What follows is a treatise on the crops Maya people cultivated, the wildlife they hunted, and the marine life they consumed. Maya peoples are placed within nature, a nature that is depicted as static across centuries. As a result, they become an extension of nature. This vision of Maya life places Maya people outside of time, denies them complex personhood, and excludes them from modernity (Castellanos 2010b).

The guidebooks also mark transitions in branding practices. What was once called the "Mexican Caribbean" is now envisioned as the "Maya Riviera." This name change speaks to shifting tastes in the tourism industry. When Cancún was first established in the early 1970s, hotel owners were oriented toward the Caribbean with its cruise ship industry. But as tastes moved away from mass tourism, hotel developers sought ways to distinguish this region from popular tourist places in the Caribbean such as Jamaica. To capture the attention of tourists who were interested in luxury ecotourism, the area was rebranded as Maya Riviera. In his introduction, Martos narrates the history of this transformation, making the transition from pre-Hispanic settlements to Maya Riviera appear seamless.

VISUALIZING TOURISM

Like maps, photographs are also synonymous with tourism (Robinson and Picard 2016). Both *The Mexican Caribbean* and *Maya Riviera* include over 150 photographs that take us on a visual tour of the region. Despite the three decades separating the publication of these guidebooks, the photographs are remarkably similar. Both present us with vibrant images of sunsets, empty beaches, and azure ocean waters. Both provide a glimpse of the region's diverse flora and fauna, along with its developed coastline and archaeological ruins. Both include heteronormative white couples or families enjoying this scenery. Both stage hotels and their amenities for our consumption. Since photographs are taken as fact, as realistic impressions of objects (Barthes 1981; Lutz and Collier 1993; Sontag 2001), these comprehensive collections work to make the peninsula familiar, a "known" object that tourists can discover from their hotel rooms before trekking through jungle or wandering through ruins. Indeed, the ubiquity of tourism photographs has converted these staged images into stable signifiers that construct a universal experience of discovery, spanning three decades and multiple rebranding campaigns. Name change aside, this region is recognized globally for its Maya ruins and white sandy beaches. Hurricanes may damage hotels and corporations may buy out or sell hotels, but the beaches and ruins remain iconic, as fixed objects that invite discovery.

Photographs also serve to naturalize and certify events and authenticate landscapes (Barthes 1981; Vergara 1995). The photographs in these guidebooks reinforce a vision of Quintana Roo as a modern, tropical paradise that ignores the peninsula's history of Indigenous insurrections and socialist governments. In *The Mexican Caribbean*, Cancún is represented by the governor's palace, the pruned landscaping of the hotel zone, and large modern hotels. Similarly, the *Maya Riviera* includes panoramic shots of miles of coastline filled with condominium towers and hotel structures, reminiscent more of Miami than Mérida (see figure 8.2).

These images offer a visual representation of a settler colonialism based on whiteness where pristine beaches and luxury hotels stand in for Mexico, displacing a history of frontier politics and invasions of Maya and ejido lands. With a few exceptions, the people captured enjoying this landscape are white heteronormative tourists and families, bolstering the idea of the region as a white settler and heteronormative space. Only the flora, fauna, and archaeological sites represent a Mexican landscape. In both guidebooks, Mexicans and Maya people are included in a few photographs as laborers, as performers, and as living mannequins for traditional textiles. In the *Maya Riviera*, for example, Maya men are shown enacting a ritual that involves rowing a canoe while bare chested and wearing pristine white head bandanas (see figure 8.3). Once again, we are presented with an image of Maya peoples that reduce them to legible types. Juan Castillo Cocom (2021) suggests that beginning in the nineteenth century, ethnographic photographs of Maya people created this fantasy of immutable Mayanness that continues to be reproduced today.

Tourist imaginaries depend on photographs to construct worlds that are spectacular yet at the same time, accessible and consumable. Photographs of the peninsula are familiar because they reproduce narratives of discovery based on a white fantasy of the tropics. This familiarity homogenizes space in order to make these landscapes legible to Anglo tourists. Transnational hotel chains and restaurants such as the Hyatt, McDonald's, and the Hard Rock Cafe also mark these landscapes with recognizable brands that lend credence to this sense of the familiar. One of the key

Figures 8.2 and 8.3. Photos of Cancún and "timeless" Maya culture (Martos 2013, 9 and 43).

selling points and critiques of Cancún is that you can experience Mexico and still have access to Walmart (and other US brands). The demand for familiarity also erases the specificity of place and thus ahistoricizes cities such as Cancún. It's not surprising that Cancún has long been touted as a city of "immigrants," of settlers who arrived to colonize a vast empty space (Martí 1991). Like cartographic routines, photographs erase specificity, making places like Cancún ahistorical. As Raymond Craib points out, "the places people have actively created—the transformations of *space* into *place*—appear preformed and preordained, detached from meaning and experience" (2004, 3). This homogeneity renders places such as Cancún into extensions of a US settler colonial imaginary.

TRANSNATIONAL MAYANNESS

It is important to note that the Mexican government also deployed settler colonial tropes to build its tourism infrastructure, but the settler colonialism visible in *The Mexican Caribbean* and *Maya Riviera* is distinct from the Mexico's approach of inviting settlers to build an urban utopia in the peninsula (Castellanos 2021). The Mexican government considered Cancún an attractive site to create a tourist pole because of its proximity to vast beaches, Maya archaeological ruins, *and* cheap Indigenous labor. While the Mexican government relied on the settler colonial narratives of terra nullius and imagined constructing a city populated by settlers, these settlers included mestizo settlers from Cancún's middle class. In contrast, the guidebooks propagate a transnational Mayanness that is rooted in US settler colonial discourses of discovery, terra nullius, *and* whiteness. What we are presented with is a simple version of Maya culture and history, one that is infinitely consumable and nonthreateningly exotic. *The Mexican Caribbean* reminds tourists that "until recently, the Yucatán peninsula was a virgin land, accessible only to daring, adventurous travelers" (Green 1984, 4). Tourists are invited to once again populate the landscape with their daring. This outlook embodies an American experience of frontier making that is not contingent on Indigenous elimination because ironically it does not acknowledge the Mexican vision of 1960s Quintana Roo as a "frontier" ready to be tamed and occupied. The history of Maya insurrection and the Caste War are not referenced here, even though they play a central role in heritage tourism in the western and central regions of the peninsula (Córdoba Azcárate 2020).

The US fantasy of "adventure" in *The Mexican Caribbean* and *Maya Riviera* also does not hinge on the trope of the encounter. Tourist encounters have mobilized national development projects that invite tourists to engage with local people (Babb 2011). These types of encounters are not visible in *The Mexican Caribbean* and *Maya Riviera*. As a result, these guidebooks preserve the image of Maya peoples as historical figures with a monumental presence embodied in archaeological sites such as Tulum. Contemporary Maya peoples are visible as spectacles in adventure parks such as Xel-Ha and as vendors in marketplaces. *The Mexican Caribbean* also portrays them as innocent and exotic: "Even the beautiful mixture of races has produced a happy, healthy, beautiful people" (Green 1984, 4). We are presented with a caricature of Maya culture and history fixated on craft production, an ancient past, and innocent exotic Others.

CONTESTING TOURIST IMAGINARIES

In the *Atlas de turismo alternativo en la peninsula de Yucatán*, cartographic routines become the means by which to reveal the complex layers that make up tourism in the peninsula. Published by scholars Ana García de Fuentes, Samuel Jouault, and David Romero, in coordination with the universities CINVESTAV and UADY, the *Atlas* is guided by an anthropological lens that attends to the complexity of daily lives in the peninsula. Through its focus on the peninsula, it shifts our gaze away from the sun, sand, and sea topography that dominates *The Mexican Caribbean* and *Maya Riviera*. Instead, its focus is on alternative tourism—broadly defined to encompass ecotourism, low-impact tourism, nature tourism, sustainable tourism, responsible tourism, rural tourism, and community-based tourism. The ubiquitous photograph is replaced with close to eighty maps of the peninsula. Following traditions set by guidebooks such as *The Lonely Planet*, the *Atlas* includes case studies that showcase tourism in Campeche, arts and crafts in Yucatán, and so forth. The *Atlas* offers a counternarrative by presenting tourism as complex, as geared to multiple audiences, as positive and negative, as financial endeavors, and as interconnected with traditional beach and mass tourism. A hardcover tome consisting of 170 pages, the *Atlas* is not a guidebook per se, nor is it available in hotel bookshops. I was gifted a copy by the editors, but anyone can download a PDF copy via Samuel Jouault's page on academia.edu.[9] I compare it to *The Mexican Caribbean* and *Maya Riviera* because editors Ana García de Fuentes, Samuel Jouault, and David Romero are writing against the settler tropes that animate beach tourism. Ana García de Fuentes is a geographer and a faculty member at CINVESTAV who examines regional development. Samuel Jouault is a French anthropologist and a faculty member at the UADY who focuses on tourism and rural development. David Romero is a faculty member in the Energy Laboratory at the UADY who studies sustainable energy. Their diverse backgrounds and perspectives are layered into the *Atlas* to create a complex and regional picture of tourism development.

A peninsular focus disrupts US settler colonial tropes of terra nullius. Each maps details multiple scales of tourism's impact on the entire peninsula. We are shown

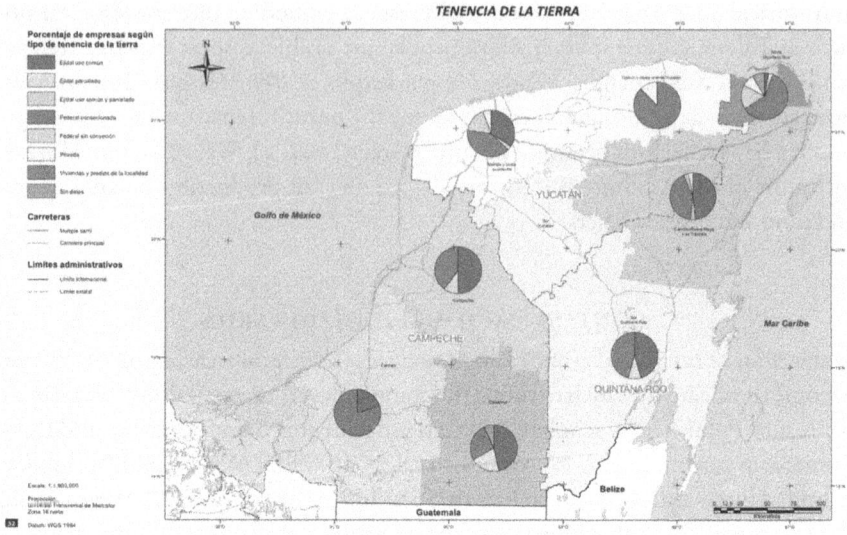

Figure 8.4. Map from Atlas de turismo alternativo en la peninsula de Yucatán.

maps that detail land tenure practices, occupation by gender, the distribution of workers' monthly incomes, the prevalence of financial institutions and cultural sites, access to telecommunications, and so on. The map on land tenure, for example, shows us the percentage of lands made up of ejido land held individually and/or collectively; which lands were expropriated by the government; which lands are private; which lands are locally controlled; and which lands have yet to be mapped or incorporated (see figure 8.4). We are presented with a peninsula that is occupied by multiple actors, institutions, and companies, whose occupation is a product of local and global histories and of the intersections of gender, race, and class. We are also presented with a multitude of facts and references that negates narratives of homogeneity and familiarity.

What the *Atlas* cannot escape is the settler trope of discovery. By relying on cartographic depictions of tourist scales and by acknowledging that alternative tourism forms part of the nexus made up of beach tourism and mass tourism, the *Atlas* remains constrained by tourist conventions. Each map conveys a new world of tourism relations to explore. On the other hand, each map offers a familiar medium by which to explore tourism relations that have been opaque to the tourist gaze. The two photographs included in the *Atlas* aim to highlight community-based tourism—one photograph shows a local boat tour led by a Maya guide and the other photo shows a Maya woman teaching a tourist how to make a hammock.

These images showcase Maya peoples as agentive and as knowledgeable. However, although the tourists in both photographs may be Mexican nationals, they appear to be of Anglo or European extraction. These photographs do not disrupt settler colonial narratives of white settlers "discovering" the peninsula's natural environment and craft traditions. In her study of CBT in Yucatán, Sarah Taylor (2018) points out that archaeological sites Ek'Balam have generated a preponderance of maps that serve to attract tourists to their locations off the beaten path. However, the towns located next to these sites may be left off these maps, as is the case with the town of Ek'Balam, placing them "in the shadow" of these tourist attractions (Taylor 2018, 4). Indeed, I suggest that the lack of maps for places "off the beaten path," including CBT sites, reinforces the sense of "discovery" that tourists seek when they go "off the grid." Although the *Atlas* cannot escape these conventions, it nonetheless seeks to produce a counternarrative to settler fantasies by centering tourism as an economy and highlighting the economic and historical relations that undergird and connect the multiple industries that make up tourism.

UNSETTLING TRANSNATIONAL IMAGINARIES

On March 2, 2021, the *New York Times* published a story entitled "How to Pretend You're in the Riviera Maya Mexico, Today." Heeding the travel restrictions imposed by the global pandemic, it suggests that "with a bit of imagination you can relish the region's culture and cuisine from home," through a virtual tour of "ancient ruins and dazzling cenotes." With its focus on flora, fauna, local cuisine, and archaeological ruins, the story replicates the discovery tropes visible in *The Mexican Caribbean* and *Maya Riviera*. Guidebooks may be updated to cater to tourist demands and tastes, but settler colonial tropes remain entrenched. This story conflates Mayanness with cenotes, cuisine, and ruins. Maya people are absent from this narrative. The only referents to local people are to the musicians Los Folkloristas and Lila Downs, who are not Maya. By resurrecting these tropes, we can once again see transnational Mayanness at work.

Juxtaposing this news coverage, tourist guidebooks, and publications such as the *Atlas de turismo alternativo en la península de Yucatán* illuminates the deep entrenchment of settler colonial tropes in tourist narratives. Uncovering these tropes is essential to any critical engagement with the transnational dimensions of tourist relations and imaginaries. As Ben Fallaw and Fernando Armstrong-Fumero note in their introduction, chapter 1 in this volume, "transnational Mayanness" is an intellectual project that is based on a global imaginary and is far removed from the everyday lived realities of Maya peoples. Tourist guidebooks may claim to introduce foreigners to Maya culture and people, but what they actually do is construct a vision of Mayanness that is discoverable and consumable, and thus legible to a western audience. By illuminating how guidebooks reproduce settler colonial narratives of Indigenous erasure for a global audience, I underscore how these tropes have been used to justify extractive economies such as tourism and the continued exploitation and commodification of Indigenous communities and their culture and labor. In sum, by reading maps and other materials against the grain, it is possible to chart new approaches to US-Mexico relations that disrupt settler colonial narratives of transnational Mayanness and invite us to reassess tourism development and the intellectual projects of anthropology and history.

NOTES

1. Characterized by cheap package deals and group tours, mass tourism has been critiqued for damaging the natural environment and funneling profits to foreign corporations instead of local economies (Wilson 2008; Harrison and Sharpley 2017). To combat this image of unsustainability, tourist centers have turned to ecotourism or alternative tourism.

2. For an ethnographic analysis of settler colonialism in Cancún, see my book *Indigenous Dispossession: Housing and Maya Indebtedness in Mexico* (2021). There is a robust literature on settler colonialism in the United States and Australia. See, e.g., Patrick Wolfe (1999), Jean O'Brien (2010); Jodi Byrd (2011); and Hu Pegues (2021).

3. Armando Herrerías was the former director of the Escuela Mexicana de Turismo in Mexico City, which was founded in 1954 during the administration of President Miguel Alemán. While serving as the president of the Asociación de Holeteles en la Ciudad de México (Association of Hotels in Mexico City) in 1959, he accompanied Miguel Alemán, who had moved on to serve as the director of the Consejo Nacional de Turismo (National Council of Tourism), in the quest to find potential tourist sites in Mexico's southeastern region, which resulted in designating Cancún as a tourist pole (Sosa Ferreira, Pricila, and Jiménez Martínez n.d.). I have been unable to find information about the author M. Green.

4. The Mexican government established the National Institute of Anthropology in 1939 to protect and conserve Mexico's heritage (archaeological, paleontological, and anthropological) and history. In 1988, Conaculta was established to promote and protect culture and the arts in Mexico.

5. For a rich analysis of the Caste War, see Redfield (1941); Reed (1964); and Rugeley (1996).

6. For a sample of this guidebook, see https://mapapocket.com/tag/guia/.

7. Images are not included from *The Mexican Caribbean* because I was unable to procure permission to reprint from Grijalbo.

8. The Ruta Maya begins in Cancún and encompasses five Central American countries.

9. See https://www.academia.edu/23467556/Atlas_de_turismo_alternativo_en_la_Pe n%C3%ADnsula_de_Yucatán.

REFERENCES CITED

Armstrong-Fumero, Fernando. 2013. Elusive Unity: Factionalism and the Politics of Identity in Yucatán, Mexico. Boulder: University Press of Colorado.

Babb, Florence. 2011. The Tourist Encounter: Refashioning Latin American Nations and Histories. Stanford, CA: Stanford University Press.

Baños Ramírez, Othon. 1996. "Neoliberalismo, reorganización y subsistencia rural." El caso de la zona henequenera de Yucatán: 1980–1992. Mérida: Universidad Autónoma de Yucatán.

Barthes, Roland. 1981. Camera Lucida: Reflections on Photography. New York: Hill and Wang.

Breglia, Lisa. 2006. Monumental Ambivalence: The Politics of Heritage. Austin: University of Texas Press.

Byrd, Jodi. 2011. The Transit of Empire: Indigenous Critiques of Colonialism. Minneapolis: University of Minnesota Press.

Castellanos, M. Bianet. 2010a. "Don Teo's Expulsion: Property Regimes, Moral Economies, and Ejido Reform." Journal of Latin American and Caribbean Anthropology 15 (1): 144–69.

Castellanos, M. Bianet. 2010b. A Return to Servitude: Maya Migration and the Tourist Trade in Cancún. Minneapolis: University of Minnesota Press.

Castellanos, M. Bianet. 2017. "Introduction: Settler Colonialism in Latin America." American Quarterly 69 (4): 771–81.

Castellanos, M. Bianet. 2021. Indigenous Dispossession: Housing and Maya Indebtedness in Mexico. Stanford, CA: Stanford University Press.

Castellanos, M. Bianet, and Matilde Córdoba Azcárate. 2021. "Guardians of Tradition: The Affective and Popular Geopolitics of Yucatec Maya Women on Tour." In Tourism Geopolitics: Assemblages of Infrastructure, Affect, and Imagination, edited by Mary Mostafanezhad, Matilde Córdoba Azcárate, and Roger Norum. Tucson: University of Arizona Press.

Castillo Cocom, Juan. 2021. "Visión etnográfica: Imaginar el iknal maya." Journal of Latin American and Caribbean Anthropology 26 (1): 10–24.

Contreras, Sheila. 2008. Blood Lines: Myth, Indigenism, and Chicana/o Literature. Austin: University of Texas Press.

Córdoba Azcárate, Matilde. 2020. Stuck with Tourism: Space, Power, and Labor in Contemporary Yucatán. Berkeley: University of California Press.

Craib, Raymond. 2004. Cartographic Mexico: A History of State Fixations and Fugitive Landscapes. Durham, NC: Duke University Press.

García de Fuentes, Ana, Samuel Jouault, and David Romero, eds. 2015. Atlas de turismo alternativo en la peninsula de Yucatán. Mérida: CINVESTAV, UADY.

Green, M. 1984. The Mexican Caribbean. Barcelona: Grijalbo.

Harrison, David, and Richard Sharpley, eds. 2017. Mass Tourism in a Small World. English: CABI.

Hu Pegues, Juliana. 2021. Space-Time Colonialism: Alaska's Indigenous and Asian Entanglements. Chapel Hill: University of North Carolina Press.

Juárez, Ana María. 2002. "Ecological Degradation, Global Tourism, and Inequality: Maya Interpretations of the Changing Environment in Quintana Roo, Mexico." Human Organization 60 (2): 113–24.

"La Ruta Maya." 1989. National Geographic 176, no. 4 (October).

Little, Walter. 2011. "Mayas and Tourist Markets." In Mapping Latin America: A Cartographic Reader, edited by Karl Offen and Jordana Dym, 241–45. Chicago: University of Chicago Press.

Lutz, Catherine A., and Jane L. Collins. 1993. Reading National Geographic. Chicago: University of Chicago Press.

Mclean, Megan. n.d. "Squatters in Paradise: State-Led Tourism Development in Cancún, 1970–1995." Unpublished thesis.

Martí, Fernando. 1991. Cancun: Fantasy of Bankers. Translated by Jules Siegel. Mexico City: Editora Martí.

Martos, Luis. 2013. Maya Riviera: Cancun–The Islands–Tulum. English ed. Mexico City: Monclem Ediciones.

O'Brien, Jean. 2010. Firsting and Lasting: Writing Indians Out of Existence in New England. Minneapolis: University of Minnesota Press.

Offen, Karl, and Jordana Dym, eds. 2011. Mapping Latin America: A Cartographic Reader. Chicago: University of Chicago Press.

Re Cruz, Alicia. 1996. The Two Milpas of Chan Kom: A Study of Socioeconomic and Political Transformation in a Maya Community. Albany: State University of New York Press.

Redfield, Robert. 1941. The Folk Culture of Yucatan. Chicago: University of Chicago Press.

Reed, Nelson. 1964. The Caste War of Yucatan. Stanford, CA: Stanford University Press.

Robinson, Mike, and David Picard, eds. 2016. The Framed World: Tourism, Tourists, and Photography. London: Routledge.

Rugeley, Terry. 1996. Yucatán's Maya Peasantry and the Origins of the Caste War. Austin: University of Texas Press.

Sontag, Susan. 2001. On Photography. New York: Picador.

Sosa Ferreira, Ana Pricila, and Alfonso Jiménez Martínez. n.d. "Crónica de un conflicto anunciado (o de-nunciado): El caso de Playas Delfines en Cancún." In Turismo y conflictos socio-ambientales en Centroamérica, edited by Ernest Cañada, 222–50. Managua: Enlace.

Sullivan, Paul. 1989. Unfinished Conversations: Mayas and Foreigners between Two Wars. Berkeley: University of California Press.

Taylor, Sarah R. 2018. On Being Maya and Getting By: Heritage Politics and Community Development in Yucatán. Louisville: University Press of Colorado.

Vergara, Benito. 1995. Displaying Filipinos: Photography and Colonialism in early 20th Century Philippines. Quezon City: University of the Philippines Press.

Wilson, Tamar Diana. 2008. "Economic and Social Impacts of Tourism in Mexico." Latin American Perspectives 35 (3): 37–52.

Wolfe, Patrick. 1999. Settler Colonialism and the Transformation of Anthropology. London: Cassell.

9

The Production and Archiving of a Design-Driven
Mayanness in Hacienda Tourism, Yucatán

MATILDE CÓRDOBA AZCÁRATE

In the twenty-first century, tourism has become a leading variable in the production of history.[1] Processes of memorialization, remembering, and pilgrimage to mnemonic places are vastly ruled by tourism's logics, desires, and imaginations. In many places around the world, these processes have been, moreover, only enabled by the material infrastructures created by states and transnational corporations to directly support tourism and its associated flows of capital, labor, commodities and cultural representations—international airports, railroad systems, highways and maritime routes; museums, galleries, and pop-up exhibitions; monuments, heritage sites, and hospitality services, such as those involved in booking hotel rooms, excursions, or rentals. These tourism infrastructures are actively engineering social and physical spaces; transforming ecological relations; and directly intervening in the production of stories about the past, identity and belonging. For this reason, tourism should not be accounted any longer as just a sector of the economy or as a particular form of social interaction. Tourism is a leading vector in the archiving of socioecological life.

In this chapter, I am interested in the different ways in which tourism shapes the boundaries between memory and oblivion about Mayanness. I build on extensive ethnographic research on tourism development in the Yucatán peninsula. This region has been a privileged object of Mexican and North American archaeological and anthropological knowledge production about Mayan peoples since the early twentieth century. It has also been massively transformed by state

198

tourism development and international corporate capital since the mid-1970s with the Mexican state creation of the city of Cancún and its establishment, just a few years later, as a leading international beach tourism enclave. Since then, national and transnational tourism actors—including tourism entrepreneurs and stakeholders, urban planners, designers and architects, and bankers and global corporations in the hospitality industry—have become, along with historians, anthropologists, and archaeologists, fundamental actors in the production of knowledge about Mayanness. These actors have not only become the new repositories of a shared knowledge about the region—still in the making—but they also share common goals to create experiences of encounter with "the Maya" according to their own definitions. These shared goals involve the material and symbolic transformation of the landscape, as well as producing novel popular archives in and of the region that selectively appropriate and expand the existing scholarly ones.

The chapter focuses on hacienda tourism, one of the most recent tourism ventures in inland Yucatán, which involves the costly and selective architectural transformation of old ex-henequen haciendas into boutique luxury hotels. Specifically, I look at Hacienda Temozón Sur, the pioneer of a tourism venture known as the Haciendas Yucatán, owned by an important Mexican billionaire and businessman and currently managed by the US giant Marriot Group's Luxury Collection; and Hacienda Xcanatun, currently managed by the Asian corporation Banyan Tree–Ansanga and owned by a couple of film and advertising executives linked by kin to the well-known Mexican archaeologist of the region, Alberto Ruz Lhuillier.

Far from unique, Hacienda Temozón Sur and Hacienda Xcanatun are pioneer examples of other contemporary ventures involving the restoration of historical buildings for elite cultural consumption in and around urban Mérida. Most of the restorations are made for tourism, and they demand Indigenous labor service. They are also exclusively in the hands of private wealthy families and individuals who have found in Mérida their second residence and in "the Maya" a source of self-centered spirituality. Moreover, many of these restored buildings are managed by family-owned businesses with close ties to the realms of global education and the arts. Their work is generally done through private societies and foundations, and it directly contributes to a nascent New Age international library on Indigenous wisdom and traditions as sources for holistic well-being. This emergent library is mostly conformed by what librarians would call gray literature—that is, professional and business-oriented publications that are produced outside of traditional commercial and academic publishing circuits and that are often distributed privately and for profit. Ethnographic research on some of these restorations offers light into who these individuals and corporations are as well as into the active role they play in the archiving of a particular corporate, design-driven

Mayanness for tomorrow. I use the expression of a design-driven Mayanness to signal a preliminary take into the analysis of these transnational corporate agents and the sociomaterial outcomes of their practices in the Yucatán peninsula.

Materials of this chapter are part of a larger anthropological project and long-standing ethnographic research in the Yucatán peninsula that recently led to the publication of my book *Stuck with Tourism: Space, Power, and Labor in Contemporary Yucatán* (2020). One of the chapters of that book explored in ethnographic detail the moral ambivalences that the transformation of Hacienda Temozón Sur into a boutique hotel had for the workers and inhabitants of the municipality of Temozón Sur, where the hacienda is located. In the process of doing that ethnographic research in the late 1990s and early 2000s, I learned about Hacienda Xcanatun, a nearby hacienda being restored at that same time under a somewhat different approach from Temozón Sur. As hacienda Xcanatun owners put it, their approach was "attentive to the historical specificity of the buildings," and to "local archeological knowledge," and not "mostly invested in global architectonic trends" such as they claimed for Temozón Sur. I could not elaborate on this declared discrepancy in my book. In this chapter, I bring these two ventures into conversation. I explore who and what capital are behind these transformations, and I try to make sense of what is the Mayanness that these tourism actors advocate for and/or preclude. I draw on my ethnographic field notes, diaries, and participant observations at these sites between 2000 and 2010. This fieldwork included interviews with some of the hacienda owners, with the managers, workers, and inhabitants of the localities where the haciendas are located. Through 2020 and 2021, I complemented those empirical materials with new analysis of secondary sources. This analysis has involved first, research on the history of the haciendas, their ownership changes, and labor practices; second, media analysis of international, national, and regional news on both haciendas, their new owners, their respective management hotel corporations, and their brand stories and philosophies; and, third, the identification and analysis of the publications and events on Maya wisdom that some of the hacienda owners and their relatives produced. I also paid special attention to a growing number of regional and local news on disputes on public space in the municipalities where the restored hacienda hotels are located as well as to the analysis of popular online tourism branding campaigns and travel brochures. I hope this comparison serves to illuminate the centrality of tourism as a leading actor in the production of history and to listen to and keep contesting the contours, form, and content of the colonial matrix of power (Quijano 2000) in which archiving Mayanness has always been trapped, yet now, through tourism, in such a blatantly predatory capitalist fashion.

HACIENDA TOURISM: OBSESSED WITH THE PAST
AND "THE MAYA" AS SPIRITUAL RESOURCE

Since the creation of Cancún in 1974, tourism has been a major vehicle in the reorganization of the Yucatán peninsula's landscapes, sociospatial relations, and imaginations. State tourism in earnest mostly concerned the Caribbean coast of the region. It radically transformed its built environment to accommodate Eurocentric tourist imaginaries of "escape" to paradisical beaches. Initial transformations were sustained in time through the enclosure of the beach and the engineering of all-inclusive resort hotels that secured the area for tourists at the same time as pushing migrant workers and irregular, unfettered urbanization out of tourists' sight. Archaeological tourism was soon developed in and around the well-studied archaeological Maya sites of Chichén Itzá and Uxmal—only hours away from Caribbean resorts. Protected as UNESCO cultural heritage sites since the mid-1990s, these archaeological sites promise "Mexican culture" and a sanitized "Mayanness" as part of packaged vacations at beach resorts. In these cases, Mayanness is always synonymous with the ancient Maya and the geographical location where the ruins are located. For tourists' quest for authenticity, these excursions soon proved to not be enough.

To satisfy growing consumer desires of experiencing cultural authenticity, in the mid-1990s, state-led cultural tourism reorganized Yucatán's inland landscapes around transnational tourism imaginaries of authentic cultural encounters with "living real Maya." To do so, cultural tourism moved away from sea, sand, and sun tourism models that privileged standardized, passive consumption of sites and put the emphasis on the promotion of active encounters with local Maya habitats, heritage, and histories (Smith 1989). These cultural tourism imaginaries of local encounters with "the Maya" are deeply influenced by the vast scholarly imagination of the region as a "world apart," as "a laboratory." These scholarly imaginations are driven by transnational, mostly foreign liberal, universalistic archaeological knowledge production and representational practices. Still mostly concerned with material culture restoration practices at internationally sanctioned archaeological excavations sites (Watson 2014), cultural tourism in Yucatán has put Mayanness, old and contemporary, to work for nationalist purposes through tourism (Breglia 2006; Loewe 2010; Córdoba Azcárate 2020).

Since the 2000s, cultural tourism in Yucatán has massively depended on private actors who work under philanthropic capitalist undertakings side by side with the Mexican state. Slowly, but steadily, this form of tourism has distanced itself from already too crowded and standardized tourism at archaeological zones to set its sights on nearby historical buildings such as haciendas. Hacienda tourism is a particular niche of the industry that was born because of this process.

Hacienda tourism is geographically concentrated in the areas that surround the fast-growing city of Mérida. These areas were once devoted to the agroindustry of the henequen and largely abandoned by the state since the fiber's demise. Currently they are under immense urban demographic and real estate pressures linked to Mérida's intense urban growth and to land speculation associated with the Tren Maya (Maya Train)—a megainfrastructure development by President Andrés Manuel López Obrador to further tourism in the Mexican Southeast. This situation makes of land around Mérida, and haciendas in particular, a coveted space for developers and conservationists alike. Where the first see haciendas and its landholdings as appealing infrastructure for future malls and housing subdivisions, the latter see abandoned green spaces capable of containing distressing levels of urban pollution and heat.

As a tourist product, haciendas' marketing highlights their proximity to archaeological Maya sites. They mostly emphasize this physical proximity as a vehicle into a slower and deeper knowledge of the self through an engagement with "romance," "healing," and "seclusion." This engagement is expected to happen *only* within the boundaries of the hacienda's enclosed and highly curated landscapes. Most tourist advertising revolves around desires to "experience the past," with elements from "Maya wisdom" and "traditional healing methods" that occur in "sacred places" or historically meaningful locales that have been repurposed for profit under western-centric ideas of spirituality and wellness. Emphasis is placed in the architectural curatorial work and the landscaping put in place to activate a "real sense of place" for those who look for "design-driven" experiences and aspirations to "give back" in their travel practices. For these reasons and despite being officially classified and promoted as a variant of cultural tourism, hacienda tourism is, in fact, a good representative of the recently named New Age tourism. This is a form of tourism that aims for the displacement of culture from the purely material and into the realm of the experiential. It is a form of tourism "obsessed with the past" only insofar as it can become a source of self-oriented wellness, spirituality, motivation and, satisfaction (Pernecky and Johnston 2006; Gómez-Barris 2012).

Hacienda hotels crave to procure unique experiences that are *spatially bound* to architectures already legitimized as *historically meaningful* by the Mexican state and the international community along with hegemonic processes of cultural protection and representation—in Yucatán, largely sanctioned by both Mexican and North American archaeological practices of knowledge production. Hacienda hotels appropriate these already existing archives and their canons, but they engage too in the direct modification of their immediate surrounding environments to mark continuities with European landscaping practices and, as I have argued elsewhere (Córdoba Azcárate 2020), place Indigenous bodies back in old spaces of production under similarly coercive labor dynamics as the ones observed by historians when haciendas were productive henequen spaces (Fallaw 2001). The way of operating these restorations varies for each hacienda. Yet, there are meaningful similarities that enable me to hint at the growing role that these restored buildings are playing in the larger tourist driven reproduction of a colonial Mayanness—understood here as a place-based and distinct set of consumables and objectifiable elements occurring in contemporary Yucatán. In this reproduction, restored haciendas for tourism act as part of a larger sociomaterial terrain in which Mayanness becomes bound to nostalgic colonial pasts, and to hegemonic stories of land interventions, and in which they are done entirely for private profit. A few words about haciendas are in order before delving into the processes of their renovation for tourism and the selective archives that these economic and intellectual infrastructural interventions are both building on and contributing to create.

DESIGN-DRIVEN COLONIALITY IN SEMI-INDUSTRIAL ABANDONED BUILDINGS

Haciendas in Yucatán worked as plantations (Wells 1991).[2] They were specialized in the production and commercialization of henequen—Mexico's "green gold" and the region's monocrop from the last quarter of the nineteenth century until the mid-twentieth century. Haciendas not only structured the economic life of Yucatán. They also articulated its sociopolitical organization and cultural dynamics.

Henequen haciendas' social organization was comprised of the hacendados, or landowners, who were mainly creoles (persons born and naturalized in Yucatán but of European origin), and the peones, or land workers, mainly Indigenous Maya and for some time, migrant workers from Korea and other parts of Mexico, mostly Yaqui *indígenas* from Sonora. Neither hacendados nor peones were homogeneous social groups; they varied greatly according to their origins, cultural and racial backgrounds, commercial interests, and ideologies. Yet, both collectives shared several characteristics that make it possible to conceive of them as distinctive social groups (Ancona Riestra and Universidad Autónoma de Yucatán 1996). First, hacendados shared what Allen Wells (1991) defines as the "hacendado elite mentality" guided by the principle that "no expense is too great." The result of this mentality was sumptuous material consumption, including ostentatious homes, ornate carriages, grandiose parties for "la gente decente de Mérida" (literally, "decent people" from Mérida), and frequent trips to Europe (Wells 1991, 134–35). Second, hacendados had total control over the processes of production and distribution of the henequen until the Mexican Revolution arrived in the region (Backlanoff and Moseley 2008). Third, they exercised severe political and repressive power over the peones; and fourth, peones were subjected to what has been defined as helpless peonage or regimes of semislavery (Alston, Mattiace, and Nonnenmacher 2009; Katz 1974).

During the henequen times, haciendas used a system of hereditary debts and loans aimed at controlling labor, mostly through housing and job incentives and marriage, to discourage Maya workers from fleeing (Mattiace and Nonnenmacher 2014, 367). These coercive methods were crucial in establishing a dependent relationship that tethered peones to hacendados, who were themselves tied to regional political elites (Nickel 1997). Haciendas' architecture was an important contributor to organizing, sustaining, and reinforcing this asymmetrical social organization. Buildings and infrastructures featured spatially segmented and architecturally distinct population settlements and domestic units, and they were designed to maximize productivity and inscribe hacendados' power in the landscape (Peniche Rivero 1999).

Although their composition varied across the region, the architectural design of haciendas, referred to as *hacienda style* in global circuits, is defined as eclectic (Witynski and Carr 2008). It is mostly known for the rich architectonical features and unique heterogeneous styles of Casas Principales. Casas Principales, however, were only part and parcel of haciendas, usually the largest building where the hacendados kept their living quarters and in which most of the administration took place. But the hacienda had other spaces too, including Maya vernacular houses, where resident peones lived; and other major constructions under hacendados' administration and control such as the *tienda de raya*, or company store; the *casa de maquinas*, or machine house, where the henequen processing took place; the *casa del mayordomo*, where the foreman lived and where the administration took place when the hacendado was away; a *calabozo*, or jail; and the *capilla*, or chapel, which stressed the importance of the hacienda as a population center. This collection of spaces is known as the *casco* of the hacienda. In addition to the casco, the hacienda also included the fields where henequen was planted and harvested, as well as the population's settlements and workers' living quarters.

Restored haciendas in contemporary Yucatán mostly refer to *Casas Principales*, which still stand out in the landscape for their eclecticism and grandiose structures if compared to the buildings around them. Their traditional gated entrances, made of *pilares de acceso* (large pillars) still inscribe in rural Yucatán a clear socioeconomic and spatial hierarchy between haciendas' owners and the rest of the municipalities or *comisarías* (smaller populations) where they are located. This is a socioeconomic and spatial hierarchy that hacienda tourism not only reproduces but has perfected. It has done so by anchoring nostalgic representations of Mayanness to areas close to those with an existing and documented history of western archaeological excavation such as Chichén Itzá, Tulum, and Uxmal, all added to the UNESCO

World Heritage List in 1997. Yet, while these archaeological sites have also become agglomerated and packed with the same "passive hordes" as beach resorts, semi-industrial buildings such as haciendas repurposed as colonial architectures and with holistic wellness in mind, claim to offer the real Mayanness, one that is approached through connection, spirituality, and "magic."

Hacienda hotels capitalize on the promise to deliver heritage as something old and monumental rescued with "good taste" (Kirshenblatt-Gimblett 1998) and not accessible, price-wise, to all pockets. Landscape and architectonical repurposing have been done through "imperial eyes" (Pratt 2007) and reactivate what, for many in Yucatán, is but "imperial debris" (Stoler 2013). This return is done through internationally sanctioned western discourses on cultural heritage and historical preservation as well as through transnational public-private and philanthropically orchestrated responses to an increasingly global awareness about the rights of Indigenous peoples, environmental sustainability, social responsibility, and holistic well-being. For these reasons, hacienda hotels seem to be part of larger transnational intellectual and economic infrastructures that exemplify larger trends in philanthropic capitalism, according to which capitalism can be philanthropic in and of itself.

Despite specific differences, hacienda tourism shares several important interventions in inland Yucatán regarding land ownership and management, labor organization, and the production and distribution of cultural representations. Notably, they also share a common way of producing and distributing knowledge about Mayanness as well as a common agenda in their goals regarding how to put Mayanness to work for profit.

First, hacienda tourism involves an ownership change of the hacienda—its buildings and land—from the state or from a private family generally linked to the henequen oligarchy, to public-private or private owners with transnational networks in the economic and cultural fields as well as shared transnational corporate management. This form of mixed ownership and transnational corporate management is not exclusive to Yucatán. It has been described in other parts of the world as part of larger global trends in philanthropic capitalism that is conducive to increased financialization and commodification of cultural practices for the global market.

Second, hacienda tourism involves selective and costly architectonical restoration practices. These practices have targeted casas principales and their immediate environmental surroundings, specifically gardens and housing. Restorations involve expert and disciplinary exchanges among architects, archeologists, and designers. They involve the production and circulation of curated, nostalgic, static, and reductionist stories about Mayanness as a luxury commodity. These stories are colonial stories, and they are primarily shared through a growing body of New Age gray literature. This literature contributes to a particular shared transnational language that communicates to the public what "the Maya is" along with liberal, universalist knowledge production practices and canons already dominant in the history of the region as an object of scholarly attention. Besides, the expertise of those in charge of restorations also resides in their capacity to use the knowledge produced through these intellectual networks to fashion a physical environment where tourist expectations of encounters with Maya cosmology are fulfilled.

Third, hacienda tourism demands the offer of lived experiences of cultural otherness that expand traditional scholarly definitions of Mayanness as place-specific archaeology only. At haciendas, this experience is offered mostly through a curated transnational promotion of selective culinary and body healing experiences claimed to be done the "Maya way" yet produced and reproducing colonial ideas about Indigenous bodies as inferior to and at the service of those of western tourists. At hacienda hotels, tourists are invited to step into the romance of Yucatán's Gilded Age with "Maya features" (Meyers 2012, 170), which involves the active erasure of discussions on labor, land struggles, and heterogeneity of Indigenous identities *at the same time as* selectively remembering certain aspects of them, those that refer to an alternative, holistic cosmology. On a global scale, this holistic Mayanness is curated as part of family- and privately driven education institutions and for-profit art initiatives. These practices directly contribute to and expand colonial practices of silencing subaltern Indigenous stories that might pose misunderstandings, or slippages of meaning with respect to the official representation of the region as "the land of the Maya," a "playground" for global tourism consumption. In doing so, hacienda tourism seems to be fostering the state's historically documented project of fixing and flattening Indigenous temporalities, spaces, and bodies for global consumption (Craib 2004)—that is, "forging uniform regional and local landscapes as well as reifying cultural difference for the benefit of global consumption" and, in so doing, eliminating "the possibility for eventualities or rebellion, and the instigation of a temporality of just-in-time production that enables the enclosure of land as well as the uneven movement of capital and the privileged classes across geographical space" (Castellanos and Córdoba Azcárate 2021, 232).

These similarities and the far-reaching extent of their economic and intellectual practices make me think of them as conforming to a nascent transnational tourism archive for the region and beyond. This tourism archive that hacienda tourism seems to be pointing at has its own logic of *accumulation of historical records* as well as its own *compositional logic*. It is an archive because the transformations that it points at and that constitute it are not ephemeral and because they undoubtedly hold the capacity to reorient our relationship to the past and to the future in the land and beyond. As the haciendas' restoration addressed here show, the *accumulation of historical records* in the tourism archive is privately driven, is market oriented, and involves vast, yet selective, material transformations of the built environment for tourism purposes only. It also demands a curated intervention in the realm of popular culture and content production for for-profit education venues. The *compositional logic* of the tourism archive participates in what Fernando Armstrong-Fumero (2009, 300) calls a "nondisruptive ambiguity" about Mayanness. That is, it aims—with different gradients—to incorporate vernacular stories yet "does not disrupt official projects" of hegemonic state formation or colonial knowledge production practices about the region.

In the surroundings of Mérida's expanding urban sprawl, new hacienda owners have become powerful agents in political decisions regarding the fate of housing, transportation, service provision, and leisure. They have become gatekeepers and direct mediators in municipal urban planning. Xcanatun, in the north of Mérida, and Temozón Sur, south of Mérida, have both seen their municipal development plans encroached upon by private and for-profit tourism calculations that oftentimes work directly against the future well-being of the communities and directly in favor of hacienda owners and their corporate partners. I see these ongoing displacements as part of the material traces of this uneven tourist archive in the making. Despite their differences, particularly in regard to the dismissal or embrace of existing archaeological liberal canons about the Maya, both cases show how hacienda hotels have become pivotal intellectual and economic infrastructures in charge of producing a transnational and tourist-oriented archive of a "feel good history" (Meyers 2012, 171) that is materially and culturally carving up the local and regional landscape as well as memories of inland Yucatán and Mayanness, for profit, and under clear colonial legacies.

HACIENDA TEMOZÓN SUR

Hacienda tourism in Yucatán is almost synonymous with a particular tourism venture named the Haciendas Yucatán. This is a private-public partnership between the state and the private and nonprofit sectors united in a rhetoric of heritage preservation, Indigenous empowerment, and social responsibility that burgeoned in inland Yucatán after Hurricane Isidore in 2002.

The Haciendas Yucatán is a group of five repurposed ex-henequen haciendas located in the states of Yucatán and Campeche, and of which Hacienda Temozón Sur, south of Mérida, is the flagship property. The Haciendas are owned by one of Mexico's richest businesspeople. It is important to mention that they have become the loci for the creation and maintenance of a series of lucrative associations and programs directly related to education and infrastructure development that have a direct say in how Mayanness is currently defined in Mexico, the United States, and beyond.

As part of the Marriot Corporation's Luxury Collection, the Haciendas Yucatán are branded as part of historical heritage preservation discourses, mobilizing the nearby UNESCO World Heritage sites of Uxmal and Mayapan, and, more recently, Izamal. Within the collection, Hacienda Temozón is promoted as having "small-town charm" which is "set deep in the Yucatán and not too far from the fabled Mayan site, Chichén Itzá" (Córdoba Azcárate 2020, 123). To create and secure this image, the architectural firm in charge of renovations and related by kin to the new owners rebuilt the former hacienda walls and gates originally created to keep a sense of isolation but also to prevent workers from fleeing (Ancona Riestra and Universidad Autónoma de Yucatán 1996). They replaced the old layout of streets and houses close to the Casa Principal with an idyllic row of traditional Maya vernacular huts at the hacienda's main entrance, which are currently used as crafts workshops. The Casa Principal has been transformed into a twenty-eight-room luxury retreat. The building has been carefully painted with its traditional colors. Original materials—such as iron, stone, and wood—were maintained for major visible structures, while the furniture and decorations in common areas and rooms re-create the European Renaissance style of the hacienda's former owners (Ancona Riestra and Universidad Autónoma de Yucatán 1996). The rest of the buildings within the hacienda were retrofitted to serve tourism consumption purposes too. The old machine house, for example, was converted into a museum space in which restored everyday objects are exhibited together with a collection of black-and-white images from the hacendado's private albums. In all these pictures, the hacendado and those around him, wear European-style clothing and accessories. The objects on display (e.g., bicycles, lady's umbrellas, children's toys) reflect the luxuries of the hacendado's life, and there are no references to the hacienda as being a highly inegalitarian socioeconomic system. The spaces that were used for drying and storing henequen have been transformed into tennis courts, jogging tracks, swimming pools, and conference rooms.

The hacienda's thirty-seven-hectare gardens have been curated as an imitation of the formal gardening or "gardens of order" of the Palace of Versailles, near Paris, with the clear intention to revive the region's hacendados' reimagined consanguinity with Europe. Guests can linger in carefully planned shaded spaces where they are soothed by the rhythmic sounds of water fountains and artificial pools. There is a botanical garden, in which clients can read, in English and Maya, the labels that describe several of the most important medicinal plants collected by the architectural group in charge of renovations. Here, Maya medicine matters because it is another signifier of a commodifiable Mayanness—as tradition. These plants are later sold at the local workshops and the haciendas' boutique stores as "Indigenous folk plants" by Maya women working for the hacienda hotel.

As a way of creating an elite tourist experience of the past, "ancient," "traditional," and "holistic mystical" treatments promise to put guests in touch with "Maya ancient culture." Following New Age tourism trends on spirituality and personal discovery, at Temozón Sur, these treatments typically consist of therapeutic body massages that revitalize, energize, and purify the self, and they are promoted as spiritual encounters with the self through Indigenous others. Massages and spa rituals take place in the "cave spa," in the village's cenote, privatized and removed from its communal uses as a religious, spiritual, and recreational family spot (Ruz 2006; Stone 2010; Marín Guardado 2008, 2012). The spa has trained young native women from Temozón to perform these *sobadas* (massages). Using sobadas as massages has required to resignify the meaning of the still active work of rural Maya *parteras* (midwives), *sobadoras* (healers), and *chamanes* (shamans) for tourism consumption. Inside the hotel, sobadas have lost their meaning and symbolism as a practice still performed by either old women to help other women in labor or by male shamans to heal the sick body. The hacienda hotel also has an on-site shaman, originally from Switzerland, who specializes, as promotions put it, "in mystical medicine, Mayan rituals and traditions."

These on-site practices are well connected with the owner's "spiritual motivations" and "mystical connection to the Maya culture," as a Mexican journalist once described them to me. They transcend the hacienda hotel's immediate grounds. In fact, Hacienda Temozón Sur Hotel stands as a node in larger global intellectual infrastructures of knowledge production about the region. It is just a player in a broader game of geopolitical interests in which Mayanness becomes but a branded economic asset. This role is evident when looking closer at both the hacienda hotel's role as a site and symbol of binational dialogue, as well as at the for-profit educative ventures directly and indirectly related to it.

Images of the hacienda's casa principal are extensively used as part of a Mexico invested in cultural heritage and dialogue both at a national and international scales. In February 1999, three years prior to its opening to the public, Hacienda Temozón Sur hosted Presidents Ernesto Zedillo and Bill Clinton. A private heliport was built for the occasion. In March 2007, Presidents Felipe Calderón and George W. Bush met for their first Mexico–United States presidential summit also at Hacienda Temozón Sur. In preparation for the presidential summit, the electricity network and paved roads were extended in Temozón Sur, and, additionally, the six Maya vernacular huts that serve as workshops were refurbished and painted bright red and white to match the hacienda hotel's walls in so doing, creating an idyllic Indigenous village that forms a polished corridor leading to the hacienda's gates. This romanticized staging of political dialogue stood in stark contrast with journalists' reports at the time who described both the hacienda hotel as "a bunker hotel" and its surroundings as quasi-militarized areas in preparation and during the presidents' visits.

Talking to the people of Temozón during my fieldwork a few years after the 2007 summit, it soon became clear that the militarized atmosphere conveyed in journalists' accounts was far from exceptional. It pointed at the strategic situation of the Hacienda Hotel as a node in a broader infrastructural network of economic and political relations. "Sites of exception" is what happens, they told me, each time the hacienda hotel receives "important guests," such as presidents and politicians, but also pop stars, film and television idols, and families from the Mexican and Yucatecan elites. These guests book the hacienda hotel to film and record albums and telenovelas, or to celebrate weddings, quinceañeras, and other special events. On these occasions, hacienda hotel workers must wait inside the hacienda's gates and "the town is under siege." Workers are on call twenty-four hours a day to respond to the guests' desires and needs, and often they say they are treated "like servants" just as they were years ago when the hacienda hotel was not a tourist space but a productive agroindustrial site devoted to henequen extraction. As some of its inhabitants have shared with me over email, WhatsApp, and Facebook messages, the COVID-19 pandemic and the militarization of Tren Maya's construction have only exacerbated these feelings since 2020.

In our conversations over the years, managers at Hacienda Temozón Sur have taken pride in affirming that most of the hotel workers at the hacienda hotel are Maya Indigenous and native to Abalá and Temozón Sur and that many of them, or someone in their families, had been previously employed as peones in the henequen hacienda. These managers believe there is intrinsic value in employing Yukatek Maya workers who have an historical relationship to the place, and they present the hacienda hotel as a tourist venture that honors a lifetime of Indigenous work. When put in context within these other larger networks of power, capital, and knowledge production, it is at least questionable the extent to which their voices have been invited in the process.[3]

Most of the social projects that the hacienda hotel is engaged with involve the material transformation of the built environment adjacent to the hotel through infrastructure provision. Tasks that used to belong to the state and municipal governments, such as designing urban space, are now granted *to* the hotel and hence often planned with profit in mind. These projects entail a top-down approach to building housing and roads. Paving roads, providing housing, and servicing electricity have improved Temozón Sur inhabitants' commutes and everyday lives, but these amenities are also pertinacious material reminders of the new owners as the new *patrones* in town.

The Mayanness advanced by the Hacienda Hotel's novel infrastructures and social venues in inland Yucatán gets curated not only through architectural firms, professional chefs, or professionalized Indigenous service workers at the hacienda itself but, significantly by the educational venues directly associated with the Hacienda Hotel's owners. Examples of these educational venues are the social enterprises La Vaca Independiente, the DIA Institute, and, more recently, the Transformation, Art, and Education (TAE) Foundation.

La Vaca Independiente, for example, is a social enterprise with an .edu domain founded in 1992 by the hacienda hotel's owners. The enterprise has its own laboratories, conducts consultancies, does editorial work, and publishes its own manuals and books. What these practices, spaces, and labs mean in practice deserves ethnographic research that I have not been able to conduct at this point. However, trying to understand the relationship between hacienda hotel's material interventions in inland Yucatán and these educative venues, I learned how far kin networks expand into the realms of archiving Mayanness for tomorrow. La Vaca Independiente, for example, offers education through the DIA Institute. The latter is a center of higher education for professionals created by the same people with the support from the Secretaría de Educación Pública (SEP) from Mexico. As it says on its website, it is invested in pedagogical innovation and the formation of its own method, the so-called Metodología DIA, as well as its own community, Comunidad DIA, "a group of mediators in search of growing as educators and human beings."[4] The DIA methodology, which is copyrighted, uses visual art to promote dialogues that become generative for self-discovery and growth. These are forms of self-discovery and personal growth that the DIA Institute itself certifies. Since 2013, the institute has had its own educators and *mediadores* (mediators) who, trained in its practices and methods, act in communities and Escuelas Normales around Mexico educating on Indigenous cosmovision, community development, and personal growth. According to its data, the DIA Institute already has a presence in over thirty-two federal entities and has over 35,000 active educators who offer a wide range of courses, workshops, and talks in public schools and art centers around Mexico. Since 2020, it also has had an international presence. Interestingly, the DIA Institute claims to be financed through selling its own products, and according to its public data it invests annually over $1 million in its educative programs.[5]

Closely related to the DIA Institute and La Vaca Independiente, yet with clearer roots in the Maya region, the same relatives of the hacienda hotel's owner founded the TAE Foundation in 2021. This organization aims to expand the boundaries of art, integrating creative processes in Maya villages in Yucatán. Part of the foundation's work is to organize public talks that call for the co-creation of spaces for transformative experiences building on Maya wisdom and tradition—knowledges and practices whose contours it is actively curating and archiving for tomorrow. One such event was, for example, "The Human in the Cosmos: The Mayan Cosmos," which was organized with the support of the Mesoamerican Center and the Los Angeles County Museum of Art (LACMA) and at which relatives of a Hacienda Temozón Sur owner spoke alongside the world's leading figures in Maya epigraphy, museum curators, and artists. Interestingly, this event had the name given by Dr. Linda Schele and collaborators, respected US archaeologists, and authors of the 1993 *Maya Cosmos: Three Thousand Years on the Shaman's Path* (Freidel et al. 1993)—which researches Maya mythology and religion—who take positions in direct opposition to Mexican archaeologist Alberto Ruz Lhuillier, whose kin, as I show in the next section, oversaw restoring Hacienda Xcanatun as a boutique hacienda hotel too, albeit through a slightly different way than Temozón Sur.

Considering these ventures, Hacienda Temozón Sur seems like just the tip of a larger iceberg, where wealth, power, and family rule in the definition of a novel transnational Mayanness, that whilst invoking self-discovery and personal growth has generated a tangible and spatial network of seemingly profitable enterprises in the realms of education and real estate in Yucatán. It is the combination of both the translation of what Mayanness is and the material infrastructure interventions in the landscape that makes me think of this venture as much more than just an isolated tourism endeavor but as part of a larger intellectual and economic infrastructure of tourism archiving.

HACIENDA XCANATUN

Hacienda Xcanatun is in the periphery of Mérida's increasing urban sprawl, about twenty-five minutes from Mérida's city center by car. The hacienda is part of the Comisaría Xcanatun, one of the over twenty subcommissaries of the municipio of Mérida made up of rural medium-sized population settlements once dependent on the agroindustry of henequen and engaged, since its demise in the late 1970s, in mixed urban-rural economies. Defined by Instituto Nacional de Estadística y Geografía (INEGI) as a modest rural enclave of 1,425 persons, Xcanatun is the perfect example of what María Cruz Rodríguez (2002) and José A Lugo Pérez and Lizbeth Tzuc Canché (2019) have defined as Yucatán's "new ruralities"—places where rural cosmologies rule but where people are economically dependent on urban wages.

The hacienda was built in the eighteenth century and was founded by Manuel Zapata y Bolio, a well-known hacendado related by kinship ties with the Spaniard Francisco de Montejo—the leading conqueror and captain general of Yucatán. Xcanatun was active as a henequen hacienda until the 1970s, and like many others it lay abandoned until 1994, when it was bought from the Sra. María del Rosario Solís Marcín de Palomeque, kin to Manuel Zapata y Bolio, by Jorge Ruz Buenfil and Christina Baker. Their intention was, from the start, to build a hotel. At that moment, they were not the only ones looking to buy into old haciendas with the intention of remodeling, but ever since then, they have been among the few public figures who have invoked existing archaeological knowledge about Mayan peoples as a legitimizing force in the process. As it happens, they had it in the family.

Jorge Ruz Buenfil is one of the two sons of Alberto Ruz Lhuillier, a well-known archaeologist of the region since his discovery of the Tomb of Pakal the Great in Palenque (see Watson 2014), and Christina Baker, better known as Tina, his wife. The couple stands for a new social type of residents in Mérida who include world-renown artists, designers, and culture entrepreneurs and who are locally known as "the expats" (the expatriates).

By 1993, Hacienda Xcanatun, like many other buildings in inland Yucatán, had been seriously damaged by Hurricane Gilberto (1988) and almost a decade of complete abandonment and state neglect. Looking for entrepreneurial venues that enabled them to give back to communities endangered by the hurricane, Ruz and Baker started the hacienda's restoration process in 1994. As they told me in an interview with them in 2008, in the selection process of which hacienda to choose the fact that Xcanatun was geographically proximate to Mérida and that it was not protected by the Instituto Nacional de Antropología e Historia (INAH) played a major role. Not only did the lack of heritage protections mean from the start, as the owners put it, "greater freedom in design," but also the proximity to the metropole always meant they could cater to Mérida's elites (Gregory 2019). In 2008, 80 percent of the hacienda hotel restaurant's clientele was from Mérida.

During restoration, however, as they recall, they found and realized that the main building of the casa principal had exposed stones whose characteristics seemed to point to ancient Maya temple sites. Although it has not been corroborated scientifically, the stones discovered probably come from the nearby Maya ruins of Dzibilchaltun, whose population was known to inhabit "not only the *pueblo* of Chablekal, but also those of Komchen and Xcanatun, and a number of large haciendas" (Andrews 1960, 257). As Christina put it in numerous publications: "3 feet thick and over 20 feet high we thought these stones would have probably been stolen from Maya temple sites."

The discovery of the stones and the couple's declared passion for both archaeology and architecture understandably slowed the hotel plans to open. As Baker explained in many international media interviews, once they suspected the Mayan origins of the stones, they tried to keep them there in an attempt "to make ancient past a visible presence" (*Boston Globe*, March 30, 2014). Unfortunately, in the meantime, Hacienda Temozón Sur opened its doors as a boutique hotel "gaining the label of the pioneer," "getting all the buzz," when, as Christina lamented in an interview with me, "we had been doing the hard work" earlier on.

Xcanatun opened as a hacienda boutique hotel in 2000 with eighteen rooms. The reconstruction of the casa principal was overseen by an architectural firm owned by a local architect—by then director of the school of architecture of a well-known elite regional university. The firm, it was later found, was by then involved in various scandals for favoring family while doing business with private investors—a disclosure that can be read as just one more testimony of the remarkable frequency in which family networks seem to rule both centers of knowledge production and real estate developments in the region.

In the hacienda's reconstruction process, as the architectural plan described, the architects aimed at a combination of rehabilitation and new construction. Specifically, the plan rehabilitated the area of the Casa Principal, the machine house, and the chapel. The intention was to reconstruct according to codes from colonial architectural styles as well as Maya architecture.[6] The transformation of the capilla as a room for social events and the casa de maquinas into a restaurant have been widely celebrated in architectural and travel magazines such as *Condé Nast Traveller* and *National Geographic*. They have granted the hacienda hotel a place in the prestigious Historic Hotels Worldwide Network and different architectural tours in Mérida and beyond. As it was new construction, the architects built an area for the hotel suites and accommodation, pools, gym, and spa.

Just as at Hacienda Temozón Sur, the remodeling at Xcanatun privileges the gilded age of henequen times, emphasizing the European consanguinity in design, landscaping, and taste. As promotional materials put it, the hacienda hotel offers an "appealing combination of Mexican and Far Eastern antiques, colonial Caribbean hand-carved furnishings, hand-woven textiles and original oil paintings"; "it is steeped in colonial architectural detail." The property has "nine acres of tropical gardens and manicured lawns [to] showcase the local flora and surround two swimming pools," and its restaurant known for the "fusion of French techniques with the freshest Caribbean and Yucatecan ingredients." Furthermore, and fully in line with New Age tourism trends, its spa offers the possibility to "indulge in an ancient Mayan treatment from a therapist schooled in holistic healing practices by her shaman grandfather." Tourists are invited to experience her healings in their rooms or in a Maya palapa that has been created anew for this purpose.[7]

The number of daily excursions—or "escapes," as they prefer to call them—that Xcanatun offers surpasses those in the Haciendas. They are also more closely curated according to their clients' different interests, which generally include archaeology, ecology, revitalization, and/or golfing. The Hacienda Hotel offers, for example, an "All things Maya" day escape "chauffeured and guided" to Chichén Itzá, Ek' Balam, Uxmal, or Dzibilchaltun. These four archaeological sites become read in a hierarchy of well-known "ancient Maya cities" and complexity in their ceremonial buildings.

Generally, they are catered to according to clients' level of comfort with cultural differences. As part of their revitalization packages, Xcanatun offers "Maya ancient wisdom and healing packages" that also include "cleansing and chakra alignment" ceremonies. This is a clear resignification of central rituals that are still alive in Maya rural areas and that are, however, not part of the hacienda hotel narratives, which seem more devoted to market beauty products from the Spanish brand Germaine de Capuccini Collection with which they work. Hacienda hotel guests also received discount passes to the exclusive and very private Jack Nicklaus Signature golf course, El Jaguar (Mitchell 2009).

In 2007, Xcanatun's restaurant hosted Presidents Bush and Calderón and their wives for dinner, just like Hacienda Temozón did. At dinner, both presidents celebrated a pledge to "enforce the rule of law, and to crack down on organized crime and drugs, and reform the judicial system." They celebrated their friendship and neighborly relations and declared themselves to be "strategic partners" with "common goals for development" and shared values "such as democracy, freedom, and respect for human rights and the law." They did so, as press releases attest, amid toasts for health, well-being, and binding claims of family and commerce (White House Office 2017).

For the dinner to take place, the comisaría of Xcanatun, just as it happened in Temozón Sur, was under siege. Protests against "the leader of the Western World," as one of the leading news media described President Bush, were held at a distance, and Yucatán's remoteness *and* Mérida's strategic geographic position for commerce and investment once more highlighted as a security and economic decision—one enabled, fully, by tourism.

In summer 2020, during the global COVID-19 pandemic, Ruz and Baker partnered in the management of Hacienda Xcanatun with the Banyan Tree Resorts, an Asian hospitality corporation created in 1994 whose owner is among the fifty richest peoples in Singapore, according to Forbes. As a result, the hacienda hotel is currently known as Hacienda Xcanatun *by* Ansagna, one of the five distinctive brands of the corporation. This partnership exemplifies the role of hacienda hotels as part of larger economic and intellectual infrastructures of philanthropic capitalism with the means and power to produce and use a branded Mayanness as a selective economic asset. As a result of this partnership, for example, Hacienda Xcanatun plans to create fifty more rooms, and remodel public areas in and around the hacienda, as well as to build full-service private residences and more hotel rooms.

At a local level, with pressure from the Tren Maya and a global pandemic, the management of the hacienda through this Asian firm results in a meaningful shift toward corporate control and a move toward securing stronger partnerships and alliances in the negotiation table for real estate investments in the outskirts of Mérida. Corporate control seems already overwhelming on social media, where Ansagna-branded logos, typographies, colors, and language make it clear to the public that this Asian corporation will become a direct driver of land and labor change in inland Yucatán. Some of the pressures have already been felt by Xcanatun's inhabitants.

Since the hacienda opened as a hacienda boutique hotel, the Comisaría Xcanatun has regularly welcomed Ruz and Baker's offering to take care of beautification projects and other public services in exchange for the control of yet one more bit of land. In a context of historical state abandonment, many in the community regularly reported being grateful about the hacienda hotel's consideration of the comisaría's well-being. Yet, in March 2021, a dispute over paving a large part of the public sports field to generate a direct vehicle entrance to the hacienda hotel in exchange for beautifying the community's playground exploded in conflict, when the hotel's offer was fiercely rejected by neighbors. In different media interviews, neighbors claimed to be "fed up" with the hotel, which had encroached on the popular expressions of the comisaría's cultural and religious life in favor of tourists. In the local newspaper *Reporteros Hoy*, a neighbor claimed: "We are not interested in this project. We just want them to remodel the playground as they said. We want them to build a kiosk and that they fulfil their promise to cover the sports arena, to build seating and bathrooms." Another neighbor also added: "Before (the hotel) we held popular dances and *corridas* [bull fights]." Now we can't do them because "they damage the image of the hotel" (Reporteros Hoy 2021; translation by author).

Corridas and *vaquerias* (popular dances) never qualified as part of the corporate design-driven Mayanness that hacienda tourism is engaged with. Maybe they never will. Since its management by the Asian hospitality giant, Hacienda Xcanatun has become certified as a COVID-19 Safe Sanctuary for well-off tourists. Further health and safety regulations concerning noise, smells, and foods are in the making, and meanwhile in a country with a fast-growing number of COVID-19 deaths, hacienda Xcanatun's further enclosure and desire to privatize yet more public land for tourism development have been felt unfair by locals and taken as a warning sign of the yet more corporate control to come. The gross inequalities that such private and for-profit tourism and health coalitions might open in inland Yucatán in the name of "the Maya" but without Mayan people are not hard to imagine. After all, there are historical precedents for this type of tourism governance practice in the region. What will these corporate coalitions entail in Yucatán is worth further reflection, empirical research, and consideration.

CONCLUSION

This chapter has examined tourism ventures and tourism actors as pivotal history-making agents. As Ben Fallaw and Fernando Armstrong-Fumero state in the introduction to this volume, this chapter has drawn on less conventional 'archives' of information to invite the consideration of newly wealthy families and transnational corporate actors that, *from* and *for* tourism, are delineating the boundaries and content of a design-driven Mayanness that is strongly pushing the boundaries of traditional archival practice. They are doing so because in their direct interventions in the realm of knowledge production and the transformations of the built environment, they are producing new economic and intellectual infrastructures and communities of meaning around Mayanness that will become part of the archive of tomorrow.

In Yucatán, tourism infrastructures are predicated on colonial systems of knowledge production and social and racial hierarchies, and they rest upon uneven geographical development premises. State-led forms of cultural tourism have become a privileged terrain for the reproduction of selective representations about Mayanness, not only at a regional or national level but well beyond. This is a Mayanness that, as Ben Fallaw demonstrates in chapter 4 in this volume, is transnationally produced. Yet, as the restoration of haciendas for tourism helped me show, the Mayanness that restored haciendas for tourism help produce not only involves science and politics, but also the United States and Mexico, Yucatecan revolutionaries and North American researchers modifying national Indigenism to represent Maya's pre-Columbian past as distinct from and in some ways superior to the rest of Mesoamerica. It also involves transnational tourism corporations, philanthropic venues, the state, international desires to encounter cultural difference, and curated efforts to fabricate a branded, corporate design-driven Mayanness with material traces to colonial pasts that hold spiritual and wellness benefits for a few. These have become meaningful historical actors in deciding what stories to tell, what pasts to recover, and how to do so. Their fabrications wield a heavy hand in dictating the form and shape of the Indigenous commons of tomorrow not only because they strategically tell stories about the past but also because they are becoming lasting intermediaries in housing, transportation, education, and public policy interventions. As such, backed up as they are by large transnational capital from the hospitality world and by the Mexican state, they are becoming a direct force in the making and/or silencing of *comunidad* where the haciendas are located.

Both Hacienda Temozón Sur's and Hacienda Xcanatun's processes of restoration for tourism purposes have shed light on the emergence of transnational philanthropic capitalists as actors driving the process of history production about Mayanness in Yucatán. These private and self-declared philanthropic processes for tourism purposes point at salient and ongoing archival practices of future making about "the Maya" that are mostly driven for-profit and that are worthy of consideration in the intellectual recognition of the "gringo" perspectives and "transnational" legacies (to use the terminology from the editors of this volume) that so pervasively still characterize this region and that this book is concerned with. Both advance the creation and reproduction of a "feel-good history" within the growing niche of New Age gray publishing and ventures. Both activate kinship ties with historically recognized liberal approaches to knowledge production about Mayanness. And, yet, there seem to be important differences too.

The Haciendas Yucatán venture instrumentalizes the past and nostalgic notions of Mayanness according to standardized global market trends and accommodations. Their partnership with the Marriot Group's Luxury Collection is an example. Its Haciendas are shaped and are significantly involved in larger ventures in the realms of art and education, which transforms them into real estate pieces of larger processes regarding knowledge production about Mayanness. Ruz and Baker's attempts and desires to articulate expert archaeological knowledge in and about "the Maya" in Hacienda Xcanatun seem to point to a more reflexive and inclusive path to reclaim the past for tourism, at least in discourse. This is a smaller-scale example of hacienda restoration for tourism if compared with the Hacienda's growing empire but one that recent events might well turn into a bigger business. The COVID-19 pandemic and the developmental promises of Tren Maya seem to have influenced the couple's decision to partner with the Asian management corporation the Banyan Tree, whose exclusive, design-driven and, private holistic wellness mottos have been already proven to work in the Riviera Maya as well as to more recently inspiring the design of Tren Maya's future *paradores* (stations).

Hacienda tourism tells selective histories about the past, about place, and about Mayanness. Its restorations, inscribed in the physical and symbolic landscapes of the region, participate in larger economic and intellectual infrastructure networks that are producing and becoming the archive of a design-driven Mayanness for tomorrow. Yet, because they have power and the media and international spotlight, they could also hold the possibility of redressing errors of the past, of fighting partial remembrance, of raising questions about selective forgetting (Meyers 2012, 169), and of otherwise serving to archive. They could do so by engaging with the region's large academic literature on land and labor discussions that makes visible the hacienda as a historically contested space (see Baklanoff and Moseley 2008). From these discussions they could learn from historians, archaeologists, and anthropologists who have already reflexively grappled with the transnational power dynamics of their own research in the region while simultaneously exposing both the qualities and inequalities of Mayanness today. Those in charge of hacienda tourism restoration today could also redress some of these inequalities by engaging directly with

Yukatek Maya literature written in Maya and Spanish and by thinking critically and reflexively about their own restoration choices, management practices, and role as interlocutors and cultural translators in public spaces. They could make a conscious, informed effort not to erase but to bring forth the voices and stories of Maya inhabitants themselves. Making these changes will entail a conscious effort to move away from grand narratives of the Yucatán's golden age in favor of plural stories of struggle told *in collaboration with* and not extracted from Yucatán's inhabitants. These efforts might have been once most viable in reconstruction processes as those seen in the earlier Hacienda Xcanatun, where there was, at least, the declared intention to redress the inequalities of the past. Yet, thus far, hacienda tourism's driven restorations still mobilize partial knowledges and reinstate instead the colonial and modern stories that archaeology once helped to denounce in the region (Meyers 2012). When Indigenous voices are not brought to the table unless as "accents"— romantic or nostalgic punctuations of larger, transnational philanthropic endeavors but not in their own right—tourism endeavors become formidable extensions of colonial ones.

NOTES

1. Acknowledgments: Special thanks to Fernando Armstrong-Fumero and Ben Fallaw for our fruitful and fun conversations that have invaluably forever strengthened the historical aspects of my ethnographic research in Yucatán. I am also grateful to Matthew C. Watson for a generous reading on an earlier draft of this chapter.

2. See Córdoba Azcárate (2020, chap. 3), for an in-depth discussion into haciendas' labor organization as plantations in the past in their present reality as tourist attractions.

3. Different sources highlight that the 2007 hacienda meeting was in fact the incubator for the Plan Mexico, or Mérida Initiative. This was a security cooperation agreement signed into law in 2008 among the United States, Mexico, and countries in Central America to combat drug trafficking, money laundering, and transnational organized crime, which made Mexico the number one recipient of US military aid in Latin America, surpassing Colombia (Delgado-Ramos and Romano 2011; Seelke 2011).

4. Instituto DIA: https://institutodia.mx/que-es-la-comunidad-dia/.

5. Portafolios Artes y Medios BlogSpot, Programa DIA: http://portafolioartesymedios .blogspot.com/2013/03/programa-dia.html.

6. "Another World in Merida: Hacienda Xcanatun," Journey Mexico, https://www.jour neymexico.com/blog/another-wold-in-merida-hacienda-xcanatun.

7. Kensington Tours Mexico: https://kensingtontours.com/tours/mexico-and-the-carib bean/mexico/hotels/hacienda-xcanatun.

REFERENCES CITED

Alston, Lee J., Shannan Mattiace, and Tomas Nonnenmacher. 2009. "Coercion, Culture, and Contracts: Labor and Debt on Henequen Haciendas in Yucatán, Mexico, 1870–1915." *Journal of Economic History* 69 (1): 104–37.

Ancona Riestra, Roberto, and Universidad Autónoma de Yucatán. 1996. *Arquitectura de las haciendas henequeneras.* Mérida: Universidad Autónoma de Yucatán.

Andrews, E. Wyllys IV. 1960. "Excavations at Dzibilchaltun, northwestern Yucatan." *Proceedings of the American Philosophical Society* 104:254–65.

Armstrong-Fumero, Fernando. 2009. "A Heritage of Ambiguity: The Historical Substrate of Vernacular Multiculturalism in Yucatán, Mexico." *American Ethnologist* 36, no. 2 (May): 300–316.

Backlanoff, Eric N., and Moseley, Edward. 2008. *Yucatán in an Era of Globalization.* Tuscaloosa: The University of Alabama Press.

Breglia, Lisa. 2006. *Monumental Ambivalence: The Politics of Heritage.* Austin: University of Texas Press.

Castellanos, Bianet, and Matilde Córdoba Azcárate. 2021. "Guardians of Tradition: The Affective and Popular Geopolitics of Maya Women on Tour." In *Tourism Geopolitics,* edited by M. Mostafanezhad, M. Córdoba Azcárate, and R. Norum. 231–51. Tucson: University of Arizona Press.

Córdoba Azcárate, Matilde. 2020. *Stuck with Tourism: Space, Power, and Labor in Contemporary Yucatán.* Oakland: University of California Press.

Craib, Raymond. 2004. *Cartographic Mexico. A History of State Fixation and Fugitive Landscapes.* Durham, NC: Duke University Press.

Cruz Rodríguez, María S. 2002. "Procesos urbanos y 'ruralidad' en la periferia de la Zona Metropolitana de la Ciudad de México." *Estudios Demográficos y Urbanos* 17, no. 1 (January–April): 39–74. Mexico City: El Colegio de México.

Delgado-Ramos, Gian Carlo, and Silvia Romano. 2011. "Political-Economic Factors in US Foreign Policy: The Colombia Plan, the Mérida Initiative, and the Obama Administration." *Latin American Perspectives* 38 (4): 93–108.

Fallaw, Ben. 2001. *Cárdenas Compromised: The Failure of Reforms in Postrevolutionary Yucatán.* Durham, NC: Duke University Press.

Freidel, David A., Linda Schele, Joy Parker, Justin Kerr, Macduff Everton, and Jay I. Kislak. 1993. *Maya Cosmos: Three Thousand Years on the Shaman's Path,* edited by First Quill. New York: William Morrow.

Gómez-Barris, Macarena. 2012 "Andean Translations: New Age Tourism and Cultural Exchange in the Sacred Valley, Peru." *Latin American Perspectives* 39 (6): 68–78.

Gregory, Lidya. 2019. "Yucatán's Hacienda Xcanatun Signs 'Serendipitous' Alliance with Banyan Tree Group." *Travel Pulse.* July 22. https://www.travelpulse.com/news/hotels

-and-resorts/yucatns-hacienda-xcanatn-signs-serendipitous-alliance-with-banyan-tree
-group.html.

Hervik, Peter, and Hilary E. Kahn. 2006. "Scholarly Surrealism: The Persistence of Mayanness." *Critique of Anthropology* 26 (2): 209–32.

Katz, Friedrich. 1974. "Labor Conditions on Haciendas in Porfirian Mexico: Some Trends and Tendencies." *Hispanic American Historical Review* 54 (1): 1–47.

Kirshenblatt-Gimblett, Barbara. 1995. "Theorizing Heritage." *Ethnomusicology* 39 (3): 367.

Loewe, Ronald. 2010. *Maya or Mestizo? Nationalism, Modernity, and Its Discontents.* Toronto: University of Toronto Press.

Lugo Pérez, José A., and Lizbeth Tzuc Canché. 2011. "Las comisarías y subcomisarías del municipio de Mérida: Entre la tradición y la modernidad." *Estudios de Cultura Maya,* 37:179–98. https://doi.org/10.19130/iifl.ecm.2011.37.18.

Marín Guardado, Gustavo. 2008. "Territorio de resistencia, integración mercantil y producción del espacio turístico en Quintana Roo: Trayectorias y transformaciones del mundo maya." In *Turismo, identidades y exclusión,* edited by Alicia Castellanos Guerrero and Jesús Antonio Machuca, 97–142. Mexico City: Universidad Autónoma Metropolitana-Unidad Iztapalapa.

Marín Guardado, Gustavo. 2012. "Los tristes trópicos del turismo en México: Industria, reflexividad y otras ficciones." In *Turismo, globalización y sociedades locales en la península de Yucatán, México,* edited by Gustavo Marín Guardado, Ana García de Fuentes, and Magalí Daltabuit, 17–44. Tenerife: Asociación Canaria de Antropología.

Mattiace, Shannan, and Tomas Nonnenmacher. 2014. "The Organization of Hacienda Labor during the Mexican Revolution: Evidence from Yucatán." *Mexican Studies / Estudios Mexicanos* 30 (2): 366–96.

Meyers, Allan. 2012. *Outside the Hacienda Walls: The Archaeology of Plantation Peonage in Nineteenth-Century Yucatán.* Tucson: University of Arizona Press.

Mitchell, John. 2009. "Mexico Premier Hacienda Xcanatun." July 2. http://www.mexicopremiere.com/hacienda-xcanatun-offers-revitalization-based-on-ancient-maya-wisdom-maya-healing-package-includes-a-4th-night-free/.

Nickel, Herbert J. 1997. *El peonaje en las haciendas mexicanas: Interpretaciones, fuentes, hallazgos.* Mexico City: Universidad Iberoamericana.

Peniche Rivero, Piedad. 1999. "La comunidad doméstica de la hacienda henequenera de Yucatán, México, 1870–1915." *Mexican Studies / Estudios Mexicanos* 15 (1): 1–33.

Pernecky, Tomas, and Johnston Charles. 2006. "Voyage through Numinous Space: Applying the Specialization Concept to New Age Tourism" *Tourism Recreation Research* 31 (1): 37–46.

Pratt, Mary Louise. 2007. *Imperial Eyes: Travel Writing and Transculturation.* London: Routledge.

Quijano, Aníbal. 2000. "Coloniality of Power, Eurocentrism, and Latin America" *Nepantla Views from the South* 1 (3): 533–80.

Reporteros Hoy IM. 2021. "Condicionan una obra de vecinos para beneficiar a la hacienda Xcanatun." March 12. https://reporteroshoy.mx/noticias/condicionan-una-obra-a -vecinos-para-beneficiar-a-la-hacienda-xcanatun/.

Ruz, Mario Humberto 2006. *De la mano de lo sacro: Santos y demonios en el mundo Maya*. Mexico City: Universidad Autónoma de México.

Seelke, Clare Ribando. 2010. "Mérida Initiative for Mexico and Central America: Funding and Policy Issues." *Congressional Research Service*. April 19.

Smith, Valene L. 1989. *Hosts and Guests: The Anthropology of Tourism*. 2nd ed. Philadelphia: University of Philadelphia Press.

Stoler, Ann. 2013. *Imperial Debris: On Ruins and Ruination*. Durham, NC: Duke University Press.

Stone, Andrea J. 2010. *Images from the Underworld: Naj Tunich and the Tradition of Maya Cave Painting*. Austin: University of Texas Press.

Watson, Matthew 2014 "Listening in the Pakal Controversy: A Matter of Care in Ancient Maya Studies." *Social Studies of Science* 44 (86): 930–54.

Wells, Allen. 1991. "From Hacienda to Plantation: The Transformation of Santo Domingo Xcuyum." In *Land, Labor, and Capital in Modern Yucatán. Essays in Regional History and Political Economy*, edited by Jeffrey Brannon and Gilbert Joseph, 112–42. Tuscaloosa: University of Alabama Press.

White House Office of the Press Secretary. "President Bush and President Calderon of Mexico exchange Dinner Toasts." March 13, 2017. https://2001-2009.state.gov/p/wha /rls/rm/07/q1/81705.htm.

Witynski, Karen, and Joe P. Carr. 2008. *Hacienda Style*. Layton, UT: Gibbs Smith.

Index

About the Authors

Fernando Armstrong-Fumero is an associate professor of anthropology at Smith College. His published work includes *Elusive Unity: Factionalism and the Limits of Identity Politics in Yucatán, Mexico* (UPC, 2013), as well as a range of articles and chapters on Mayan identity politics, cultural heritage policy, and the history of American anthropology. Two upcoming projects focus on rethinking the chronology of neoliberalism in Mexico, and on tracing the links between US-based Mayanist research and the expansion of New England capital in the nineteenth century.

David Carey Jr. holds the Doehler Chair in History at Loyola University Maryland. In addition to writing more than thirty peer-reviewed articles and essays, he is the author of *I Ask for Justice: Maya Women, Dictators, and Crime in Guatemala, 1898–1944*, which was the corecipient of the 2015 Latin American Studies Association Bryce Wood Book Award. His most recent book is *Oral History in Latin America: Unlocking the Spoken Archive*. He has authored three other books and has edited or coedited three volumes. Among other entities, the Fulbright Program American Philosophical Society, and John Simon Guggenheim Foundation have supported his research and scholarship.

M. Bianet Castellanos is professor of American studies at the University of Minnesota. Her works include *Indigenous Dispossession: Housing and Maya Indebtedness in Mexico* (SUP, 2021) and *A Return to Servitude: Maya Migration and the Tourist Trade in Cancún* (UMP, 2010). Her current research analyzes national and familial reckonings with Indigenous erasure and anti-Blackness in Mexico.

Matilde Córdoba Azcárate is an associate professor in the Communication Department at the University of California, San Diego, where she also codirects the International Institute, Nature, Space and Politics faculty and graduate group. Her research examines tourism, capitalism, and crisis. She is the author of *Stuck with Tourism: Space, Power, and Labor in Contemporary Yucatán* (UC Press, 2020) and coeditor of *Tourism Geopolitics: Assemblages of Infrastructure, Affect and Imagination* (University of Arizona Press, 2021).

Lydia Crafts is an assistant professor teaching US and Latin American history at Manhattan College. In 2019, she received her PhD in history from the University of Illinois, Urbana-Champaign. She is working on a book entitled, *"Guatemala's Tuskegee": Experimentation, Ethics, and Empire in the Circum-Caribbean.*

Ben Fallaw is a professor of Latin American studies at Colby College in Maine. He is the author of *State Formation in the Liberal Era: Capitalisms and Claims of Citizenship in Mexico and Peru*, with David Nugent (Arizona, 2020), *Religion and State Formation in Postrevolutionary Mexico* (Duke, 2013), and *Forced Marches: Soldiers and Military Caciques in Modern Mexico* with Terry Rugeley (Arizona, 2012). His research has been supported by the Mellon Foundation, the American Council of Learned Societies, and the National Endowment for the Humanities. Currently, Fallaw is completing an ethnobiography of Bartolomé García Correa.

John R. Gust is a principal investigator of archaeology and project manager at Cogstone Resource Management, Inc. in Orange, California, and an independent scholar of the historic period of the Maya region. He has worked on the Yucatán peninsula since 2000.

Sheila Hernandez graduated from Smith College in 2021 with a dual major in anthropology and Spanish and Portuguese.

Julio Cesar Hoil Gutiérrez was born and raised in the Mayan community of Xcalakoop, Yucatán, Mexico. He is a native speaker of the Yukatek Maya language. He completed a doctorate in History at Centro de Investigaciones y Estudios Superiores en Antropología Social (CIESAS), and has been a professor of anthropology and history at Universidad de Oriente (Valladolid, Yucatán). He has published various articles on the agrarian history of Yucatán and is coeditor, along with Fernando Armstrong-Fumero, of *Legacies of Space and Intangible Heritage: Archaeology, Ethnohistory and the Politics of Cultural Continuity in the Americas*. He is currently a researcher and professor at the Universidades para el Bienestar Benito Juárez García and collaborates with the Tihosuco Heritage Preservation and Community Development Project of the Penn Cultural Heritage Center of the Penn Museum.

Jennifer P. Mathews is a professor of anthropology and chair of the Department of Sociology and Anthropology at Trinity University in San Antonio. Her PhD is in anthropology from the University of California, Riverside, with a specialization in Maya archaeology. She is the coeditor of three edited volumes on Maya archaeology, and two monographs that focus on the history of chicle, and sugarcane and rum in nineteenth-century Yucatán.

Matthew C. Watson is an associate professor of anthropology at Mount Holyoke College. His book *Afterlives of Affect: Science, Religion, and an Edgewalker's Spirit* was published in 2020 by Duke University Press. His essays have appeared in venues, including *American Anthropologist, Social Studies of Science, Cultural Critique*, and *Theory, Culture & Society*. He is currently writing a history of the Harvard Chiapas Project that traces the politics of race, gender, knowledge, and technology in the ethnographic field.

Meredith Whitman, history and global studies major, graduated in May 2020, after serving as Ben Fallaw's research assistant. She has a love of history, Spanish, and grammar. In her free time, she enjoys watching sports with friends and family, hiking with her dog, and cooking.

www.ingramcontent.com/pod-product-compliance
Lightning Source LLC
Chambersburg PA
CBHW070618030426
42337CB00020B/3844